GIFT
CHILDREN

BOOKS BY
J. DOUGLAS BATES

The Pulitzer Prize
Gift Children

GIFT CHILDREN

A Story of
Race, Family, and Adoption
in a Divided America

J. Douglas Bates

Ticknor & Fields
New York
1993

Copyright © 1993 by J. Douglas Bates

For information about permission to reproduce selections from this book, write to
Permissions, Ticknor & Fields, 215 Park Avenue South, New York, New York 10003.

Library of Congress Cataloging-in-Publication Data

Bates, J. Douglas.
Gift children : a story of race, family, and
adoption in a divided America / J. Douglas Bates.
p.   cm.
ISBN 0-395-63314-1
1. Interracial adoption — United States — Case
studies.   I. Title.
HV875.64.B37   1993
362.7'34'0973 — dc20   93-20005
CIP

Printed in the United States of America

AGM   10   9   8   7   6   5   4   3   2   1

Book design by Anne Chalmers

For Gloria

Children are a gift from God; they are his reward.

Psalms 127:3

The adoption of "gift children" by close friends was common among poor blacks in the South, a custom that involved generosity on both sides . . .

Nicholas Lemann, *The Promised Land*

Acknowledgments

Several of those close to me have sacrificed something precious — their privacy — so this book could be written. Throughout the undertaking I found myself moved by the openness and generosity of a bunch of basically reticent people. Most members of my family normally think our triumphs and troubles are subjects that belong within our circle of love, not shared with the world. I couldn't have told this story unless my spouse, our children, and many of our relatives had been willing to make an exception and talk openly — sometimes with discomfort — about some of the intimacies of our lives.

My family's motives were honorable. None who helped received any offer or implied promise of financial remuneration. Some cooperated mainly out of loyalty to me. Others said they feel it important that our family's story be told. We all hope it will help the thousands of American children who are being denied loving homes today because adoption across racial lines in this country has become politically incorrect.

The book owes an enormous debt to my daughters, Lynn and Liska. Their personal courage, in trusting me (and the reader) with their most private feelings and experiences, has been inspirational. Both have expressed hope that their candor will benefit others with similar adoptive backgrounds, particularly young African-American women of mixed race.

My sons, Steve and Mike, also have earned my deepest appreciation and respect, not just for their help on *Gift Children* but for their entire lives as caring brothers of Lynn and Liska. In the extended family, my brothers, Tom and Dan, and my sisters, Jill and Jamie, helped out immensely with reminiscences that caulked up many a gap in my memories of the past twenty-three years.

Two individuals outside the family made huge contributions. My agent, Richard Pine, hatched the original idea for the book, gave it vision and shape, and worked many weeks with me on refining it. John Herman, editorial director at Ticknor & Fields, nurtured the project throughout the creative process with patience, sensitivity, and professional mastery. His colleagues in New York — particularly editorial assistant Amy Hunerwadel and publicist Barbara Henricks — deserve recognition, too, as does Katarina Rice, the copy editor who worked so skillfully on the manuscript in Concord, Massachusetts.

Along the way, I received invaluable assistance from Mike and Sandy Thoele, fine people as well as good friends. I also am grateful to the *Register-Guard* photographer Wayne Eastburn, who in 1972 took the photo that appears on the cover of this book.

Above all I owe thanks to Gloria Jean Bates, my wife. In her capacity as personal assistant, she transcribed nearly one hundred hours of tape-recorded interviews and served commendably as memory-jogger, fact-checker, and proofreader, devoted to the accuracy of the book. All that aside, though, her most crucial role was the big one that began back in 1963, when she became my forever friend and partner in the adventure of our lives.

Throughout this book I have used the words "black" and "African-American" somewhat interchangeably, mainly to keep peace in the family. Like the rest of black America, my daughters are not monolithic in their views. Lynn prefers the former label; Liska, the latter. I have no objection to either.

The use of unnamed sources has been kept to a minimum in *Gift Children*, and only two identities have been concealed — those of "Bernard Lee" and "Mustafa Isfahan," whose real names were not used. I have tried diligently to double-check every fact in the book, but any chronicle of this nature faces the hazard of faulty memory. Any such flaw is entirely my own responsibility, not that of the many who helped. They deserve only heartfelt thanks.

Contents

GIFT
CHILDREN

🌿 1 🌿

Second
Thoughts

Dear Mom,
    I hope you know even though you're white and I'm black
I still love you very very much. The end. Your child, Liska.
(PS: I love you too Dad)

Note from Liska, age ten
Spring 1979

LISKA WAS THE FIRST of our children to openly ask the unanswerable question. "Dad," she began, "if the house caught fire some night while all of us were sleeping, and if you woke up in the smoke with only enough time to save one member of the family, which one of us would it be?"

Liska was always asking questions like that, probing our love from every imaginable angle. She was twelve when she came up with the house-on-fire conundrum one evening as all of us — Gloria and I, our two white sons, Steve and Mike, and our two adopted black daughters, Lynn and Liska — sat around the dinner table. All children with siblings probably ponder that awful question or a version of it at some point in their lives. Adopted children, however, can be obsessed with it, especially if their adoptive parents have "biological" children, too. In our family, the sibling bias issue carried yet another complicating factor: the undercurrent of race.

"Well, come on, Dad, who would you save?" Liska demanded. As usual, her manner was good-natured, even playful; her eyes twinkled as she bore in, ever the little prosecutor. But this was not just a dinner-table game. Deep down, she really did want to hear what I would say, and Lynn — quieter and three years older than Liska — was paying unusually close attention, too.

Gloria tried leaping to my defense. "That's not fair, Liska," she said. "No parent can answer an impossible question like that. There *is* no answer."

Liska, however, was tenacious. Whenever she took off in quest of truth and justice, usually in matters of sibling equality, she did not back down easily. "This question is for you, Dad, not for Mom," Liska said. "You have to answer, okay? Let's say you wake up and the house is burning down and you have just enough time to rescue one of us. Who would it be?"

"That's easy," I replied. "I'd save Rosie."

Rosie was our golden retriever. My flip response evoked some laughs and groans around the table — from Liska, too, although I could tell she wasn't satisfied, even after I somberly explained that I would rather not survive such a tragedy than have to choose which of my children would live. I knew that in her heart she was certain my true, secret answer was Mike or Steve. Nothing I could say would convince her that losing either of my adopted daughters would be just as devastating to me as losing one of the sons I had fathered.

Eight years later, Liska came frighteningly close to getting a real-life test of her parental favoritism theories. No fire was involved, but the circumstances were equally harrowing.

It happened three nights before Christmas in 1989, as I lay in bed at our home in Eugene, Oregon, where Gloria and I had raised our four children. For hours I had been drifting in and out of troubled sleep when suddenly I was jolted fully awake by the sound of footsteps outside. Someone was approaching the house, crunching through a coating of frozen snow on our hundred-foot-long drive-way. Out at the end, on the street, a car engine purred, idling, waiting. Instantly I knew it must be Bernard Lee, keeping his promise of vengeance against the Bates family, especially Gloria — "that ol' white bitch," as he had called her repeatedly in obscenity-laced threats left on our telephone answering machine.

Bernard Lee was a Los Angeles car thief, ex-convict, cocaine addict, and black racist. Months earlier, while passing through Eugene, he had wooed away our twenty-year-old Liska, who hated nobody and loved just about everyone, including her white adoptive parents. At the time, Liska was attending a local community college, living in her own apartment, and supplementing her parental support by working part-time as a cashier at Burger King. That's where she met Lee, who stopped in for something to eat. He was good-looking and charismatic. In our community of one hundred thousand, with barely a sprinkling of people of color, Liska had never met anyone quite like Bernard Lee. He engaged in clever conversation with her at the cash register, then returned to meet her when she got off work. They went out together. He flattered her and talked about L.A. and told vague stories about his business dealings there. Liska was thoroughly charmed. Before long, he was staying at her apartment.

Much later, by the time Gloria and I found out about Lee, after he had returned to Los Angeles, Liska had made up her mind to join him there. We were horrified at her decision but were unable to stop her. That was Liska: once she had charted a course or formed an opinion, there was no talking her out of it — not if you were her parent or any other authority figure. At the time, she thought Gloria and I were letting our bias show. Our son Mike, then twenty-one, had traveled to Reno a short while before to spend time with a young woman we had never met; why shouldn't Liska go to Southern California to be with a young man we similarly had yet to meet? She didn't use the R-word, but she clearly was raising the race issue. Weren't Gloria and I assigning racial stereotypes to Bernard Lee? The fact that he was a young black male from Los Angeles did not make him a bum or a gangster, right? And after all of that, Liska dropped her bombshell: she was pregnant. Bernard Lee was not the father, but he wanted to marry her and support her and the baby, she said.

So Liska went to Los Angeles, where she moved in with Lee and gave birth to a son, Terrell. As the months rolled by, it did not take her long to discover that Lee had no intention of marrying her or getting a job or being the father figure she so desperately wanted for the baby. Instead, Lee introduced her and Terrell into a life of public assistance as his steady source of food, shelter, and welfare money for drugs. When she tried to change him, he threatened her. When she attempted to leave him, he beat her. Finally, Liska, now pregnant with Lee's child, made a clandestine, urgent telephone call home for help. We spirited her out of Los Angeles on the pretext of bringing her and the baby home to Oregon for Thanksgiving.

Lee had no difficulty figuring out what we had done. For a few weeks we screened his phone calls so he couldn't get through to Liska, and Gloria finally told him to quit calling. He complied for a while, and Gloria joined me on a mid-December business trip to New York, leaving Liska and the baby at home. While we were gone, Liska let the answering machine intercept all calls. On December 20 Lee abruptly resurfaced with a string of chilling recorded messages. Liska, nearly hysterical, called us that night in New York, and we flew home the next day. I immediately obtained a new, unlisted phone number and took the answering machine tape to the Eugene police. They still have a copy of it, and so do I:

(*beep*)

Yeah, Doug, this is Bernard. I want you to call me 'cause we gonna talk about a lotta shit. Tryin' to take away my family. Take away my family, I take away your family. I don' 'preciate that shit. You wanna be white, I'll be black. I'll show you black. Bye.

(*beep*)

The white bitch don't want to answer the phone. But that's all right, Liska. I'm gonna kill that white bitch you call your mama up there. Liska, I don't give a fuck about your punk ass and I'll kill every last one of them motherfuckers. I will be up there. That's a goddamn promise from me.

(*beep*)

Go ahead, Liska. Care about them white motherfuckers up there. Care about them when you go to their funeral. 'Cause like I said, I'm for real. Okay? I'm for real. And I know where you're at.

(beep)

One of you white trash better get your shit together 'cause one of you white trash is gonna end up comin' up dead. And I think it's gonna be that ol' white bitch. Liska, you think your ass gonna hide behind one a those white motherfuckers? Call a white man daddy? What kind of motherfuckin' shit is that? Suppose to be my bitch, callin' this white motherfucker daddy. He ain't even your daddy. He don't give a fuck about you.

(beep)

Altogether, Bernard Lee left thirteen messages during several frenzied hours that day while Liska was home alone except for the baby, terrified, refusing to pick up the phone. She believed Lee was capable of carrying out his threats, and she knew he had our address, on letters she had left behind. In his thirteenth call he said all he needed was "to get up some money for the gas" and he would be on his way. Then the calls stopped.

Police were no help the next day when Gloria and I returned home. A Eugene dispatcher wearily told me there wasn't a thing city police could do about threats telephoned from out of state. Maybe, she said, I should try the Federal Communications Commission or the California parole officer who was supposed to be supervising Bernard Lee. So I tracked down the parole officer by phone, but he was hurrying to leave his office for the holidays, and he said there was nothing he could do unless Lee actually violated his parole by leaving the state — or worse, by carrying out his threats.

"What am I supposed to do in the meantime?" I asked. "Buy a gun?"

"That wouldn't be a bad idea," he replied.

Today, long after hearing those footsteps crunching toward our house in the darkness, I'm still astonished at how quickly the adrenaline kicked in that night. My mind, despite being anesthetized hours earlier by too much punch at a Christmas party, quickly began computing how much time I had to sprint downstairs and load the new shotgun I'd hidden in the laundry room.

The Mossberg 12-gauge lay across several neat, dusty stacks of old *Rolling Stone* magazines, well out of Gloria's sight on a high shelf over the washer and dryer. Never fired, the gun was still in its box with the owner's manual I had yet to read. Next to it was a box of shells, still in a plastic Bi-Mart sack with the receipt from my purchase the previous day. Gloria and I hadn't stayed married more than twenty-five years by keeping such secrets from each other, but I didn't want her to know about the shotgun. Like me, she hated guns and didn't want them in the house. The main reason I sneaked the weapon home, though, was to spare her from knowing just how seriously I was taking Bernard Lee's threats. A former newspaper colleague, as a favor to me, had obtained a police background check on Lee and had found him to be a bit more of a felon than he had led Liska to believe. Besides his sentence for grand larceny, he'd served time in California's penitentiary at Chino for nonfatally shooting a white man in a street fight with apparent racial overtones. So I understood, while neither Gloria nor Liska did, what Bernard Lee meant by one of his more ominous threats:

(*beep*)

We gonna see now who got the upper hand, 'cause I got a precedent fuckin' with these white motherfuckers [who] fuck with me . . . And now we're gonna see who take away who. Like I said, I got a precedent.

(*beep*)

Liska had shown me a picture of Lee, photographed while he was in the penitentiary. Scowling at the camera and wearing a sleeveless T-shirt, his arms bulging from months of prison weightlifting, he looked menacing enough. Behind the scowl, though, he also appeared sad, and I felt pity for him. By Liska's account, he'd had a wretched life. Bernard Lee did not grow up with any of the advantages Liska Bates enjoyed, but that gave him no license to wreck her life, too, or to terrorize her family. I did not hate the man, but I feared him. And I knew he could get from Los Angeles to Eugene in fourteen or fifteen hours of hard driving.

Today I'm still faintly embarrassed when I recall that I tried initially to buy a .357-caliber Magnum, made legendary by all those Clint Eastwood movies. As much as I disliked guns, I figured that if I was going to buy one, it might as well be the most lethal handgun I could think of. So that's what I asked for when I went to Bi-Mart's gun counter. The clerk, however, frowned as he enlightened me about the state's two-week waiting period for handguns.

"What do you want it for?" he asked. His eyes and body language let me know he was sure I was a novice crook nervously planning my first convenience-store holdup.

"Personal protection," I replied. I was completely caught off guard by how flustering it was to admit that I was purchasing a gun for reasons other than hunting or target practice. This was totally out of character for me. I was a bookish author and former newspaper editor, not an outdoorsman. Other customers were watching. I pinked up like a teen-ager buying condoms for the first time.

The clerk pointed out that I *could* take a rifle home the same day, and he suggested the shotgun. "Statistically, it's much safer than a handgun, anyway," he said.

That night as the footsteps approached, I swiftly calculated that Bernard Lee would reach the house before I could possibly bolt downstairs and figure out how to load the new 12-gauge. I also made a quick mental blueprint of the house and an inventory of those in harm's way: Liska and Terrell, asleep downstairs in a guest bedroom; Mike, twenty-one, home for the holidays and sleeping downstairs in the den; twenty-three-year-old Lynn and her two little ones, Sofia and baby Zack, also home for Christmas and asleep upstairs in the loft; and Gloria, still slumbering beside me.

That totaled seven: wife, three children, and three grandchildren — all of the people I cherished most, except for Steve, our oldest child. He was twenty-four, supporting himself as a carpenter and living at his own home, only a mile or so from ours. But even with him absent, it appeared that Liska was finally going to find out whom Dad would try to save first when the house caught fire — or, in this case, when the bogeyman came.

So whom would I save first? I was ill prepared to save anybody, especially if Lee had come armed, as I was sure he had. I decided to wake Gloria, dial 911 and summon the police, then dash downstairs and do whatever I could to protect my family while waiting for help.

First, though, I considered yelling something out the open bedroom window. Perhaps that would slow Lee down, I thought. Maybe it would even discourage him, making him turn back and clear out. I put my face to the window screen and bellowed a single word, in my deepest voice, which echoed throughout our peacefully sleeping neighborhood: "HEY!"

The footsteps halted. There was no reply. I could see the lights of the idling car at the end of the driveway, swathed in exhaust, but I couldn't make out the driver behind the wheel. Nor could I see Bernard Lee on the driveway, and that made me regret I hadn't left our outdoor Christmas lights burning all night. I'd strung hundreds of colored bulbs along the house and on the fence beside the driveway, all the way out to the street. No intruder could have sneaked to the house unseen if I'd been just a little less energy-conscious.

Gloria was awake now, startled and sitting up in bed. Relief swept over me as I realized my outburst had apparently stopped Lee. Emboldened, I bellowed a second time, bluffing: "I've called the cops! They're on their way!"

No reply. And still no footsteps. Not a bad sign, I thought. As I picked up the telephone and began to dial 911, a voice called up from the driveway, not far below the bedroom window, "It's just me."

It was not the same baritone voice I'd heard on the answering machine tape. This intruder was younger, and after a pause he called up again: "I'm the paperboy."

Gloria grabbed our alarm clock and looked at it. "It's five-thirty A.M. He always comes at five-thirty!"

Oh, God, I thought. And that must be his father out in the car, taking the kid on his route because of the icy streets. Numbly I watched as Gloria leaned to the screen and yelled into the darkness, "It's okay. Never mind."

She switched on a light and eyed me with concern as I silently put on a robe, feeling partly ridiculous but mostly outraged at the element of fear that had violated our home. As I headed downstairs I checked on Lynn and her kids in the loft. They had slept through all the yelling. The house was cold, but Sofia was half out of her sleeping bag, as usual. I covered her and put an extra blanket on Zack, who was wheezing a little with a nasty cold. Lynn was suffering from the same virus. Poor Lynn. She had been dealing with all sorts of adversity lately, particularly her separation from her husband, Mustafa.

Downstairs, I looked in on Mike, still asleep in the den. Then I softly entered the spare bedroom and found Liska and Terrell, both sleeping soundly. Terrell, five months old, was in a bassinet. He was an adorable baby, and I wanted to pick him up and hold him but thought better of it. That might wake him, which would mean a diaper change, and I was never a dedicated person in that regard. In the glow from his night light, Terrell was a tiny, doll-like version of his mother, and I guessed that he looked strikingly like Liska as an infant. We have no baby pictures of Liska, an injustice that saddens her whenever she looks through our family albums. Gloria and I had taken scores of snapshots of baby Terrell, perhaps unconsciously compensating for the missing photographic record of Liska's first years of life. And she seemed to appreciate our compulsive camera-clicking as a sign of our acceptance of her out-of-wedlock baby.

I gently closed the bedroom door and went out to the kitchen. As I made coffee, my hands shook slightly. The aroma of the freshly ground beans was overpowered by the scent of the Douglas fir I'd put up on a stand the day before in the living room. The Christmas tree fragrance — for all of my forty-three years associated with the happiest times of life — was now disorienting. Next year, would the familiar evergreen scent trigger fear and dread?

Our golden retriever was scratching on the door of the laundry room, where she slept every night. I put her outside, realizing she hadn't barked at the intruder. Of course not, I thought, upset with myself. The paperboy always comes at five-thirty.

Back in the laundry room, I reached high and pushed the new firearm farther back out of sight. Then I poured some coffee and took it to a kitchen nook overlooking our back yard, where the dog was enthusiastically exploring the frozen landscape, her breath visible in vaporous puffs. As I sat there watching her, with the long winter night gradually turning to light, I glumly assessed what had become of our twenty-year family experiment in race relations.

Let's see, I said to myself. Today is the last day of Hanukkah, two days before Christmas, and a dangerous felon is heading for my home with homicidal intentions. Our two adopted girls have grown up and multiplied and come back to us in misery, so now we have a house overflowing with children and an additional one on the way. What else? Oh yes, I'm not wealthy enough to provide for all of these people, and to be frank, I'm terribly worried about what's going to happen to them.

Sick with guilt and self-pity, I pondered how we had reached this point. Gloria and I were far from perfect parents and had made many mistakes. But we had tried hard to make the girls feel loved, to help them be proud of their ancestry, and to give them many privileges of the American middle class: a stable and comfortable home, a safe neighborhood, excellent schools, summer camp, annual vacation trips, and the opportunity to go to college with financial support from home. We had envisioned successful careers for Lynn and Liska, along with happiness and wonderful sons-in-law — probably black, and that was just fine. In a private fantasy born of 1960s liberalism, I even imagined all of us — with beautiful grandchildren in tow — someday traveling to Africa to see the great land of our daughters' ancestors. I had always thought this exotic pilgrimage, financially impossible for us while we were raising our family, would come later in life as a spiritual and symbolic capstone on the Bates family's interracial adventure.

Now it was achingly clear to me that few of my treasured dreams for Lynn and Liska had come true, and they did not seem likely to. Instead of airplane tickets to Africa, my biggest expenditure for the family this Christmas was for a shotgun hidden in the laundry room.

What, I wondered, had gone wrong for my daughters? For that matter, what had gone wrong for our country? Two decades earlier, when Gloria and I adopted the girls, race relations in the United

States seemed to be brimming with hope and promise. The civil rights movement had scored tremendous victories. Black nationalism was fading fast as a viable cause, the peace movement was sweeping the land, a new "war on poverty" was under way, the urban riots seemed to have awakened white America, and our nation appeared to be ready, finally, to address the social needs of its oppressed minorities.

All of it had been a mirage, I realized as I brooded in the kitchen nook that December morning in 1989. Instead of entering an age of enlightenment, our society had lost its way and now was exhausted by its racial difficulties. Anyone who read newspapers was aware of our litany of woes: inner-city poverty was worse, unemployment and crime and drug abuse were soaring, family breakup was rising, education was deteriorating, and, in the most widely reported statistic of all, more young African-American men were in jail than in college. The saddest part, I thought, was that the nation's white leadership, instead of trying to heal and unify the separate Americas, was at best indifferent to minority issues and was at worst cynically exploiting them, blaming the victims and perfecting the politics of race. In my darkest thoughts, I felt that our neglectful leaders had created the Bernard Lees of this land and now were calling attention to them to fuel the racial fears of white America.

George Bush was using the black rapist and killer Willie Horton to win votes, no matter what the cost to American race relations. In the meantime, at one end of the country, New York was engorged with racial hatred and fear after a gang of black youths had raped and savagely beaten a twenty-nine-year-old white jogger. And at the other end, Oregon was no oasis of brotherly love, either; white skinheads with baseball bats had fatally beaten a black man in Portland around that time, and white supremacists with assault rifles were target-shooting in the woods.

I was disappointed in the leaders of black America, too. How could they have allowed the historic civil rights momentum of the 1960s to slip away? Where was the next great leader, the next Martin Luther King, Jr.? Why were his would-be successors so ineffective, so divisive, so content to blame whites for all African-

American problems? And how, I wondered, could our black leaders stoop to anti-Semitism, anti-Asian rhetoric, and the same politics of race that white leaders were exploiting?

I felt betrayed. It seemed to me we had made hardly any progress as a people since 1970, and in many ways we had actually gone backward. This was not the kind of society I had anticipated for my children.

The coffee in my cup, untouched, had turned cold as I bitterly mused. I realized the house was freezing. As I got up to turn on the heat, I felt disgusted with my thoughts. Lots of parents — black or white, adoptive or "natural" — end up disappointed in the way things turn out for their children. I decided to think more positively and to quit feeling sorry for myself. But as I poured more coffee, all the old doubts — ones Gloria and I had wrestled with twenty years earlier — came roaring back, along with some new questions.

Why would a white professional couple, already raising two young sons of their own making, adopt black daughters in the early 1970s, thereby subjecting the entire family to the racial tensions that continue to be America's most pressing social problem?

How could white parents, despite good intentions, possibly provide black children with the emotional tools they would need as adults to cope with this dual society? Is it true that only black families can give African-American children the upbringing they need? Would black parents have had better success protecting our Liska from a predator like Bernard Lee?

Is there such a thing as racial and social predestination in America? Are my adopted daughters, despite their middle-class upbringing, somehow foreordained to gravitate to the impoverished class of their biological parents? Or would environment finally triumph over biology, as the behavioral scientist B. F. Skinner was arguing at the time we adopted our girls?

I also asked myself whether black critics were correct, after all, in opposing interracial adoption, seeing it as a form of cultural genocide that robs black children of racial pride and turns them into "white niggers" who have lost contact with their heritage and the black experience. And I wondered again whether Caucasian critics were correct in questioning the motives of the white adoptive parents. Did we adopt our daughters to flaunt our liberalism? to resolve our racial guilt? to settle some other personal or social problems? Did we naïvely set out to build world brotherhood without recognizing the personal consequences for the children?

Maybe, I grimly reasoned, it had been a terrible mistake. After all, Gloria and I had been dead wrong in 1970 about the nation's prospects for racial harmony. Perhaps we had been equally wrong about the wisdom of interracial adoption. The critics appeared to be right: Gloria and I had been ill equipped to raise black children. We had reared our girls in a sheltered white world, and now they were young women stepping forth into a hostile, fractured society that defined them almost solely by the color of their skin. They were hardly prepared for the full force of white rejection, they were naïve about the realities of the black community, and they were sitting ducks for the likes of Bernard Lee.

On that dreary winter morning in 1989, I had no way of knowing that my real showdown with Lee was only hours away. He was, at that hour, unbeknownst to me, stealing a car for his mission to Oregon. Nor did I have any inkling that the events of that gloomy holiday season would set me forth on a bumpy spiritual journey of sorts. Over the next three years, as American race relations would horrendously worsen, this odyssey would carry me through some grit and heartbreak on the way to understanding what I had done over the past twenty years. Eventually I would discover that love is the only thing that's real, that my children were special gifts, and that I'd do it all again.

❧ 2 ❧

Small-Town Kids

Dear Mr. and Mrs. Bates:

Your application to adopt a child through the Oregon Public Welfare Division was received in this office on April 3, 1970. It will remain on file for one year. When children become available to this agency for adoptive planning, certain applicants will be selected for study who appear to meet the needs of these children. If your home is selected, you will be notified.

Letter from Barbara Davis, Adoptions Supervisor
April 1970

WHEN GLORIA AND I LOOK BACK, we see only one extraordinary thing about our otherwise ordinary, white, middle-class lives: we were the parents of two black children by the time we were twenty-five years old, but neither of us had ever had a truly meaningful conversation with an African-American. Our early exposure to black people was so utterly limited that both of us still remember those few occasions with great clarity today — proof, if any is needed, that we were a most unlikely couple to undertake the cross-racial commitment that has dominated most of our years together. Understanding why we took Lynn and Liska into our lives requires a glimpse at who we are, where we came from, and what we experienced long before such a notion ever occurred to us.

Gloria and I have similar roots. Knowing the background of one of us almost suffices for comprehending that of the other. Both of us were born in October 1946, only twenty-five days apart, in small towns separated by eighty miles of lush farmland in Oregon's Willamette Valley. Our fathers had just returned safely from the war, making us part of the nation's first class of baby boomers. Both of our dads became small-town businessmen with typically conservative Republican leanings, and our mothers were homemakers. None of our parents had a college education, yet they provided us with a level of affluence far beyond what they had known as Depression-era children. We grew up in virtually all-white communities, attended public schools, went to church on Sunday, and never questioned that we were expected to go on to college and represent the first generation of Bateses and Burtons to do so.

Oregon, at the time we were born, had yet to reach its first million in population. The state had only a few thousand African-Americans, most of them in Portland, the only Oregon city of substantial size. Neither Gloria nor I can remember seeing a black person in the flesh until we were teen-agers.

Gloria grew up in Junction City, a lovely, quiet farm town of about four thousand people near the southern end of the Willamette Valley. Grass seed and mint are the major crops there today, although the area's rich bottom land also is known for bountiful orchards, sweet corn, green beans, and berries. Named for the convergence of two railroads, Junction City attracted large clans of Swedish, Finnish, Danish, and Norwegian settlers in the nineteenth century. Their descendants still heavily populate the area today, giving the community a regional reputation for its annual Scandinavian Festival. Gloria, however, descended from Anglo-Saxon farmers and shopkeepers. She was the older of two daughters born to the Junction City natives Merle and Mildred Burton. They were a civicly active couple who prospered throughout the 1950s and early 1960s from Merle's successful Chevrolet dealership and used car business. Gloria's upbringing was as WASPish as any child could have. She cannot remember any discussion involving race, or even any remarks about the subject, as she was growing up.

"I never saw a black person, except on TV, until I was in junior high school," she says. "It sounds hard to believe, but I didn't even realize they were real until a black girl moved to Junction City when I was in the eighth grade.

"That's probably why I didn't know what the words meant in some of our childhood games and rhymes, like 'Catch a nigger by the toe,' or Ring Around the Rosy, which always ended with 'Last one down is a nigger baby.' I literally didn't know what a nigger baby was. I didn't know what nigger meant, or what it meant to use such a word. My parents always put out a big bowl of 'nigger toes' — Brazil nuts — at Christmas. And in high school my best friend's black cat was named Nig. We'd go out in the neighborhood and call, 'Here, Nig! Here, Nig!' "

But Gloria found herself pulled toward children from other ethnic and cultural backgrounds. One school year her best friend — "my *only* friend, actually," she recalls — was a tall, shy Native American girl, who later moved away. Another year her best pal was a Mennonite girl who felt like an outcast because she had to wear plain clothing and put her hair up in an unfashionable manner. Later, toward the middle of Gloria's eighth year in school, a beautiful new girl enrolled at Junction City. She was black, the first African-American Gloria had ever seen. They quickly became friends.

"I don't know exactly why I was drawn to her," Gloria says. "She didn't have a lot of self-confidence, and neither did I, so maybe that was the reason. I didn't think of her as 'Negro.' I just thought of her as pretty. I liked the way she looked, the color of her skin. She also seemed a little frightened, kind of alone, and really nice. We sat together every day at lunch and talked. And then she was gone — moved away, after just a couple of months."

Gloria never saw her again. Nor did she have occasion to speak to another black person for many years to come — unless you count her fellow white students made up in blackface for a high school minstrel show that Gloria declined to join. She did not know why at the time, but something about white kids painting their faces black, singing plantation songs, and acting goofy made her uncomfortable.

In 1963, during her junior year of high school, Gloria's father announced that he was buying a lucrative new Chevrolet dealership and moving the family to another Oregon town, named Oakridge. For Gloria, the news of being uprooted just before her senior year came as a shock, one of those bigger-than-life traumas that make teen-agers briefly think they hate their parents. But given no choice in the matter, she went along with the move, sulking all the way and having no idea that this twist of fate would soon introduce her to the young man she would marry.

Oakridge, the Cascade Range town where I grew up, was known for its big sawmills and plywood plants and vast logging operations in the surrounding forests. The community's setting was gorgeous; the town was framed by emerald green mountains, snowcapped Diamond Peak, and several sparkling streams prized by anglers. The Chamber of Commerce promoted Oakridge as "the tree-planting capital of the world." Citizens celebrated that boast in a community festival each spring by trekking into nearby woods to plant thousands of Douglas fir seedlings. In reality, Oakridge was America's tree-*cutting* capital. More timber was harvested annually from the surrounding national forest than from any other in the United States.

In the decade following World War II, as troops came home and the nation's need for lumber to build houses soared, Oakridge's population doubled, to about four thousand. In the late 1950s the town swelled even more as large construction crews arrived to work on a major flood-control dam nearby on the middle fork of the Willamette River. Just as Gloria's father located in Oakridge to sell Chevy pickups to all those laborers, my father went into business there to sell them work boots and wool socks.

I was the second of the five children of John and Patricia Bates. They, like Gloria's parents, were prominent in civic affairs and enjoyed modest prosperity. My father's store was small but successful.

Unlike Gloria's girlhood community of well-to-do farmers, Oakridge was a rough, blue-collar town. That probably explains why I discovered fairly young what "nigger" meant. I also learned at an early age that my parents did not want me saying that word or any other racial epithet, at home or anywhere else. Even "nigger toes" was an unacceptable expression around the Christmas nut bowl. My parents were not necessarily more racially sensitive than Gloria's. Rather, our parents' racial views and vocabularies simply mirrored the sensibilities of their white peers in the communities they lived in. "Nigger" was everyday language among Oakridge millworkers but not among merchants and the town's handful of professional people. My parents and their circle of friends considered that label vulgar and redneck. Their acceptance of racial diversity, though, was probably not much more highly developed than that of the millworkers and loggers.

Oakridge was just like Junction City in one respect: it was not a town where African-Americans were made to feel welcome. In fact, the absence of nonwhites was celebrated by the local newspaper, the *Oakridge Telegram*, in a weekly column called "Shangri-la of the Cascades." Every Thursday the column reminded Oakridge readers of the virtues of living in our Cascade mountain community. I especially remember one late-1950s piece pointing out that our town was "close-knit" and had none of the racial unrest that plagued some large U.S. cities. This was certainly true; it's hard to have racial unrest where there's no racial diversity. It was during the summer of my thirteenth year, when I was hosing off the sidewalk in front of my dad's store, that I began to understand the racial homogeneity of the Shangri-la of the Cascades.

I hated waiting on customers, so for twenty-five cents an hour I spent as much time hosing the sidewalk as I could get away with, being careful to shut off the spray whenever somebody walked by. One day that summer I had to shut off the spray for a man who came trudging up First Street, the town's main business thorough-fare, with a shabby suitcase in one hand and a crumpled paper bag in the other. Each of us said hello, and it was no big deal, except that the fellow was black — the first African-American I had ever spoken to and the first nonwhite I'd ever seen walking past John's Shoes & Sportswear.

The novelty apparently wasn't lost on the Oakridge Police Department, either. By the time the stranger had walked a block and a half past me, the city's lone police cruiser pulled up beside him. I stopped spraying again as I watched the officer get out and question the man, then put him in the car and drive off.

I might have forgotten the incident if it hadn't been for the next edition of the *Oakridge Telegram*. It proclaimed, in bold headline type: NEGRO ARRESTED ON FIRST STREET. The story beneath the headline said police had stopped a "suspicious-looking colored man" and had charged him with vagrancy. Naïve sidewalk-hoser that I was in those days, I did not know what vagrancy was. At the dinner table I asked about it and my dad explained. I listened, thought about it a while, and replied that it did not seem fair to arrest people and put them in jail just because they had no home or job. And even if it *were* fair, how did the officer know this stranger was a vagrant? What made him "suspicious-looking"?

He was a Negro, my dad replied.

I was barely aware of the concept of racial prejudice and discrimination at that stage. But I clearly remember being bothered. "That doesn't seem right," I said.

"It isn't," my dad responded.

And that was it. Just two words, probably the most enlightened thing I ever heard him say on the subject of race. But it had an enormous impact on me. I idolized my father, a tall, always composed man whose distinguished good looks remind many people of the actor Sean Connery. And here he was, agreeing that I — a skinny little teen-ager going through my most awkward years — had figured out a basic truth, all by myself. Inside, I swelled with pride. Long forgotten by everyone else at the dinner table that night, the moment remains lucid for me as one of a handful of boyhood incidents that probably helped set my moral compass.

It would be misleading, though, to paint my father as some sort of small-town civil rights champion like Atticus Finch, the fictional dad in *To Kill a Mockingbird*. Harper Lee's novel about racism in a small Alabama town found its way into our home in 1960, when my parents belonged to a book club. My mother read it and praised it. So did some of us five kids, but my dad did not read it. The books were for us, not for him. He worked mind-numbing hours to support the family and had little time for reading anything beyond the daily newspaper. That was his primary source of information about matters of race.

Like Gloria's father and both of our mothers, John Bates had lived his entire life in small Oregon towns devoid of people of color. He seldom mentioned the subject, other than to voice respect for Negro athletes, musicians, and entertainers. Once I heard him express scorn for the Ku Klux Klan and Southern bigotry. Another time, however, as we watched a professional football game on our old black and white Zenith, I heard him refer to Negro players as "smokes." My father was no Atticus Finch, but like my mother, and like Merle and Mildred Burton, John Bates was a fair-minded person. Usually his actions revealed far more about him than his words.

A year after the stranger walked by my father's store, a black woman settled in Oakridge. She and her four children lived in a run-down rental house on a side street. Her name was Ann. Around the first of the month, Ann would sometimes bring her children into the store and buy a few things for them. Occasionally, if her public assistance check arrived on a Saturday, when the town's only bank was closed, she would ask my father to cash it for her. But one summer day Ann and her brood came into the store in the middle of the month. My dad had gone to lunch, leaving me in charge for an hour, so I waited on Ann. Her shabby shoes were falling apart — literally splitting open at the seams and soles. She said her feet hurt. But Ann had no check to cash, no money at all. She asked if she could charge a pair of shoes and make monthly payments for them.

I remember the incident particularly well because it made me feel so many different emotions. One of them was compassion. I wished I could simply give the woman some shoes and tell her to take her time paying for them. But I wasn't allowed to open new charge accounts; that was business my dad always handled. I had to ask Ann to wait for him to return from lunch.

For me, the wait must have seemed a lot longer than it did for Ann's children, who ran sort of wild around the store for the next half-hour or so. I felt considerable apprehension, knowing my dad was going to have to turn Ann down. A short time before, he had been forced to tighten up on credit because the business was in crisis over an ad he had placed in the *Oakridge Telegram*. Instead of buying a conventional weekly advertisement, my dad wrote a column, called "Feet First," which always ended with a plug for the store. He was a fine, clever writer, and his weekly ruminations were easily the best-read item in the town paper. (In fact, his flirtation with journalism did much to influence me in choosing a newspaper career.) But that summer, as unions at the mills threatened to strike, my dad had unwittingly created a nightmare for himself and our family by publishing a column opposing a walkout. He was not antiworker, just antistrike, arguing that a walkout would irreparably harm the community. But millworkers were outraged and organized a boycott of Dad's store. By the time Ann and her children came in that day, survival of the business required cash flow, not new charge accounts.

When my dad finally returned from lunch, I nervously explained Ann's request. He looked over at her and the youngsters she had somehow managed to calm down. They were a scruffy bunch, with clothes and shoes just about as shot as Ann's. But they all sat reasonably still beside her in a row of chairs facing the fitting bench. Dad sighed and told me he would deal with her. I was only too happy to distance myself from the unpleasant matter. There were no other customers in the store, thanks entirely to the boycott, so I took my turn and went home for lunch.

An hour later, when I returned, I was surprised to find Ann and her kids streaming out of the store. Ann was wearing a big smile and a new pair of shoes. So were all of her kids — with new stockings, too.

My dad never said a word about the episode. Eventually Ann moved away before accounts had been completely settled, but it didn't matter. John's Shoes & Sportswear survived that summer.

For me, the shoe store was much more than a learning ground; it was the place where I met Gloria in 1963, in our senior year of high school. After her transfer that year from Junction City we had seen each other at school and around town, and I had noticed her at her father's Chevrolet dealership, just across the street from my dad's store. From that distance, I perceived her to be (1) beautiful, (2) stuck up, (3) already taken by some guy in Junction City, and (4) too rich for me anyhow, because she had her own new Chevrolet 409 and I had no car at all.

That fall I had a chance to test all four of those perceptions when Gloria came into the store after school while I was working. She was shopping for a plastic rain slicker. As I waited on her, I discovered I had been right about two things: she was very nice looking, and she had a steady boyfriend back in Junction City. But I was wrong about her owning the gleaming new 409 and being conceited. The car was her dad's, and she was quite down-to-earth, friendly, and witty. As we talked a little about school, her remarks revealed an outsider's mild contempt for the popular elite of Oakridge High. She had not been made to feel welcome, she didn't *want* to feel welcome, and she couldn't wait to graduate and kiss this place goodbye. I was stunned. That was precisely the way I felt.

Gloria stayed in the store for nearly an hour. As my dad darted amused looks at us, I assisted her with picking out a rain jacket. Then a pair of fur-lined boots. And a pair of black slacks. And some nylon stockings. And a plastic rain bonnet. All of it, of course, she charged to her parents' account. By the time she left, we had discovered something else in common: her younger sister, Marilyn, was pals with one of my younger sisters, Jill. Soon afterward, Gloria and I communicated our mutual attraction in the most traditional and logical of ways: she told Marilyn and I told Jill.

Gloria and I quickly became best friends and were practically inseparable throughout our senior year. If it's true that the churn of world events can help shape personal relationships, ours was influenced that year, 1963–64, by some earth-shakers. The slaying of Medgar Evers and the huge march on Washington by black and white Americans sharpened our awareness of the nation's moral slumber on civil rights. "I have a dream," the most famous words of Martin Luther King, Jr., resonated in headlines and over the airwaves. The Vietnamese coup against the Diem regime heightened our concern about U.S. military involvement in Southeast Asia. And the assassination of John F. Kennedy, announced over school loudspeakers as Gloria and I stood together in the cafeteria lunch line, shattered all of our snug, secure feelings about the future.

In the fall of 1964 we enrolled together at the University of Oregon. With about ten thousand students then, it was the state's largest liberal arts school, located in Eugene, downstream from Oakridge on the banks of the Willamette River. Gloria majored in sociology and I chose journalism. Both of us were good students, but we were less than competent in certain subjects, most notably the intricacies of birth control. By the end of our freshman year, we were married and the parents of a handsome baby boy whom we named Steve. Thanks to scholarships, low-rent student housing, and a part-time job at the Eugene newspaper, I was able to continue in school. Gloria chose to stay home with Steve, to earn money providing childcare, and to defer her formal education — informally, though, she learned much by helping me with my studies and simply by living on campus during that turbulent time.

Eugene was then a cozy college town of about seventy thousand people. It was only forty-three miles from Oakridge, but for us two small-town kids it was light-years away. We were suddenly exposed to ideas and people we had never dreamed existed. University life became a steamy broth stirred by antiwar fervor, flower power, civil rights activism, and black nationalism.

Both Gloria and I began learning that there was far more to black America than TV celebrities, the Oakridge vagrant, the family on welfare, or even the angry young Black Panthers who were marching on campus. I found myself totally entranced by a black literature class. It introduced me to the works of Ralph Ellison, Richard Wright, James Baldwin, Margaret Walker Alexander, Langston Hughes, and many other great African-American writers I had never heard of. Later, after a chain of racial disorders in Detroit and twenty-two other American cities in the summer of 1967, I enrolled in a course called "Black Power and Urban Unrest." Required reading included *The Autobiography of Malcolm X* and the Kerner Commission Report, spawned by the 1967 riots.

It ominously warned that America was becoming "two societies, one black, one white — separate and unequal." Ironically, I was sitting in that class, discussing that chilling prophecy, on April 4, 1968, the day Martin Luther King, Jr., was shot to death in Memphis.

By the time my graduation neared, two months after the assassination of King, Gloria and I were not the same people who had left sleepy Oakridge four years earlier. As the country had changed, we had changed. We bitterly opposed the war in Vietnam, we supported Robert F. Kennedy for president, and we wanted an end to racism in American society. As we reached age twenty-one that year, we discovered we could not politely discuss any of those views — or any others related to war, politics, or race — with our parents. They, along with the rest of what was called "the establishment" in those days, were appalled by the noisy uproar from our generation. Instead of being influenced positively, they reacted with fear and disgust. In our view, they prolonged the war and further polarized the nation by putting Richard Nixon in the White House. His ascendancy, of course, got an enormous, tragic boost just three days after I received my bachelor's degree in journalism, when the assassin Sirhan Bishara Sirhan removed Kennedy from Nixon's path to the presidency.

Gloria and I were angry young adults, but we were not activists or even active protesters. We were far too busy working, caring for Steve, and getting me through school. Gloria's father gave us a 1955 Chevy from his used car lot, but otherwise we fully supported ourselves from the day we got married. Thus my only contribution to any social cause my senior year was a letter published in the campus daily — a piece my older brother, Tom, a *real* antiwar protester and leftist, ridiculed.

I wrote the letter to the *Oregon Daily Emerald* after being impressed by an incident at an Oregon–UCLA basketball game. As a soloist sang the national anthem, a large cluster of African-Americans in the student section refused to stand with the rest of the crowd in sold-out McArthur Court. Instead, the blacks loudly heckled the singer, mocking the lyrics with catcalls and shouts such as

"Go, LBJ, go!" At the conclusion, after many whites in the arena booed, a young black man who *had* stood for the anthem, a few rows down in front of the demonstrators, turned and scowled up at them. "You all keep on like that," he yelled, "and you'll *never* be set free." For that, he was jeered by his fellow blacks. In my letter describing the incident, I expressed admiration for his courage. I also agreed with him that the demonstrators' conduct would do more harm than good, though I shared their hate for the war and racism.

After the letter was published, I sent a clipping to my brother Tom, then a graduate student at the University of Wisconsin. He wrote back that he found my piece well-written — "and just about as fascist" as some of his own writings as an undergraduate. I was hurt. Tom was my hero. He was everything I felt I could not be — a gifted athlete, a Fulbright scholar, a talented writer, a peace advocate with enough courage to go to jail for his convictions. I had not expected his put-down. Nor had I expected another, quite different reaction to my letter: a compliment from the university's dean of journalism. Not long after praising the piece, he recommended me, without my asking, for employment as a beginning reporter at the *Daily Chronicle* in Spokane, Washington. I went to work at the *Chronicle* two weeks after graduation and one day after Gloria gave birth to our second son, Mike.

We enjoyed life in Spokane, a beautiful small city of many parks and thundering waterfalls near Washington's northeastern border with Idaho. But Spokane was also a highly conservative city, far more so than Eugene, and the newspaper that employed me was the most vocal protector of the community's resistance to change. The *Chronicle*'s news policies and editorial positions, particularly those involving the war and civil rights, made me cringe. I kept a personal journal during our year in Spokane, and many of the entries reveal how out of place I felt. On January 4, 1969, I wrote:

Found out *Chronicle* society desk won't run pictures of racially mixed marriages. White college girl and black African student came in today to get marriage announcement in paper. Editor lady let them fill out the forms, accepted their photograph. They asked when it would appear and were told *story only* would appear within two weeks. Picture was "against company policy." Couple were incensed, withdrew the announcement and left. I witnessed this and felt bad rest of day. Later I asked society editor why such a policy. Reply: not felt to be in best interest of community, as black and white marriages usually ill-founded. I said: with this kind of discrimination, it's no wonder! Also, was told that "regular" society people and news contacts would be offended to have their photos appear alongside those of racially mixed couples.

Later that year, thirty-six African-Americans and six whites from the Spokane area were arrested in an incident in the tiny farm town of Colfax, south of the city. Police moved in on them after they peacefully blocked, for twenty-four hours, the jailing of five Washington State University black students arrested in a campus melee. I covered the trial, in which all forty-two were convicted of unlawful assembly. Each was fined $25 and placed on probation. Although their attorney had referred to defendants as "blacks" throughout the trial, *Chronicle* editors changed all those references in my stories to "Negroes." That did not bother me nearly as much as the newspaper's subsequent editorial page stance, criticizing the sentences as too light. There was no acknowledgment whatsoever that the protest had been nonviolent and based on legitimate concerns about justice and race.

The paper's ultra-hawkish position on the Vietnam War was also troubling to me. Even on the news pages, the *Chronicle* skewed reality in its slanted selection, editing, and play of war reports. YANKS MAUL RED UNIT was typical of the misleading, jingoistic headlines placed on the front page day after day by editors treating Vietnam as if it were World War II. While much of the rest of the news industry was slowly beginning to question the war, the *Daily Chronicle* was only digging in.

The newspaper's hidebound practices embarrassed me. After a frustrating year there, I applied for work at the Eugene paper, the *Register-Guard*, a much more progressive publication in a considerably more liberal community. The Eugene editors offered me a reporting job in their suburban Cottage Grove bureau. So in mid-

1969 Gloria and I moved back to Oregon with our two little boys and felt, with great relief, that we had come home.

By 1970 Gloria was beginning to talk about having another baby. Steve was almost five, Mike was one and a half, and Gloria wanted a daughter. I was not enthusiastic about the idea. It seemed to me that our first five years of marriage had been a stifling life of final exams, maternity clothes, and babies in diapers. I'd had enough of it. Selfishly, I felt that I had sacrificed the traditional fun part of college life by being a young parent while getting my degree. I was ready to stop with the two boys and begin enjoying our newfound freedom to go on fishing trips and other family outings in which infants only get in the way.

Gloria disagreed. She didn't mind at all the notion of more babies. She deeply wanted a daughter, and she was enamored of the idea of a larger family, like the one I came from. Gloria had been charmed by Bates family reunions. Whenever she saw me and my two brothers and two sisters and the rest of our big Catholic family all together at once, we seemed to have fantastic fun compared with the more staid gatherings of her small clan of Methodist teetotalers.

I, too, liked the idea of a big family, but not if it meant more babies. I also pointed out, quite correctly, that there was no guarantee that Gloria would end up with a daughter. "Look at my parents," I argued. "It wasn't till their fourth try that they got a girl — first Tom, then me, then my brother Dan, and then finally Jill and Jamie." It was possible, I said, that Bates sperm was male-dominated, and maybe we'd have to have seven or eight babies before a girl would show up.

It was at that point that the earth shifted and our lives took off in a different direction. "Okay," Gloria said. "I want a daughter, and you don't object to the concept, but you don't want to be tied down with another baby. So maybe we should adopt a girl — an older child."

What was going on in the world at that time certainly helped shape the personal decisions Gloria and I were making. The Vietnam War continued to rage, and dozens of soldiers from the Eugene area were being killed. Part of my job as a reporter involved going to dead soldiers' homes and asking for photos to publish in the paper. Both Gloria and I were more outraged by the fighting than ever before. The My Lai massacre had been exposed around that time, and the University of Oregon campus was erupting in violence. Meanwhile, across the nation, cities were fighting court-ordered school integration; the Black Panthers were self-destructing, their leaders in exile; the FBI was searching for Angela Davis, implicated in the Soledad Brothers shooting in California; the Elks organization had voted nationally to keep its whites-only rule; Richard Nixon had nominated Harrold Carswell, a segregationist, to the Supreme Court; and the White House was standing behind U.S. ties to South Africa even after that country had denied a visa to the black tennis star Arthur Ashe. In America, the civil rights movement was plainly dying, and we were chagrined.

Not long after Gloria had raised adoption as a possibility, we mentioned the idea over dinner at the home of our closest friends, Mike and Sandy Thoele. Like me, Mike was a *Register-Guard* reporter; he was assigned to the paper's bureau in Junction City, where Gloria grew up. We had much in common with Mike and Sandy, who had a baby daughter named Tiffan, yet we were astounded at their response. They, too, were considering adoption! And Gloria and I were particularly impressed by their statement that it didn't matter to them whether their new daughter turned out to be white, black, Asian, Indian, or Eskimo. Race was not a factor. They would love her regardless.

We were tremendously influenced by our friends the Thoeles, and by current events that made us want to do things to help America's tattered society as well as ourselves. Today, that admission may sound pious, or at best hopelessly idealistic. But it was exactly how we looked at the world in 1970, and we were not alone.

A few weeks after visiting the Thoeles, Gloria and I contacted the Oregon Children's Services Division and asked them to begin adoption proceedings. We told them our reasons were not complicated. We wanted a daughter — an older child, preferably one who badly needed permanent parents. Race, we told the agency, did not matter.

Setting the wheels in motion was surprisingly easy. The state bureaucracy was no slow train but a speeding locomotive. Within four months it brought us a daughter who turned out to be healthy, beautiful, and black.

Looking back, Gloria and I are still amazed at how little questioning went into our decision. We never talked to any African-Americans about our intentions. We did not consider possible negative outcomes. We didn't even think about the economic expense of raising an extra child. In those days, like many of our friends from that era, we were guided by a much less complicated notion: if it feels right, do it.

Compared with our adoption decision, Gloria and I would expend far more time and energy a decade later researching the purchase of our first VCR.

❧ 3 ❧

Lynn, the Pet Shop Girl

Your petitioners, J. Douglas Bates and Gloria J. Bates, husband and wife, respectfully petition the court for an order of adoption and change of name of Regina Lynn Garrett and in support of this petition, state as follows:

That your petitioner, J. Douglas Bates, is a member of the Caucasian race . . .

That your petitioner, Gloria J. Bates, is a member of the Caucasian race . . .

Petition for Adoption
Lane County Circuit Court, Eugene, Oregon
October 1971

NOT COUNTING TIME in the womb, Regina Lynn Garrett's relationship with her biological mother lasted less than seventy-two hours. On the third day after her birth, the baby was taken from the young woman, who was promptly returned to prison. The birth was recorded at 10:22 A.M. on February 13, 1966, at Salem General Hospital, not far from the Oregon Women's Correctional Center, where the mother was serving a sentence for drug possession. The father was nearby in the men's penitentiary on related charges. Pending the couple's release, Regina Lynn Garrett was placed in temporary foster care.

The foster parents lived in a tiny rural community a few miles outside Eugene. They called the infant Lynn. She was expected to stay in the home only a few months, until her parents were paroled. When they eventually left prison, however, they quickly disappeared without claiming their baby. So Lynn remained in foster care while the Oregon Children's Services Division tried to track down the absent parents and reunite them with the child. The reunion would would never happen.

Lynn today knows little about the troubled couple who created her life. State officials have described the birth mother only as nineteen years old, white, pretty, and addicted to heroin. While serving time for drug offenses at Oregon's Hillcrest juvenile home, she was let out to attend a beauty school. During her release, she became pregnant with Lynn and was arrested for possession of heroin along with Lynn's father, a young, light-complexioned black man whose last name was Garrett. The couple were not married, but the mother gave Lynn the name Garrett on her birth certificate, anticipating marriage after release from prison. That lone surname is Lynn's only clue to her biological parents' identities. Their names remain secret today, in sealed records.

The young woman was incarcerated early in her pregnancy, so the heroin addiction had no discernible effect on Lynn, who was born healthy, alert, and at normal weight. She was a darling baby with large brown eyes, skin like extra-light café au lait, and lots of soft, exceedingly curly, chestnut-colored hair.

Shortly after her parents left prison, they did get married. Then they vanished, inexplicably. After more than a year of unsuccessful attempts to locate the couple, state authorities began the laborious process of seeking a court order terminating the birth parents' rights and clearing Lynn for adoption. But as Lynn approached the age of two, the procedure was thrown off track when officials received a letter from the mother, in a neighboring state, requesting pictures of Lynn. That stalled the legal proceedings and rekindled the effort to reunite Lynn with her mother, but she quickly disappeared again. Eventually, the move for termination of rights was resumed, only to be interrupted twice more when Lynn's mother resurfaced — on both occasions when she was jailed in other states. Each time, she slipped away again upon her release without claiming her daughter.

Today, when Lynn analyzes her early development, she realizes how significantly her life was affected by her long wait for permanent parents. "There was a lot of anger in the foster home," she recalls now. "They were really angry people. I remember there was yelling all the time. There were several other foster kids who were a little older than me. I felt like an outcast. The love towards me — I never sensed any.

"I don't remember the foster mother very well. She was never really there. I don't know if she was working or just didn't pay any attention, but she really didn't seem *there*. What I do remember is that she just kind of stayed to herself. There was a lot of fighting. Of course, I thought it was all about me. I was always excluded from everyone else. They'd put me outside all the time. They would all be inside and I would be outdoors in this little walker thing. I could walk, but I'd always be in that walker."

A snapshot of Lynn at age seven months shows her with her foster parents, a somber, plain-looking middle-aged couple, both white, and five other children, also white, posing in front of a mobile home. One of the youngsters in the photo, a girl who looks about sixteen, was the only member of the family whom Lynn recalls warmly. "She was the older sister, the only one I can remember ever helping me or picking me up. She paid the most attention to me. I felt safe around her."

Until she was twenty-six, Lynn suppressed her unhappiest recollections of early childhood — her memories of rats. "My foster father frightened me," she says. "I don't remember any physical abuse. I really don't. But he really, *really* scared me." She recalls his killing rats, then dangling the dead rodents by their tails, in her face, as he threatened her. "He said that if I didn't straighten up and behave, or something — I don't remember the exact words — he would lock me in a closet with the rat. It always terrified me. The foster mother didn't do anything about it. I could see that she kind of felt bad for me, but she didn't have the power to do anything. She just went on with her business."

Lynn got used to seeing foster brothers and sisters come and go at the home. Always, she assumed they were taken away because they had done something wrong. Somehow, she reasoned, they had failed to "straighten up." So Lynn discovered very early she should avoid getting overly attached to her foster siblings; they might be gone tomorrow. She also learned to be wary of people. And she became expert at remaining quiet, staying safely within herself, thinking that her success in such behavior was what protected her from being locked in the closet with dead rats — or worse, in her young mind, being taken away like the other children.

By the time the Oregon Children's Services Division finally got the courts to terminate the birth mother's rights to Lynn, it was the winter of 1970. She had been in the foster home nearly four years. Now the state could legally put her up for adoption. Unfortunately, there were no parents waiting to take her. Lynn was what adoption workers classify as a "special needs" child — a euphemism for a hard-to-place child. "Special needs" kids include those who are nonwhite, ill, physically or mentally handicapped, emotionally troubled, or part of a family of siblings who should not be separated. This group also includes older children, beyond infancy. So Lynn was considered a "two-fer," an older, mixed-race child.

Ideally, perhaps, the state would have placed Lynn with a black family. But Oregon in early 1970 had no black couples seeking to adopt a child like Lynn through the state agency. Lynn would have to wait, possibly settling for second-best, which meant adoption by white parents.

Shortly after Lynn's fourth birthday, the Children's Services Division office in Eugene received a telephone call from a white couple, both twenty-three, who were considering adoption. They wanted a daughter, an older child, preferably a healthy little girl between one and three years of age, although that was not a hard-and-fast requirement. Race did not matter.

A few days after making that call, Gloria and I went to the agency's offices for our first formal interview. We had briefly considered going through a private agency, but when we discovered the cost — possibly amounting to thousands of dollars in fees — we turned to the state. The Children's Services Division was not the ideal source for healthy, white, newborn babies, but it was an excellent agency for parents willing to accept "special needs" children. The state charged no fees; adoptive parents were responsible only for the legal expense of getting the final adoption decree.

Gloria and I wanted desperately to make a good first impression with the state authorities. On the day of our appointment, I got a haircut and put on a shirt and tie and my best sport coat. Gloria selected one of her dressier outfits and fixed her long, auburn hair more conservatively than the way she normally wore it — hanging straight, parted down the middle, as was fashionable among young women in those days. We left our boys with a sitter at the little duplex we rented in Cottage Grove and drove the twenty miles to Eugene in silence. Both of us were nervous, but especially Gloria. This kind of pressure — requiring one to perform and be judged — was among her most dreaded experiences. I was certainly uncomfortable, too, at the idea of putting my aptitude for parenthood out on the table for close scrutiny by government employees I didn't even know. In our past, getting children was almost too easy; we simply made babies. Now, for the first time, we were going to let other people judge whether we were qualified to have a child. I thought the two of us, especially Gloria, were at least competent for the job, but I was apprehensive about convincing others. What if they rejected us? The notion was petrifying.

As it turned out, the appointment was a breeze. We met with a veteran caseworker, Leith Robertson, an exceptionally professional, calm woman who spoke slowly and chose her words carefully. She was about our mothers' age, late forties, with kindly eyes, a reassuring manner, and an air of weariness born of years in social work.

As she took notes, Leith asked a lot of general questions about ourselves, our two boys, our extended families, and our aspirations for a daughter. Answering was easy. Soon I could sense Gloria loosening up. Leith handed us one surprise, however, when she said the agency normally would not want to place an adopted child between two "natural" siblings like Steve and Mike. They were ages five and almost two, so that seemed to rule out getting a three-year-old girl. Leith said the state preferred to place children as the youngest in a family. We were taken aback slightly but said that was fine. In fact, for Gloria, the idea of a younger child, one to two years old, was somewhat more appealing.

Leith concluded our visit by outlining the adoption process facing us if we decided to continue. The next step would involve filling out formal application papers, which included providing personal and employer references willing to be interviewed. Then would come separate interviews — each spouse alone, without the other. Gloria began tensing up again at this revelation. Family members might also be interviewed, Leith said. Then would follow a "home study" in which the caseworker would visit our neighborhood, have a look at our house, see our children, and write an evaluation. This news *really* got Gloria tightened up again. And that was far from the end of the process. After the home study, we would be notified if we had been accepted for placement of a child. Then we would have to wait, possibly up to a year, for the agency to select a girl who appeared to be a good fit for our family.

Both of us were a bit dazed as we drove back to Cottage Grove. Adopting was going to be more complicated than we had thought. Neither of us had expected that we could just waltz into the agency and come home with a beautiful daughter, but we had also not anticipated so many hoops to jump through. It seemed rather daunting. That night, as Gloria and I sat up late talking it all over again, she expressed wariness about the process, especially the home study. Our two-bedroom, $100-a-month duplex was cramped already. Until we could afford a bigger place, our new daughter would have to share the boys' bedroom, where Steve slept in a twin bed and Mike in a crib. What would the caseworker say about *that*? The individual spouse interviews were also troubling to Gloria. What were they going to ask each of us that they did not want us to answer in the presence of the other? Maybe, I suggested, the separate interviews were a good way to find out if only one partner in the marriage is eager for the adoption while the other is lukewarm or even secretly reluctant. That would be a warning sign.

"Is one of us secretly reluctant?" I asked.

"Not me," Gloria said.

"Me neither."

Thus we marched bravely ahead. Over the next couple of weeks we completed the laborious written application, which required copies of our income tax returns and photos of each member of our family. We also arranged for our references. Besides Doug Wilson, my editor at the newspaper, we listed our friends Mike and Sandy Thoele, who told us they would be glad to help. As family references we listed my younger brother, Dan, and Gloria's sister, Marilyn. We pointedly did *not* want our parents contacted. Dan and Marilyn were enthusiastic about our plans when we talked to each of them in confidence. But breaking the adoption news to our parents was going to be a delicate undertaking, we felt, and we wanted to put that off until we were sure the adoption would go through. In other words, we were cowards.

We had solid-sounding reasons for procrastinating on telling our parents. Today, though, I know we were wrong. Our decisions would have enormous impact on the lives of Gloria's mother and father and mine. Leaving them out of the early adoption discussions was unfair and could have been disastrous. However, it's easy to say all that today, conveniently forgetting the huge, tragic generation gap and communication void that existed in 1970. Both Gloria and I loved and revered our parents, but the political and ideological polarity that was ripping the nation apart in those days was also tearing at the fabric of families, even the closest of them.

During the weeks of our adoption screening, the United States was rocked by war-related events we could not talk about with our parents without upsetting them. In a nationally televised address on April 30, President Nixon disclosed massive U.S. bombing raids in Cambodia and announced the invasion of that country by American and South Vietnamese troops. In response, open rebellion erupted at colleges across the nation, including the University of Oregon in Eugene, where thirteen students were indicted on riot charges. Nixon publicly denounced the campus dissenters as "bums." Within hours of that remark, four white student demonstrators were fatally gunned down and eleven were wounded by National Guardsmen at Kent State University in Ohio. A few days later two black students, protesting the disproportionate number of black college graduates being drafted and sent to Vietnam, were shot dead and sixteen others were wounded by police at Jackson State College in Mississippi. Many antiwar activists began calling for an end to peaceful protest and a shift to violence.

Our parents, meanwhile, seemed far more appalled at the civil unrest than at the fighting in Southeast Asia. Our fathers had risked everything fighting for the country in World War II — Gloria's dad as an Army tank mechanic near the battlefront in Europe, and my dad as a gunner's mate on a Navy destroyer in the South Pacific. Our mothers had made great sacrifices, too, both of them staying behind as war brides. "Their" war was the most heroic, emotional time of their lives. How could we young adults be so unwilling to support "our" war? The answer, I once suggested to Gloria's dad, was that we had more objectivity and information about it. I know my words hurt him, and I was instantly sorry I had broken my rule about avoiding the subject with our parents. Whenever we knew they were coming to our home, Gloria and I even tried to remember to take down her refrigerator poster that said WAR IS NOT HEALTHY FOR CHILDREN AND OTHER LIVING THINGS.

Nor could we safely discuss race with our parents. During the adoption proceedings, that was a huge subject in the news as five blacks were shot by police in a Miami race riot. Huey Newton, cofounder of the Black Panthers, won a new trial in the shooting death of an Oakland policeman. The FBI put the black militant H. Rap Brown on its Most Wanted list of fugitives, on charges of arson and inciting to riot. The U.S. Army reported an alarming rise in racial tension on bases throughout the world. Nixon's domestic adviser Daniel Patrick Moynihan proposed in a private memorandum, leaked to the press, that "the time may have come when the issue of race could benefit from a period of 'benign neglect.' " The NAACP blasted the Nixon White House as "anti-Negro." Meanwhile, our parents tended to lump civil rights activists with war dissenters in the same unsavory category — right alongside gun-toting black nationalists and bomb-tossing student radicals.

Gloria and I felt reasonably sure our two sets of parents, given the choice, would prefer their first granddaughter to be "natural" rather than adopted. We were even more sure they would prefer the girl to be white. Thus, we reasoned, it made little sense to upset them unnecessarily by telling them we wanted to adopt a child who might be of a minority race. She might just as easily turn out to be white. Not only that, we said to ourselves, the adoption might not even happen. We could be rejected for being too young, having too small a house, receiving poor references, or saying all the wrong things during our interviews. Why risk rattling our parents prematurely over something so tenuous?

To my surprise, the matter of our parents emerged as a major issue when I went back to the state offices, one day ahead of Gloria, for the first of our separate spouse interviews. I was also startled to discover a distinct change in our caseworker, Leith Robertson. She was still the same kindly, professional woman we had met two weeks earlier. But now her questions were much more direct. They were tougher, with an edge to them. After our exceedingly friendly, easygoing first encounter with Leith, I had come prepared for a warm one-on-one conversation. Now, I realized as I sat facing her, with her cluttered desk between us, she was playing hardball. Her blunt opening question set the tone: "Why did you and Gloria marry so young?"

I swallowed, blushed a little, and told her the truth.

"The survival rate of teen-age marriages like yours is extremely low," she replied. "Very few make it past five years."

"Ours did," I said, trying hard to come off sounding more self-confident than defensive.

Leith then wanted to know why I felt our marriage was strong, why I thought it would last. What made us any different from other young couples who wed at eighteen and ended up in divorce? To this day I can't remember exactly how I responded, other than stammering something trite about our being exceptions to the rule.

I do remember feeling I had badly tarnished our chances for adoption by the time Leith got to her next line of questioning: our financial status. She opened a folder containing our formal application papers and took out our statement of income and assets. It showed that I earned only $167 a week as a newspaper reporter and that we had only a few hundred dollars in savings, our measly nest egg for a house we hoped to buy someday.

"Is there any chance," Leith asked, "that Gloria might take a job to supplement your income?"

The correct answer, it seemed to me, was yes. But I told her the truth: "No, Gloria doesn't want to go to work or even go back to school as long as we have preschool kids. And I agree with her."

"That's good," Leith said. "We prefer to place a child in a home where at least one of the parents is normally there, at least for the first couple of years."

I tried to hide my great relief. I had successfully fielded a loaded question. Nothing like telling the truth, I said to myself. Score one point for Doug and Gloria.

Then Leith surprised me by asking what I thought about my prospects for continued employment at the newspaper. Over the next sixteen years I would rise through the ranks to become the *Register-Guard*'s managing editor. But at that interview in 1970, still in my first year at the paper, I was completely unsure of my job security. In fact, I had broken a couple of stories that had made me highly unpopular in my bureau community. Cottage Grove civic leaders had closed ranks on me a short time before, cutting me off from easy access to information, after I had exposed an attempt to cover up a chemical spill that killed thousands of fish in the coast fork of the Willamette River. My page-one story, disclosing that the town's big Weyerhaeuser plywood plant had dumped hundreds of gallons of carbolic acid into the stream, led to a grand jury investigation in which I was called to testify against city and company officials. I had also alienated Cottage Grove's school administration by disclosing its refusal to allow the town's all-white high school to join in an exchange-student program with a Portland high school with a heavy black enrollment. My story, quoting off-the-cuff racist remarks by members of the school board, resulted in an official call of complaint to my boss, demanding that I be replaced by someone "less hostile to the community." Doug Wilson, the editor, told me to forget the complaint, which he construed as evidence that I had done my job. He said he was solidly behind me, but I was unsure of support from higher management. At my previous newspaper, in Spokane, I had noticed the publisher's hypersensitivity to community complaints, and I had yet to learn that I was now at a paper with considerably more spine.

"I could be fired tomorrow," I replied. "Or I could get promoted. I really don't know, so you'd be better off asking my employers about that."

"We will," she said. "Now, what can you tell me about your religious beliefs?"

That was another zinger I had not anticipated. I sputtered something like, "Gee, is that really pertinent?"

"The supervisor will want to know," she said.

"Supervisor?"

Leith explained that she, as our caseworker, would eventually offer a recommendation on our fitness as adoptive parents, but the final decision would be made by the state adoption supervisor, Barbara Davis. She would review our formal application, our references, our financial statement, Leith's report, and the results of the "home study." And yes, she said, Davis would want to know something about our religious beliefs.

"Well," I said, "Gloria was raised in the Methodist Church, and I was raised Catholic. But today we're neither. We sort of teeter between agnosticism and atheism."

Leith wanted to know what faith we were teaching our children. I told her we weren't imposing any religious beliefs on them; we planned to let them make up their own minds and form their own beliefs. She responded that children reared so loosely often grow up to be vulnerable to religious cults.

"Okay," I said. "Put down that we're teaching our children Judeo-Christian values without participating in organized religion." And that's exactly what she wrote down, leaving me reconsidering the wisdom of being so forthright. At that point, I judged our chances of adopting to be, at best, about 50–50.

Next, Leith wanted to hear my views about parenting. This part of the interview went smoothly until she asked how Gloria and I handled discipline. "Well," I said, "we don't believe much in spanking, if that's what you mean. Positive reinforcement of good behavior seems to work best for us — although once I gave our son Steve a pop on the bottom when he needed it."

Leith seemed concerned. "With what?" she asked. "A paddle? Your hand?"

Now I knew I had blown it. "No," I confessed. "With a rolled-up newspaper." She looked at me sternly. I tried to lighten things up. "I'm a reporter, remember?" I laughed at my cleverness. Leith did not laugh with me; she just kept watching me, silent, as I stumbled on. "It really didn't hurt the little guy. It just sort of startled him. He had run out in the street, in front of a car. It almost ran over him. I had to get his attention." She maintained her steady gaze, letting me convict myself. "It worked," I added, about as lamely as I ever sounded.

Leith was expressionless as she wrote something down. I was pretty sure it said "child abuser." Odds for the adoption now seemed closer to 30–70.

Then came the coup de grâce. She wanted to know about our parents. I gave her a totally unvarnished description of their views and our parental relationships, figuring there was nothing to gain by lack of candor at this point. I told Leith the adoption might be hard for our parents to accept if the child turned out to be nonwhite. But I also described them as fundamentally good people who would try very hard and probably succeed. Leith cautioned that failure of an adopted child's new grandparents to accept the youngster can have a destructive impact — on the child and on the adoptive couple's marriage as well.

After a sobering hour and a half with the caseworker, I went home thinking I had overdone it with honesty and had clumsily sabotaged our hopes for adoption. Fortunately, though, Gloria was next up at bat. I figured she could salvage us with some deft damage control. I considered her to be an impressive, instinctively strong parent, while I was the bumbling, weaker one who relied a lot on her strength and common sense.

That evening, of course, Gloria wanted to hear every sad detail of my interview. As she listened, she became increasingly distraught. I was describing exactly the kind of critical inquisition she dreaded most. She was appalled at the prying nature of some of the questions, such as the circumstances of our young marriage. And she could hardly believe some of my responses.

"Why on earth did you even mention the rolled-up newspaper?" she asked. "Your gentle little swat probably saved Steve from getting run over in the street. But you made it sound like we beat our kids."

A sense of doom settled over our home that night. Gloria could not go to sleep, and by the hour of her interview the following day she was extraordinarily tense and defensive. She went into the one-on-one session grimly assuming that Leith would ask her many of the same questions she had asked me, probing for disparity of views and for conflict in our marriage. Instead, Leith had an entirely different agenda, putting Gloria off balance as much as I had been.

"When you and Doug found out you were pregnant with Steve," Leith asked, "did you discuss having an abortion or putting the baby up for adoption?"

That was the opener, and it made Gloria bristle. She replied that we never considered such options. We had already talked about getting married after college, she explained. Steve merely speeded things up.

After dwelling on that subject longer than Gloria appreciated, Leith switched to another sensitive matter, which dominated the remainder of the interview: Gloria's relationship with her mother. Did Gloria feel that Mildred loved her? Did Mildred ever *tell* Gloria she loved her? Exactly *how* did Gloria know she was loved?

"I told Leith I was pretty sure my mother loved me," Gloria recalls today, "although I couldn't remember Mom ever using those words, 'I love you.' I said I had always felt secure, although there wasn't a lot of physical affection shown in our family. Not many hugs. That part of the interview really bothered me and brought up all kinds of things and feelings that probably needed to be dealt with. I guess Leith asked me those questions to find out what kind of mother I would be. It really upset and flustered me. She hit one of my buttons."

I knew Gloria and her mother loved each other, but their relationship was always somewhat taut, and neither could understand why. Most of the problem, I thought, rested with Mildred, who was stiff and incapable of showing her feelings. I never heard her praise Gloria or compliment her in any way.

After Gloria's session with the caseworker, she came home and shut herself in our bedroom. Her interview had been a disaster, she told me through the locked door.

Today Gloria recalls, "I was sure Leith would say, 'Well, forget it. You can't have a daughter. No way. You don't even know if your own mother loves you.' I figured there was no way we'd get a little girl now."

Glumly, with little hope or self-confidence, we began preparing for the next step in the screening process, the dreaded home study. This hurdle loomed on our calendar like oral surgery — or worse, actually. Both Gloria and I had impacted wisdom teeth removed over the next two weeks. And both of us agreed we preferred the painful dental work to having Leith Robertson inspect our home. We briefly considered canceling her visit and withdrawing our application to adopt. But when Leith called to set the time for her visit, she was so unexpectedly upbeat and friendly that we decided to go ahead and have her come.

Our tiny rented house was part of a duplex in a tidy neighborhood on a fairly quiet street in Cottage Grove, a mill town of about seven thousand people south of Eugene on Interstate 5. Our tranquility, however, was disturbed once each weekday afternoon by students squirreling around in cars after getting out of classes in a nearby school — hence my fabled episode with little Steve, the car in the street, and the rolled-up newspaper. We were careful to schedule Leith's visit in the morning, so she would not be alarmed by speeding Cougars and Camaros out in front of our house.

Fortunately, the place had a spacious, fenced back yard, where we had set up one of those assemble-it-yourself swing sets. And our neighbors were first-rate. A Forest Service family with two little girls occupied the other half of our duplex. A state trooper and his wife and baby lived on the other side of us. Gloria and I figured Leith would judge our neighborhood as safe and acceptable, but the small size of our house — the shortage of bedrooms — greatly worried us. To give our kids more space to play, Gloria and I slept in the smaller of our two bedrooms, which had to double as my office. The newspaper gave me a monthly housing allowance of $25 for operating the news bureau out of our home. That meant cramming a desk and all my office equipment into the bedroom, where Gloria and I would jam pillows over our ears many nights as midnight messages came clattering over my teletype machine beside the bed.

Over the weekend prior to Leith's visit, we got rid of Mike's crib and splurged on a bunk bed for the boys. We kept the twin bed, hoping Leith would see that our new daughter could at least have her own bed, if not her own room.

We also bought a few dozen bedding plants — white and purple petunias — and planted them in front of the duplex. I mowed and edged the lawn, and Gloria cleaned house like a maniac, making sure there were no fingerprints on the woodwork, not a single hair in the bathtub, not even any dust balls lurking under the beds.

On the day of the home study, we rose at dawn, bathed and dressed Steve and Mike in their best clothes, and went over the whole house again. Gloria arranged things in the kids' room in the most ridiculously orderly way she could think of — educational toys prominently displayed, stuffed animals in neat, obedient rows. Meanwhile, I was equally obsessed in the living room. I made sure all of our most sophisticated books were at eye level and our Jimi Hendrix and Iron Butterfly record albums were safely out of sight behind Vladimir Horowitz, Artur Rubinstein, and the New York Philharmonic.

As the appointed hour approached, both of us were wound so tight we could have thrown up. Instead, it was Mike who lost his breakfast and required a frantic change of clothes as Leith's car pulled into the driveway.

This time, to our enormous relief, Leith was the warm and reassuring caseworker we had met on our first visit to the state offices. No more hard-boiled interrogation. She asked no questions at all. Instead, she complimented us on our petunias, accepted a cup of

Gloria's coffee, chatted with Steve and Mike, and admired a few toys they dragged out to show her. And that was it. End of home study.

"Uh, would you like us to show you around?" Gloria asked as Leith rose to leave.

"No, that's not necessary," Leith said. "I need to get back to the office." She thanked us for the coffee and said goodbye.

Gloria and I looked at each other in disbelief as Leith drove away. Leith hadn't even asked about bedrooms. "Darn," Gloria said. "I was kind of hoping she'd look under the beds."

I figured the easygoing visit could be interpreted as either a good sign — we had jumped successfully through all of Leith's hoops — or a bad one — we had already blown it and she was cutting things short. A couple of weeks later, we got our answer. It came in a letter from Barbara Davis, the state adoptions supervisor, informing us that our home study had been completed and we were now being considered for placement of a child.

We were thrilled. But before we could even open the champagne to celebrate, the phone rang. Leith wanted to know if we could come to her office right away. She had photographs to show us — pictures of a little girl. We jumped in the car and speeded to Eugene, hardly able to believe how fast things were moving.

In Leith's office, she congratulated us on being cleared as prospective parents for adoption. She said there were some concerns about our parents — particularly Gloria's — but our references had been quite positive, overriding any fears that the elder Bateses and Burtons would not be suitable grandparents in this situation. Later, Gloria and I would discover that one of our family references, my twenty-one-year-old brother, Dan, had not been interviewed, but Gloria's eighteen-year-old sister, Marilyn, *had* been called in. Basically, Marilyn told Leith that Gloria could walk on water if she wanted to, and that nobody should worry about Mildred, their mom, who had a big heart but just didn't know how to show it. Marilyn, as it turned out, had probably saved our adoption.

The next step, Leith told us, was matching us with a daughter whose needs we met. And that was why she had summoned us to her office: she had identified such a child. Leith explained that the girl was nearly four and a half — much older than the state would normally want to place in a family like ours — but she thought our boys were so well-adjusted that sibling rivalry would not be a problem. She said the girl had been in foster care since birth and had just been cleared for adoption by a judge, who had terminated the birth parents' rights. The child's name was Lynn.

Leith, glancing through a file that we were not permitted to examine, described Lynn to us in some detail. We learned that the mother was white, the father black. We heard about the heroin addiction. Their drug convictions. Their strange disappearance after getting out of prison.

Did we want to hear more? Leith gave us a chance to end the conversation right there. We told her to continue.

Leith told us Lynn was healthy and highly intelligent, shy, and a bit hesitant to become attached to people. She had seen several foster brothers and sisters come and go. She was a quick learner, and she was figuring out that it was best not to let herself become too close to others. "Lynn is very ready for adoption," Leith told us, understating the urgency of the situation. "We want to move quite fast on this one."

Leith asked us if we wanted to see Lynn's pictures. Of course we did. They showed a vulnerable-looking little girl with light brown skin, African-American features, and dark, smiling eyes. In each exposure she wore the same red and white plaid dress, which Leith confessed she had bought for Lynn before going out to the foster home to take the pictures. There was Lynn, sitting on a backyard swing. Then sitting on a slide next to the swing. Then sitting on a living room chair. Then standing next to the chair. Besides the dress, she wore white knee stockings and black patent leather shoes and the same wary smile in each shot. She was beautiful.

Leith talked to us about the absence of prospective black parents for Lynn. It would be extremely important for us to work hard to help her develop black pride and a black identity, both sorely needed to grapple with society and racism, Leith said. And she cautioned us that regardless of race, almost all children who are adopted at older ages, like Lynn, rebel to some extent when they become teen-agers, testing their adoptive parents' love. Gently, without the least trace of pressure, Leith instructed us to go home and think it over and let her know if we wanted to continue.

Gloria and I drove back to Cottage Grove in confusion. Could we handle all this? Was it worth it? What would our parents think? How would our boys deal with the arrival of a four-year-old black sister? That night we hashed it over so long and so earnestly that Gloria finally flopped onto our bed and burst into tears.

"I can't make any decisions," she sobbed.

"Look," I said. "Let's back up and go over how we even got to this point."

So we reexamined our motives, talking the whole thing through one more time. By the end of the emotionally exhausting evening, in which we looked at Lynn's pictures over and over, we finally decided adoption was still a good idea for us. And we agreed that it should be an older child. And that it should be a girl. And so what if she's part black?

The following day we notified Leith that we wanted to continue. She said the next step would be for us to see Lynn in person.

Leith arranged the encounter in a sensitive way. Lynn knew the caseworker well from all her visits to the foster home, so it might seem natural for Leith to take Lynn shopping with her at Valley River Center, the big indoor shopping mall in Eugene. There, at precisely 4 P.M., the two of them would be looking at kittens in the pet store. Doug and Gloria Bates, whom Lynn had never seen, would also happen to be browsing there, and that would be our opportunity to see Lynn without her knowing she was being looked over by prospective adoptive parents. If we were still interested and wanted to meet her, the plan called for us to bump into our old friend Leith and strike up a conversation. Then we'd all go to a nearby coffee shop and have a visit, with Lynn tagging along, of course. Lynn would never know the hidden agenda; after chatting with her in the restaurant, if we decided this wasn't a match, we could gracefully bow out and Lynn would be none the wiser.

That, at least, was the plan. But we arrived at the shopping center a half-hour early, and as we nervously walked around, Gloria said she was already having second thoughts. She wasn't sure she could go through with this. She wasn't Catholic like me, but she had enough Catholic guilt for the two of us. Just looking at Lynn's pictures had made Gloria feel guilty about possibly rejecting the child. Turning her down would be doubly difficult after seeing her in person, even clandestinely, Gloria said, and rejection would be just about impossible if we actually met Lynn and spoke with her. Gloria said that once we'd seen Lynn in the pet store, deciding then to "bump into" Leith would be the same as agreeing on the spot to adopt Lynn. And that was a mighty big decision to make in a split second, standing amid squawking birds and barking puppies.

As we walked and talked in the shopping center aisles, I began to feel queasy — a combination of all the butterflies I had ever experienced in job interviews, public speaking, and childhood piano recitals. Gloria was a wreck, too.

"Want to bag it?" I asked.

"Leith would understand," Gloria said. "But it's four o'clock. I can't just walk out and go home now."

Our hearts thumping, we made our way to the pet store and entered. The place was crowded, and we didn't spot Leith and Lynn right away. But as we neared the rear, we saw the two of them looking at cages filled with rabbits and kittens. Leith spotted us, too, but casually averted her eyes. Like voyeurs, we gaped at the little girl. She looked just as she did in the photographs, wearing the same red and white plaid dress and white stockings and shiny shoes that the kindly social worker had purchased for her. Leith made it as easy on us as she could by not meeting our eyes. She kept talking softly to Lynn and pointing out the animals.

Gloria was standing stiffly at my side, and I could sense she was highly upset. I gently took her arm and leaned close to her ear.

"Shall we go?" I asked.

She stiffened more and didn't reply. I looked into her eyes. They were moist.

I whispered, "We can turn around and walk right out the door."

Gloria took my hand and squeezed it a little. "No, we can't," she said.

Then she led me firmly, as she would so many times in the years ahead, toward our destiny — back to the rear of the store, back to the kittens and rabbits and the little girl who had waited so terribly long to meet her mom and dad.

𝕲 4 𝕲

Guess Who's
Joining the Family

Ten Things I Want To Do Before I Die:
1. Go to college and get a scholarship.
2. Become an excellent doctor.
3. Make lots of money.
4. Have a nice home and a good car, etc.
5. Have a good family.
6. Go to Hawaii or Florida again.
7. Go on a cruise ship in the ocean.
8. Go to Las Vegas.
9. Have my teeth straightened.
10. Get about four inches taller!

School paper by Lynn, age thirteen
1980

LYNN WAS NOT RUDELY DUMPED in our home after the encounter at the pet shop. Several highly sensitive preparatory steps lay ahead, for the benefit of the Bates family as well as for Lynn. One of these steps was to tell Lynn's prospective new grandparents. Gloria and I had no more excuses for delay.

In an ideal world, breaking the news about Lynn to our parents would not have been difficult. What should be stressful about telling a middle-aged couple they're about to become the grandparents of a bright, healthy, lovely little girl who happens to have a slightly better tan than the rest of us? But in the strained atmosphere of May 1970, our task turned out to be almost as emotionally taxing as the night nearly six years earlier when we told Merle and Mildred, and then John and Patricia, that we were going to have a baby and intended to get married. This time, even though Gloria and I were older and raising two children and advancing in the world, our same old parental-judgment phobia was creeping back. Maybe the fact that we had married so young and thought we had so much to prove contributed to our overdeveloped dread of disappointing our parents. I suspect, though, that much of our anxiety grew from simple love and respect. Both of us cared a lot about our parents. We wanted to live by our own rules, but we were sensitive to the pain they felt in those days as the generational schism widened. In their presence, we constantly found ourselves keeping quiet about our views, sidestepping potential arguments, deflecting hurtful statements. Now our plans to adopt Lynn were emerging in enormous, unavoidable conflict with our wish to avoid dismaying them.

Telling the Burtons was going to be especially formidable, as we realized after an unpleasant event during the adoption process. The incident occurred about a month before we met Lynn in the pet shop, on Easter Sunday, during a gathering of Gloria's relatives at her grandparents' big farm near Junction City. As women toiled in the kitchen, getting a feast ready for the table, Gloria's dad, grandfather, uncle, and I talked in the living room. (Later, in the inequitable labor division of that era, the men would wash the dishes.) Our conversation, as always, got around to the car business, and Merle mentioned he needed a new master mechanic and was having trouble finding one. Luring top-drawer automotive-repair talent to a remote mountain community like Oakridge was difficult. He was frustrated.

One of the other men urged Merle to place a help-wanted ad in a Los Angeles newspaper. The ad, it was suggested, could emphasize the Oregon town's fishing and hunting and the near absence of crime or pollution.

"Sure," Merle replied, "there's probably a lot of good ones who'd like to get out of Los Angeles. But what if I brought a man up here and he turned out to be colored?"

Gloria, setting silverware in the adjacent dining room, overheard the remark. She was as chagrined as I. Here we were, fully immersed in adoption proceedings that might bring us a child of color, and her dad was openly voicing his fear of hiring a nonwhite mechanic.

"Yes, your applicant might turn out to be black, or maybe Hispanic. So what?" That's what Gloria or I should have said right then but did not. Instead, Merle's words hung in the air for a moment, only to be greeted by a murmur of agreement from Gloria's grandfather. Within a few years Gloria and I would gain the courage we needed to challenge such remarks, even when they came from those we loved. But on that Easter Sunday we remained meekly silent, a memory neither of us takes pride in today.

As we drove home after the dinner, all Gloria and I could talk about was her father's comment. Did Merle really mean what he said? Was he a racist? What kind of father and grandfather would he be if our new daughter turned out to be what Merle labeled as "colored"? Could he handle it?

We agreed that yes, Merle had meant what he said, probably figuring that a black mechanic would be bad for business in a tiny white community like Oakridge. And yes, he was a racist, as all of us are to an extent, but he was not the hateful, hopeless kind. And yes, on the riskiest question of all, we decided he would learn to accept and even love our new daughter, no matter what her color. I was a more vigorous advocate for Merle than his daughter was on our drive home that Easter. Despite clinging to political views that clashed with mine, Merle Burton was one of the kindest people I had ever known. He had a good, gentle heart, incapable of malice. As I saw it, all that really tarnished his racial attitudes was a deficiency of information and experience. He would get both, and plenty of them, if our new daughter was black.

We decided not to let Merle's upsetting remarks derail our plans to adopt. However, the incident strengthened our resolve to delay breaking the news — and deepened our apprehension about the task.

After our fateful rendezvous with Lynn, we decided our boys should be the first to learn about her. That night, we gathered Steve and Mike close to us in our living room and told them we had met a nice little girl who needed a home. We described Lynn and explained that her mother and father could not take care of her and that we were thinking about becoming her new mom and dad. We said our family had lots of extra love, and maybe we should give some of it to Lynn.

We showed Leith's pictures of Lynn to the boys and asked them what they thought. Mike, approaching his second birthday, did not really grasp what was going on, but Steve, relatively mature for his five years, understood.

"You mean she would be our sister?" he asked.

"Yes," I said. "You would be her big brother, and Mike would be her little brother. Would you like that?"

"Yeah!"

Steve was easy, as we had anticipated. Gloria and I have always been proud of his unselfish acceptance of Lynn, but we don't congratulate ourselves on giving him the perfect upbringing; as young parents, we now know, we were overcontrolling with Steve in our desire to prove to the world we were fit for the job. So he was a wonderful, smart, well-behaved kid who grew up to have all those traits as a young man, lacking only in the self-confidence that would have come more naturally if Gloria and I had known a little more about parenting when we were in our teens. But we did some things right, too, and one thing Steve always had was a sense of security. He knew he was loved, absolutely and unconditionally. He felt no more threatened by the idea of a new sister than he was by the arrival of a new brother two years earlier.

Next came the gut-wrenching task, telling our parents. Gloria and I settled on a straightforward approach: we would do the job together, we would do it immediately, and we would talk to each set of parents face to face rather than over the phone. We also agreed that Gloria would pick the moment and handle most of the talking in our meeting with her parents, and I would take the lead when we met with mine.

Gloria's parents came first. On Memorial Day weekend we drove to Oakridge to join the Burtons for dinner and to see their new home. Japanese automakers had yet to bring General Motors to its knees, and Merle's Chevrolet dealership was thriving. His good business instincts, along with the community's hankering for Chevy trucks and cars, had made the Burtons one of the most affluent families in town. Their newly constructed house, high on a hill overlooking the entire community, was the biggest and fanciest dwelling I had ever visited. The opulence of the new Burton home, with its world-class view of snowcapped Cascade peaks, made our mission that day more difficult. Since the last time we had visited Gloria's parents, they had risen materially up the socioeconomic ladder; they had made it solidly into the upper middle class. Their new level of prosperity made them seem even less likely to accept a black grandchild easily.

I spent the entire day nervously wondering when and how Gloria was going to broach the subject. All through dinner, which neither of us had much appetite for, I kept waiting for her to bring it up — our adoption plans, not the roast beef. But she didn't say anything about Lynn at the table. Later, after the dishes were cleared away, I went outdoors to help Merle build a redwood deck, and that was when Gloria struck.

First, she talked to her sister, Marilyn, when the two were alone. Marilyn, home from college for the holiday weekend, already knew about our hopes for adoption, of course; her interview with the caseworker had helped make it happen. Now, Marilyn seemed pleased to learn about Lynn and to see her photos.

Then Gloria cornered her mother. Mildred was alone in the kitchen fixing dessert when Gloria came in and casually mentioned we were adopting a daughter, a healthy, intelligent girl who was almost four and a half years old. Nothing about race was mentioned.

"My mom's first reaction was negative, just as I expected," Gloria recalls. "She frowned and said, 'Oh, why would you kids want to do that?' I explained it to her, briefly, and showed her one of Lynn's pictures — the one that was somewhat overexposed, making her appear lighter than she really was. Mom looked at it and didn't say anything. That was the end of the conversation."

Outdoors, I anxiously hammered on Merle's new deck, occasionally missing nails in my nervousness and denting the boards, much to my father-in-law's exasperation. After suffering through an hour or more of my incompetence, he called it off for the day and we went indoors for dessert. It was then that Gloria caught him alone and repeated her brief news bulletin.

"Dad was quiet," Gloria recalls. "I don't think he said anything. If he did, I was too shook up to hear it. But I really don't remember him saying a word."

That evening we drove from Oakridge to my parents' summer home on Odell Lake, high in the Cascades. Both of us were feeling a mixture of relief and despair. Gloria, in particular, was despondent. She felt she had botched her part of our chore, and I was inclined to agree. Now it was time for John and Patricia to hear the news.

We waited until the following day, which turned out to be gloriously sunny at the lake — a good omen, I thought at the time. The kokanee were biting, and many of us caught our limit of the delicious sockeye salmon. At day's end, as the fish sizzled over coals during the cocktail hour, I calmly announced that Gloria and I had some wonderful news. Soon, I said, we would be the parents of a daughter, a beautiful, healthy, four-and-a-half-year-old girl named Lynn, who happened to be part white and part black.

Eyes blinked all around the campfire during the instant of silence that followed. Then my mother smiled weakly and said something like, "Why, that *is* wonderful news." My dad smiled, too. "Congratulations," he said. Then he was quiet, just as Gloria's father had been, while my mother raised a couple of reasonable questions. She wondered how Steve and Mike felt about getting a new sister. She also asked how the Burtons had reacted to the announcement. And that was about it — except that a moment later, as our news sank in, my father drained his Scotch, put a gentle arm around my mom, and addressed her with his most affectionate term of endearment: "Patsy," he said, "are you ready for another round?" Then he took her glass, went into the kitchen of the cabin, and fixed each of them a second drink. This time, I noticed when he returned, they were doubles.

"Timing is everything," I quipped as Gloria and I drove home the next day. She didn't appreciate the remark. I was feeling almost giddy with relief. But she was sensing, far more realistically than I, how difficult this adoption was going to be for the elder Burtons and Bateses.

"I think our folks were subdued because they're worried about us and wonder if this is such a good idea," Gloria said. "I also think they realized, the moment we told them, that our families are never going to be quite the same."

Big change was imminent for Lynn, too. She was over four years old and had known only one home, that of her foster family. Our caseworker, Leith Robertson, cautioned us that the inevitably jarring move from foster care must be managed carefully, with as little emotional trauma as possible. But rather than follow normal procedure and remove her gradually, with the process spread over many weeks of progressively longer visits to our home, the state wanted to move more quickly than usual. We were initially doubtful about the accelerated process. We thought about our son Steve and how devastating it would have been for him to be taken precipitately from our home and placed in another. Wouldn't it be just as crushing to Lynn? But Leith seemed to think a quick separation would be best in Lynn's case, and we deferred to her judgment and considerable experience.

The next step for Lynn was meeting Steve and Mike. The occasion was arranged somewhat similarly to our encounter at the pet shop. Leith visited the foster home again and while there asked Lynn if she would enjoy getting out of the house and going to a park with her. Lynn, of course, was delighted to go.

So Leith and Lynn drove to a Eugene city park that warm afternoon in early June, and while they were there, enjoying the sunshine, guess who just happened to show up? Doug and Gloria, Leith's friends from the pet store, came to the park with a basket of snacks and two little blond boys named Steve and Mike.

As the three adults talked, the boys and Lynn took turns behind the wheel of the park's old red fire engine and played on swings and climbed all over a big concrete brontosaurus. The three got along well.

After an hour or so, Leith took Lynn back to her foster home. On the way, the caseworker asked Lynn if she would like to go to a birthday party at the Bates home. Mike was going to be two years old in a few days, and there would be games and balloons and cake to eat at the party. In fact, Leith said, Lynn could take her pajamas and stay overnight with Mike and Steve if she wanted to. Lynn loved the idea.

Mike's birthday, June 16, 1970, turned out to be quite a day for news. The Charles Manson trial opened in Los Angeles. UCLA fired Angela Davis. Chicago Bears halfback Brian Piccolo died of cancer. And Vice President Spiro Agnew vowed to keep speaking "forcefully, factually, and fearlessly" against opponents of the Vietnam War. The biggest news in the Bates household, however, never made the papers: Lynn spent her first night with our family.

Leith brought Lynn to our home wearing the same red and white plaid dress she had worn at the pet store and at Amazon Park. By design, she and Steve and Mike were the only children at the party, but it was still a smashing success. I had set up an above-ground swimming pool in our back yard, where all three kids happily splashed around under close supervision, getting to know each other much better. During the festivities my parents dropped by, along with my sister Jill, all bearing gifts for Mike and something for Steve and Lynn as well. By nightfall we found ourselves with three tired youngsters who had no trouble falling fast asleep.

First, though, came all our family rituals, including the brushing of teeth. That was when we discovered Lynn did not know how. Leith had told us the state had taken care of Lynn's dental work a short time earlier. That night, when we checked her teeth, we were astonished to find her baby molars literally dotted with new fillings. We were also surprised to discover that Lynn had no toothbrush. She told us she had never used one. It quickly became clear that in fact she did not know what a toothbrush was. We sterilized an old one for her, and Gloria gave Lynn her first lesson in brushing.

Then came bedtime stories and our next discovery about Lynn. As Gloria and I read books to the three kids and talked about the pictures, as was our custom, we realized that Lynn did not know colors. Not orange, or purple, or green. Not basic red, blue, or yellow. She did not even know black or white. We were stunned. Child-development specialists would later confirm our suspicion that a youngster who can't name at least some of the basic colors by age four is probably behind the average child on the learning curve. That did not mean Lynn was a slow learner; she simply hadn't had enough adult attention, hadn't been exposed to the concept of color. When we gently probed the subject with Lynn, she told us she had looked at books but nobody had ever read them to her.

We had also noticed during the birthday party that Lynn could not give or accept a friendly hug. A gentle embrace by anyone, man or woman, caused her considerable discomfort. At best, she would stiffen and submit, patiently waiting to be let go; at worst, she would resist, quickly squirming to free herself. Over the first twenty-four hours in our home, it became dramatically clear to everyone that Lynn was a little girl who did not like to be touched in any way, especially by a man.

The day after Mike's party, we drove Lynn back to the state office building in Eugene. We briefly described Lynn's visit and told Leith we now wholeheartedly agreed with the accelerated placement. In fact, we wanted Lynn in our home immediately, if possible. Leith said she would see what she could do, but for the time being Lynn had to return to the foster home, as previously arranged.

So we went home to wait and worry. Fortunately, the interval was a short one. Five days after the birthday party, Leith returned to our house with Lynn and a cardboard box filled with everything the girl owned. Besides the new outfit Leith had bought her, Lynn had little clothing — all of it secondhand and frayed. Her undergarments were rags. Her shoes were hand-me-downs that did not fit. She had three toys — a rubber ball, a wooden jigsaw puzzle, and a broken plastic game. Lynn had no doll, no children's books, no stuffed animals, no pictures of herself, no swimsuit, no coats or sweaters, and as we already knew, no toothbrush.

We would give her all those things and something far more precious: a permanent family. Lynn came to us a wary, distrustful child, and she would remain that way for many years, only slowly letting herself believe the truth, that her new mother and father, brothers, grandparents, aunts, uncles, and cousins were hers, and hers forever.

5

Friends and Relatives

Dear Doug & Gloria:
   It is now legal to pass out cigars. I have enclosed a copy of the adoption decree, signed by Judge Spencer on October 28, 1971. Congratulations on becoming parents once again.

Letter from our attorney, Jim Anderson
November 1971

MUCH OF THE YEAR that followed Lynn's arrival remains locked in memory as an exhilarating time of discovery. Our home was blessed with a third child, but the experience was wholly different from having an infant. Our new daughter could speak and ask questions, grasp ideas, and form relationships. Every day brought fascinating moments as Lynn learned more about her new family and we discovered more about her. Gloria and I reveled in watching Lynn adjust to her new world, soak it up, and gradually embrace it. Although she remained cautious about letting us get close, we could see attachments forming between Lynn and her new brothers — and, eventually, between her and the extended family. Materially, we had little in those days, always operating about one paycheck away from being broke. But we look back on it as an exceptionally happy period, one of life's blissful interludes. It lasted eleven months — ending only because of a tragedy that none of us could have predicted.

At first, in the days after arriving with her cardboard box of belongings, Lynn did not seem certain she wanted her new family. She thought we were her penance for some vague sin she could not comprehend.

"When the caseworker took me away [from the foster home], I

was really confused," Lynn says. "I remember crying — not because I wanted to go back but because I didn't really know what was happening to me. It was kind of, 'Pack up your bags and leave,' and I thought I had done something wrong. I was thinking, 'Well, what did I do?' Not that I liked it there. I had been threatened a lot, so I thought being taken away was a punishment, that they didn't want me there anymore."

In Leith Robertson's car, on their final drive to our house, Lynn became distraught. Her memories remain vivid today: "I remember the caseworker trying to explain it all to me, and I was crying and throwing a tantrum. She pulled the car over and stopped along a little creek. I don't recall exactly what she said, but she told me I didn't do anything wrong. She said she was taking me to my new home. I was really frightened."

That night, as Gloria and I tucked Lynn and the boys into bed after the brushing of teeth and the reading of stories, there were no tears. Lynn almost never cried. Her eyes were tremendously expressive, though, and we could tell she was in turmoil when she looked up at us from her pillow. "I want to go back to my other home," she said, her tone almost matter-of-fact. Leith had prepared us for such a plea, but its effect on us was no less heartbreaking. We knew we could only guess how it must have felt being abruptly taken at age four and a half from the only home she had ever known. Our joy at having Lynn was dampened by realization that her life, despite what we considered to be a turn for the better, had been suddenly wrenched upside down.

Leith had suggested a soothing, reassuring response. "Yes, Lynn, we'll all go visit your other home very soon," Gloria told her at bedtime that night. "But now it's time to go to sleep, because we have many fun things to do tomorrow."

In the darkness of the bedroom, Gloria softly sang to the kids, lulling them into sleep with folk songs of the sixties. Those lyrics seem incredibly cloying today, but in 1970 they somehow did not come across that way, and they worked with rapid, magical, almost narcotic effect on our three sleepyheads. That night, sappy songs about a better world became part of the evening ritual.

The next night, shortly after we put the kids to bed, Lynn surprised us by tiptoeing into the living room in her nightie. "When can I go back to my other home?" she asked. Again there were no tears. She seemed to accept our reassurances that we loved her and would soon take her on an outing to the foster home. We meant it, too, and would have arranged a visit if Lynn had kept up her requests. But after her first full week in our home, she dropped the subject. She never again asked to go back — not even when we gently broached the idea. In fact, all Lynn would tell us about the foster home, when we asked about her life there, was that she missed her older sister and that the place had lots of "big mice."

A couple of weeks later, when the caseworker returned to see how we were doing, we mentioned Lynn's earlier requests to return to her "other home." Leith speculated that the plea was actually a little girl's cautious way of asking a painful question: "*Am I going to be sent back to my other home?*" Leith did not think a return visit was a good idea. Today, Lynn agrees with that assessment.

"It was the only place I knew, but I didn't have any wish to go back," she says. "I didn't really like it there. I liked my new home. There was a whole garage full of toys, and a swing set and swimming pool in the back yard, and it was exciting. I'd never seen that many toys in my life. And my adoptive mom — I felt comfortable with her. I also felt safe around my new dad. I was treated real well, but I was almost afraid to enjoy myself. I thought I'd be moving on. Maybe that's why I was so shy and quiet.

"I remember that my new parents both tried so hard to make me feel welcome and secure. I just wanted to jump out and say 'Okay' and relax and have fun, but I was afraid I'd do something wrong and be sent back to the foster home. Part of me still felt like the little girl curled up on the couch, scared of being put in the closet."

Gloria and I had no idea Lynn was experiencing such fears. We knew only that she was deeply unsettled, so we responded in the only manner we could conceive: deluging all three kids with affectionate attention of an intensity we probably were never able to duplicate in our years of rearing children. If my newspaper publisher had known how many assignments I rushed, how many public meetings I skipped, so I could do things and go places with Steve, Lynn, and Mike that year, I might have lost my job. Fortunately for us, my suburban bureau was many miles from the watchful eye of the city desk, so I could take the family on outings to parks and campgrounds and fishing spots during the day, then stay up late into the night banging out news items and feature stories based on interviews I conducted over the phone after the kids were in bed. At the time I felt guilty about my work habits, but when I look back today at my clippings from that period I'm surprised at the quality. The reporting was some of the best work I ever did — proving, perhaps, that in the latter years of my newspaper career, when I began putting job ahead of family, my new priority was as unnecessary as it was wrong.

Gloria and I wanted so desperately for Lynn to love us that we would have tried buying her affection if we'd had the money. Our meager savings, though, were eaten up by the new bunk beds, some badly needed clothes and shoes for Lynn, and a down payment on a new Chevrolet, sold to us at cost by Gloria's dad. Our little Corvair Monza was suddenly too small for us, so we replaced it with a family-sized van. We also started looking for a larger house to rent and quickly discovered we had failed to consider the full economic impact of adding a daughter. The rental market was extremely tight that year in Cottage Grove, and the few houses that were available were beyond our reach.

Luckily for us, however, a lot of good people surprised us that summer with help we had not expected. Our next-door neighbors brought over gifts for Lynn. Mike and Sandy Thoele invited us to a dinner in Lynn's honor. A fellow reporter at the paper, Bill Lynch, and his wife, Viola, held a welcome party for Lynn, and my co-workers showered her with a pile of presents, mostly clothes and toys.

Even our landlord responded. When I went to Bob Bowser's lumberyard to pay our rent two weeks after Lynn's arrival, I told the elderly gentleman about the adoption and our search for a larger house. "We're having trouble finding anything we can afford, but when we do, I'll be giving you at least thirty days' notice," I told him.

A day or two later, Mr. Bowser showed up at our home with a carpenter and started taking measurements. He said he had always wanted to add a couple of bedrooms to the house. "It's hard finding renters who'll plant petunias and take such good care of the yard," he told us. "If you'll stay, I'll add the bedrooms and try to keep the rent within reason." He was as good as his word. Within sixty days our little duplex became a four-bedroom home, and Mr. Bowser raised our rent by only $35.

Relatives pitched in, too, with an outpouring of gifts and emotional support that helped enormously. We had sent out homemade cards announcing Lynn's arrival in our family, along with pictures I took of Lynn as she played in the backyard pool. The warmth of our relatives' response, which lasted for many weeks, came as a bit of a surprise. An unhappy experience about two weeks before Lynn's arrival had jarred our faith in the family's ability to accept her and had left us expecting the worst.

The incident occurred at a Eugene pizza parlor where Gloria and I had arranged to meet with a favorite uncle and aunt. This was our perfect opportunity to spring the news about Lynn to them, and we had looked forward to the occasion with special excitement. Compared with most of our aunts and uncles, this couple was younger and seemed more in tune with our generation and the changes that were buffeting the country in 1970. We felt we had much in common with them, especially since they had an adopted daughter of their own. Theirs had been an infant, and white, but Gloria and I did not see that as fundamentally different from what we were about to do. We felt confident we could count on these people for the heartfelt blessing we so badly wanted from our extended families.

As the four of us sipped beer, waiting for our pizzas, I couldn't wait any longer and blurted out our news. Beaming, Gloria and I sat back and waited eagerly for the expected response, but there was none. After a few moments of silence, my uncle cleared his throat, looked down at the table, and addressed us coldly. "I've got to be honest with you," he said. "What you two have now is like a clear, pristine mountain stream. Why would you want to spoil something so pure by mixing it with polluted, muddy water?"

The crude response shocked and sickened us. I mumbled some sort of dumb, defensive reply that I can't clearly remember, but my uncle's words, and my aunt's silent complicity, hurt too much to forget. When the pizza arrived, Gloria and I took one or two bites and left in a huff. As we drove away, Gloria could barely speak, she was so outraged. "I can't believe they could sit there thinking their adopted white baby is a wonderful thing while telling us Lynn is pollution." Over the years both of us found ways to forgive my uncle and aunt, who later bestowed many kindnesses on our family, almost as if in search of absolution, but there was never an apology or any healing. My uncle had expressed his views in brutal honesty, and his words could not be withdrawn. We never were close again.

The sobering pizza parlor encounter, which happened shortly after Gloria and I had drawn subdued responses from our parents when we told them about Lynn, left us leery about the rest of our relatives. And none loomed more forbidding than Grace Bates, my Tennessee-born grandmother, the family matriarch. Grandma Grace, as we affectionately called her, was a highly opinionated, outspoken widow who was known to hold some traditionally Southern views about race. As a girl she had known and respected a number of former slaves. She told us stories of such black men, hired for odd jobs at her parents' house. Grace's views might have been more enlightened than those of many Southerners; I had heard her say segregation was wrong and even "stupid." But she also felt strongly that whites and "colored people" — a label she always insisted was more respectful than "blacks" — should not inter-marry. Toward the end of our adoption proceedings, I often thought about Grandma Grace and felt fairly confident she would have no trouble accepting Lynn. But after that dash of cold water at the pizza parlor, my confidence in my relatives was badly shaken.

The arrival of Lynn, after all, meant that Grace's first great-grand-daughter would be a child viewed by society as black. I began worrying that my grandmother's views about interracial marriage would extend to adoption.

Before mailing out our announcement cards and photos of Lynn, Gloria and I agreed we needed to tackle the delicate task of notifying Grandma Grace. Letting her receive the news by mail or telephone or the family grapevine seemed cowardly to us. We decided that if Lynn were to stand any chance of being accepted by Grace, it would be most likely to happen face to face. So we loaded the kids into our new Chevy van and drove to McMinnville, the little Willamette Valley farm town where my grandmother had lived for fifty years in a cozy bungalow beside a lovely creek bordered by oak and ash trees.

With Steve, Lynn, and Mike bunched around us on Grandma Grace's front porch, Gloria and I knocked on the door and ner-vously waited. We had come unannounced, reasonably sure she would be home, because that was where she liked to be. Grace had never learned to drive a car, never traveled far, had not gone to college, had not even made it to high school. But she was not ignorant. She was a highly intelligent and surprisingly well-read woman, enlightened on a broad array of subjects. As I stood there on the porch, hearing her footsteps approaching through the tiny living room, I fervently hoped her enlightenment extended to the news she was about to receive.

The door opened, and there she was, squinting at us through her thick eyeglasses, then beaming and squealing with delight as she recognized Gloria and me and the boys. Hugs and kisses were exchanged all around until Grandma came to the shy little new-comer among us.

"Lynn, this is your Grandma Grace," I said as an awkward silence fell over the greetings on the doorstep. "Grandma, this is our new daughter, Lynn. Sorry to surprise you like this."

Grandma Grace took a look at Lynn, then at Gloria and me. And then she just chuckled. "Surprised? I'm seventy-eight years old.

Nothing surprises me anymore." With that, she stooped over and gave her newest great-grandchild a grandmotherly embrace.

The response enormously relieved both Gloria and me. Grandma Grace was going to be okay. And for years afterward, the old woman's salty rejoinder was our private joke: "Nothing surprises me anymore." It was always good for a laugh that only Gloria and I would understand.

Both of us are aware that we will never know what it feels like to be black. After Lynn's arrival, though, we quickly began discovering what it feels like to be the parents of a black child. Every day brought us another surprising lesson in the countless ways in which racially isolated whites have trouble dealing sensitively with their African-American counterparts. Our white friends and relatives, despite the very best of intentions, bombarded us with racial affronts throughout Lynn's first few months in the family. One well-meaning relative, for example, assumed she was handing us a compliment when she exuberantly told us she thought Lynn was quite beautiful "and much, much lighter than I had expected" — clearly implying that we should take comfort in that fact. Another relative, after meeting Lynn for the first time, cheerfully exclaimed that our new daughter wasn't really "Negro," she was "mulatto — a lovely mulatto girl!" A friend who was obviously trying to offer praise and support suggested we get Lynn into music lessons right away, to nurture her "natural abilities."

At first Gloria and I bristled at these comments. "Good grief," she said to me after politely brushing off one such faux pas. "If these are the kinds of remarks black parents have to deal with every day, it's no wonder there's so much tension in this country." Almost overnight, though, we began to see that we were going to be miserable — and without any friends — unless we learned to be a little less sensitive and a lot more patient and tolerant. Lynn's well-being, in fact, depended on our ability to toughen up. We correctly sensed that uninformed, stereotypical comments by well-intentioned whites were now a part of our life, and just like black parents, we were going to have to deal with it every day. Within our family and circle of friends, such remarks would quickly diminish and virtually disappear as all of us learned and matured. But in the early going, Lynn's arrival brought forth an epidemic of foot-in-mouth disease that we never dreamed existed.

Even our own mothers, who learned to love Lynn and became devoted to her, made early comments that dramatized their inexperience with people of color. My mother, Patricia, after Lynn's first visit to my parents' home, could not help noticing that Lynn had much difficulty pronouncing the letter *r* and certain vowel combinations. "They talk that way, don't they?" my mother whispered to Gloria and me as we discussed Lynn's problem. "Nah," I replied, trying hard not to take offense. "Lynn just needs a little help with her pronunciation." I was right, of course. A few months of speech therapy in first grade would help Lynn get over the problem, but until then my mother sincerely believed that "they" did indeed "talk that way."

Gloria's mother, Mildred, seemed uncomfortable around Lynn at the beginning. I suspected that Mildred, too, thought "they" talked "that way," because Mildred never mentioned noticing anything different about Lynn even though Lynn's speech problem was blatant, making her difficult to understand some of the time. If my hunch was correct, Mildred mistakenly linked Lynn's speech defect to race, just as my mother had done. But Mildred could never bring herself to acknowledge, in word or deed, Lynn's racial heritage. Over the remaining twenty-two years of Mildred's life, she never said or did anything in our presence to reveal that she accepted, rejected, or even comprehended the African-American part of Lynn's ancestry. To me, it was always clear that this was not a noble transcendence of race but a denial of race: Mildred could not admit that her first granddaughter was part black. Yet Gloria and I knew Mildred was sensitive to the fact. It showed in subtle ways from the day Lynn joined the family.

One such glimpse came our way when Gloria's grandfather died, not long after we adopted Lynn. Harold Edwards had been one of the most prominent farmers in Junction City, and his funeral was packed with the community's most respected people. Afterward, the wives of neighboring farmers put on a big potluck for Harold's survivors at the Edwards farm. During the luncheon Gloria's mother introduced us and our children to many different people. Whenever it was Lynn's turn to be introduced, however, Mildred referred to her as an "adopted granddaughter." Gloria and I winced at this. It was not good for Lynn's sense of belonging to hear herself labeled that way, and it signaled to everyone that Mildred could not bear to have Lynn mistaken as her biological granddaughter. We said nothing to Mildred but found a good way to deal with the matter. From that day on, *we* took the lead in introducing Lynn to strangers, always with pride as "our daughter Lynn." Mildred surely noticed. Never again did we hear her attach the qualifying "adopted" label.

Despite that sort of awkwardness in the early days, it would be misleading for us to characterize our parents' response to Lynn as anything but generous. Accepting interracial adoption can be easy for college-educated white liberals who came of age during the sixties. But for people like our parents, with entirely different backgrounds, acceptance can be much more difficult. Today, looking back not just at the early days but at the entire two-plus decades, we give our two sets of parents extremely high marks. We know many other white couples who adopted nonwhite children, and some have told us stories of grandparents rejecting the child, at one extreme, or offensively flaunting the child, at the other. Our parents succumbed to neither temptation. In fact, over time, which seems to smooth out so many rough edges in life, the elder Bateses and Burtons began to see through color and genes and accepted Lynn as just another member of the brood.

Lynn agrees with that judgment today. Her earliest memories of her new grandparents and great-grandparents make her think of kindness, not awkwardness. She remembers no ill-chosen remarks, just warm embraces, sitting on her grandfathers' knees, watching her grandmothers cook, romping on the Edwards farm, playing with Grandpa Burton's old toys, and learning to fish in Grandpa Bates's boat.

"Right from the start, I felt at ease," Lynn says. "Everyone treated me fine. But I was overwhelmed with all my new relatives. I wasn't used to being around so many people."

Gloria and I were sensitive to Lynn's new challenge, learning who was who and keeping them all straight. We coached her a lot by showing her the family photo albums. She seemed enthralled by her new relatives and spent hours gazing at their pictures — hundreds of them, from blurry old black and white shots to sharper recent color prints. As she pored over them, Lynn could not help noticing our great number of photographs of Steve and Mike, from birth on. Lynn's envy was poignantly obvious to Gloria. She picked up the phone one day and called our caseworker, asking if the foster family could provide any baby pictures and any other information, such as birth weight, that we could add to a special photo album for Lynn. A couple of weeks later, Leith forwarded to us the following terse letter from Lynn's foster mother: "Lynn's birth weight was seven pounds, nine ounces. She smiled first at three weeks. She walked, pushing a footstool ahead of her, at seven-and-a-half months. Her first words were daddy, mama, bye-bye and no. If there is anything else Lynn's parents want to know about, please let us know and we'll try to remember." Along with the letter were seven photographs of Lynn at various ages and an ink impression of her tiny footprints at birth. Today those items — the only visual record of her first four years of life — occupy the opening pages of a large album filled with hundreds of pictures taken after the adoption.

As Lynn studied the photos of her extended family members, she took pride in learning to distinguish them and memorize their names. I recall being amazed at her quick mastery of the subject — a huge challenge for a child her age, considering that she now had two great-grandmothers, four grandparents, seven aunts and uncles, twenty great-aunts and great-uncles, and untold numbers of cousins.

Lynn's two new uncles seemed to fascinate her the most; at least, they remain most vivid in her memories of meeting the family. There was my older brother, Tom, just back that summer from a year of graduate study in Italy. "Uncle Tom was like a big grizzly bear, kind of a huge hippie," Lynn recalls. "He was a rugged, big, strong man, but laid-back and cool. I remember him being fun and really nice to me." And then there was my younger brother, Dan, a struggling car salesman who Lynn sensed was uncomfortable in the shadow of college-educated older brothers. "He was a really nice man — quiet and reserved, shy like me," Lynn says. "I think he felt like the black sheep of the family, and that's how I felt sometimes. We had a lot in common."

Lynn quickly became close to her new aunts, too. There was Tom's wife, Eloise — "a really sweet lady, always caring, then and still today," Lynn says. And there was Dan's wife, Sally, whom Lynn "liked and admired," and my two younger sisters, nineteen-year-old Jill — "real pretty and tall, a lot of fun to be with," and eighteen-year-old Jamie — "like a goddess to me, a beauty queen with long, blond hair, which I wished I could have."

Foremost, though, was Gloria's nineteen-year-old sister, Marilyn, who had done so much to help our adoption go through. Gloria and I felt that all of our siblings were tremendously open and helpful after Lynn joined the family, but if there had been a trophy for support that went above and beyond, Marilyn probably was the champ.

With five years' difference in age separating them, Gloria and Marilyn were not particularly close when I first knew them. Gloria was absorbed in high school activities, studying for exams, preparing for college, and going out with me, while Marilyn was drifting through her awkward early teens, participating in athletics and the marching band, and doing a lot of things with their dad, often playing the role of the son Merle never had. The two sisters' differences were physical in nature, too. Gloria was born with the petite features and small bones of one side of the family, while Marilyn inherited a large frame and chunky figure. Gloria was the homecoming princess; Marilyn could have been the fullback if they had let girls suit up. The two were so opposite in almost every way that their mother occasionally felt she needed to order Gloria to spend time with Marilyn.

But after Gloria and I got married and began having babies, the two sisters found a common bond — Steve and Mike. Marilyn seemed to love being around our boys and playing the role of "Auntie Marilyn." For years she was always available to us as a free-of-charge, overnight-if-needed baby sitter. She enjoyed buying things for the boys and often took them on outings. The more Marilyn saw of young Steve and later of Mike, the closer she and Gloria became. The sisters even resurrected their old childhood nicknames for each other: Marilyn was Mouse and Gloria was Big G. I could not help noticing the blossoming of their relationship at the time, and I was pleased for both of them. My own two sisters, Jill and Jamie, were always close, but I had never seen sisterly love as deep and poignant as the feeling I saw growing between Mouse and Big G. Jill once described Marilyn as "the kind of person everybody wants for a best friend" — loyal, funny, generous, and without a trace of envy. Those qualities helped make her Gloria's best friend, too.

By the time Lynn joined our family, Marilyn was a college student, driving her own new 1970 Chevrolet Camaro (a high school graduation gift from her dad) and living in her own trailer house out at the Edwards farm. Marilyn often came to our home in Cottage Grove and took care of the three youngsters — so many times that I now realize we took advantage of her kindness, probably taking it for granted. A number of times she also gathered up all three kids for outings to the farm. Lynn looks back at those occasions with special warmth.

"Marilyn was really good to me," Lynn recalls. "She gave me rides on the tractor, and sometimes she let me drive her car around the farm, sitting on her lap, steering it. She was like a tomboy, very nice and down to earth. To me she was a complete opposite from Mom. Marilyn wasn't into wearing dresses or makeup. I don't even know if she had any boyfriends. I think she was probably lonely."

Eleven months after we adopted Lynn, Marilyn agreed to drive to Cottage Grove and stay with our kids so Gloria and I could go to a Sly and the Family Stone concert in Eugene. At the last minute, though, Marilyn came down with a bad cold and had to back out.

We hired a local high school girl to baby-sit that night and went to the concert with some friends. A week or so later, Gloria's mother phoned us with the news that Marilyn was very ill and had more than a cold. It was bronchitis — a severe case, but she was under a doctor's care and was taking medication, Mildred said.

A few days later, Mildred called to say that Marilyn's symptoms had gotten worse and that the doctor had had her admitted to Sacred Heart General Hospital in Eugene. We were concerned about the news, but it was somewhat of a relief to know that Mouse was finally getting proper medical attention.

The following day Gloria and I talked about visiting Marilyn at Sacred Heart. We left our plans loose, though, because first we had to deal with a rather awkward obligation. One of our next-door neighbor couples, the state trooper and his wife, had become involved in the Amway organization. They had been pressuring us for weeks to come over for a sales presentation, and Gloria had finally agreed to do it that afternoon, just to get them off our backs. I refused to go. "I'll buy some laundry detergent or something," she said, "but don't worry. I won't get involved in their program."

So Gloria dutifully went next door while I stayed home to work on a news project and keep an eye on the kids. She had not been gone long when our phone rang. It was Gloria's uncle, Bud Edwards, in Junction City. He said he had just received a call from Mildred at the hospital. Marilyn was dead.

"What?" Stunned, I didn't know what else to say.

"She passed away a few minutes ago," Bud said.

Later, we would learn that Marilyn's "bronchitis" had been misdiagnosed: she had a severe case of mononucleosis — a rare form of the disease that, left untreated, can lead to death. But all Bud knew at that moment was the bottom line, that we had lost Mouse.

After hanging up, I said a silent prayer for Marilyn and tried to compose myself. It fell to me to break the news to Gloria. I was only twenty-four and had never dealt with anything like this. How would I handle it? Gloria was sure to be hysterical. She would need her mother. Maybe a doctor. Tranquilizers, even. What words could I choose to soften the blow, to comfort her? I did not have a clue, but I knew instinctively that it was somehow obscene to let her sit through one more minute of that Amway presentation at the house next door. I telephoned the trooper and asked him to send Gloria home in a hurry. "It's a family emergency," I said. He seemed a little irked but agreed to do it. I hung up, ran into the bathroom, and pressed a cold washcloth over my face.

A few moments later, Gloria was standing before me in our living room, out of breath and slightly pale. I sat her down and held both her hands. "Honey," I said, "it's Marilyn. She's gone."

I had to choke back the emotion as I told her the little I knew, but Gloria — though shocked — was oddly composed. There was no hysteria, not even any tears. Her voice shook a little as she asked me some questions, but she was far more controlled than I expected.

I never saw Gloria cry in the days after that phone call — not even at the funeral. Knowing how much Marilyn meant to her, I could only guess that my wife had somehow found a way to vent her sorrow without showing it.

Months after Marilyn's death, on a summer day, I learned how wrong I had been. Gloria and I had gone to a movie matinee with my brother Tom and his wife, Eloise. Afterward, all of us went to dinner at my parents' home, where Gloria shut herself in a bedroom and would not come out. My mother delayed dinner for a long time but finally went ahead without Gloria. I was confused and embarrassed. I had no idea what the problem was and assumed everybody suspected some sort of marital rift. As hard as I tried, I could not get Gloria to come out of the room or even tell me what was upsetting her. At the dinner table, Eloise said she might be able to help. She excused herself and went to see Gloria as I trailed sheepishly behind.

Peeking through the bedroom door, I saw Eloise sit down beside Gloria on the floor and put her arms around her. "I'll be your sister now," Eloise said.

And that unleashed everything. Gloria began sobbing uncontrollably. Stunned, I watched her bury her face on Eloise's chest and weep with great, grief-stricken convulsions of release.

Eloise saw me gaping through the crack in the door. "It was the movie," she whispered.

I finally understood. We had seen the film version of *Fiddler on the Roof.* In a scene near the end, one of the five daughters of Tevye, a poor Jewish milkman in czarist Russia, leaves for a Siberian labor camp, never to see her father or her sisters again. The utter finality of their separation was highly moving and triggered a response in Gloria, bringing forth her long suppressed feelings of loss. Perceptive Eloise, who has always been able to sense what is not obvious to others, stayed in the room with Gloria for another two hours.

Not long after that day, Gloria surprised me again one evening after the kids were in bed. "I've been doing a lot of thinking lately," she said, "and I'm convinced Lynn needs a sister."

I had been quite happy with our family the way it was, and I had no idea she was harboring such thoughts. "Honey," I said, groping gently for the right response, "that won't bring Marilyn back. And it's the wrong reason for having another kid."

Gloria insisted that Marilyn's death had nothing to do with it. "Every girl should have a sister — especially Lynn," she said. "Lynn ought to have a sister who is adopted like her, so they have a lot in common."

We discussed her feelings for hours that night and continued the talks over many days. During this period our friends Mike and Sandy Thoele adopted a seven-month-old girl who was part black, part white, and part Native American. They named her Leith in honor of the state caseworker who had worked hard for both of our families. Gloria and I were enchanted by baby Leith, and I think her arrival nudged me toward consensus with Gloria. Eventually I came around to agreeing with her about adding a daughter. Aside from wanting a sister for Lynn, we had reasons that sounded much like those we had in our first adoption: we wanted a bigger family and we chose to have it by adopting another child, preferably a girl between the ages of one and three, and race didn't matter.

For a long time Gloria continued to deny that Marilyn's death had any connection to her longing for another girl. But early in 1972, when we finally did get a sister for Lynn, I knew it was no coincidence that Gloria insisted on changing our new daughter's middle name to Maril.

✤ 6 ✤

Liska,
the Bouncing Baby

Recipe from the Bates kitchen:

1 little girl named Liska
2 brothers and 1 sister
1 pr. of parents
1 c. friendship
1 pinch of tenderness
10 lbs. of patience

Mix ingredients often. Spice with a child's delight. Simmer only when necessary. The above is a guaranteed success. Congratulations.

Note from our friends Kay and Larry Bacon
February 1972

TINA LYNN JACKSON suffered daily neglect and physical abuse for the first eighteen months of her life. Scars from those early days are still visible on her body today. They will always be there, along with whatever healed-over wounds to the psyche lie hidden within.

She was conceived at a migrant labor camp in eastern Washington state by a fourteen-year-old white girl and a man she would not, or perhaps could not, identify to state welfare workers. Her parents reported only that he was "a good-looking dark man" who had worked in the fields and orchards along with their daughter.

While pregnant, the young woman married a different man, whose last name was Jackson. Tina Lynn was born on January 1, 1969, at Saint Elizabeth Hospital in Yakima, Washington. Within a year the woman had a second baby, also a girl. Both children were dangerously neglected, and at least one of them, Tina Lynn, was physically abused by the husband. When she was eighteen months old, state authorities took custody of both girls and flew them to a foster home in Oregon.

Tina Lynn found considerable love and caring in her new home. The foster parents snapped many photographs, all showing a happy, smiling toddler with pretty, light-russet skin, curly black hair, sparkling brown eyes, and teeth as white as ivory. The foster mother's obvious attachment to Tina Lynn was recorded in a baby book filled with affectionate entries such as these:

Christmas 1970 — I got a black baby doll, some educational toys, a Fisher-Price pocket radio and a doll with a raincoat on. I really love the Christmas tree, but was scared to death of Santa Claus.

January 1, 1971 — Today I was two years old and we had about forty people at my house for dinner, and I had two birthday cakes. I got a brown and white knit dress, a top and a couple of other toys. My foster mommy thinks I had a light case of chicken pox, but I wasn't sick with them.

Tina Lynn Jackson spent a year in the foster home waiting for the state to terminate her birth mother's rights and find permanent parents for her. At age two and a half she was placed for adoption. Her new mother and father were a white couple who lived in a tiny mountain community in Oregon's Coast Range. The husband worked for the Forest Service. He and his wife had two young sons of their own making. It might have been a fine home for Tina Lynn, but the placement did not work out. After a short time her new mother made a courageous, emotionally wrenching decision: she could not go through with the adoption. Neighbors in the close-knit community had not gracefully accepted the arrival of a black child, and the adoptive mother felt she could not cope with the rejection. She and her husband agreed to continue taking care of Tina Lynn, but only until the state could find another couple willing to be her permanent parents.

Thus commenced another period of waiting. At that time Oregon's Children's Services Division did not have any families, black or white, seeking to adopt a girl who fit Tina Lynn's description.

A few months later, when her third birthday arrived, Tina Lynn's fate was still uncertain. The Forest Service couple put on a small party for her, and she received many gifts, including new clothes and a gleaming new tricycle. But the girl's true birthday present arrived a few days later when state caseworkers in Corvallis learned that the agency's Eugene office had been contacted by a young couple seeking to adopt a child like Tina Lynn. The man and woman were both twenty-five years old and white. Luckily, they were prequalified for a speedy placement, because two years earlier they had been thoroughly screened for the adoption of another older child — a mixed-race girl now named Lynn Regina Bates.

Gloria and I rushed to Leith Robertson's office after receiving her call about Tina Lynn Jackson. We could hardly believe she was summoning us for a meeting just two weeks after receiving our application to adopt a second daughter.

This time, our drive to Leith's office took only a few minutes. We now lived in Eugene, a move that resulted from a second tragedy that occurred within a few months of Marilyn's death. After a series of heavy rainstorms in the Cascades, four Eugene men went up in a light plane to look at spectacular slides that had closed a mountain highway. The aircraft disappeared on snow-blanketed Wolf Mountain, not far from Oakridge. The following day, my fellow reporter Mike Thoele and I were with the search party that located the wreckage. Only the pilot survived. One of the passengers was our editor and good friend Doug Wilson, who had served as a valuable reference to help both of us adopt our daughters.

At the newspaper, in the gloomy staff realignment that followed Doug Wilson's death, I was assigned to a reporting job in the main office. That meant moving from Cottage Grove to Eugene. The adoption of Lynn had drained our paltry savings account, so we had no nest egg for buying a house. To our good fortune, however, we learned of a new subdivision being developed with federal loans for first-time home buyers who had low or modest incomes. Getting in required only a $200 down payment and an agreement to paint the new dwelling inside and out. Gloria and I qualified. And by the time Leith Robertson telephoned us with news about a child we might want to adopt, we were living in our own heavily mortgaged house in one of north Eugene's working-class neighborhoods.

In Leith's office, she told us about a three-year-old girl who had bounced from home to home and still needed permanent parents. The child was part white, part black, and possibly part Native American, Leith said. She said the girl was healthy but had experienced abuse and neglect, and had been hospitalized with pneumonia at the age of three months. The child also had significant learning disabilities, Leith said.

"Steve, Lynn, and Mike are all pretty bright kids," she commented. "How would they respond to a new sister who might not always be able to keep up with them?"

We thought all three siblings would be able to accept and love such a sister. We said we would like to see her.

Leith showed us some photographs and said that if we chose to move ahead, there would be no need for separate spouse interviews, a home study, or many of the other hurdles we had faced in adopting Lynn.

"This child has been moved around way too much, so we really have to make this placement go fast," Leith said. "We don't want to draw it out or it's going to have an adverse effect."

A week or so later, we left Steve, Lynn, and Mike with the Thoeles in Junction City and drove to Corvallis, about forty miles north of Eugene, to meet Tina Lynn Jackson. No subterfuge was arranged for this visit. We were introduced to her at the Children's Services Division office, where she was playing with toys in a reception room.

"The first thing I noticed," Gloria recalls, "were these gigantic, sparkling brown eyes. She also had incredibly white-white teeth and wore a cute red corduroy jumper with a white blouse. She looked like an adorable doll."

We also could not help noticing a large white bandage and protective splint on one of her fingers. She had injured it a few days earlier while playing on a folding chair that collapsed, severely pinching her. A physician, who later was proved wrong, had predicted that her finger would not be able to grow a nail anymore.

A caseworker introduced herself, chatted with us briefly, and asked Tina Lynn if she would like to go out with us for ice cream. She was an extremely cuddly little girl who instantly warmed up to Gloria. And yes, she wanted some ice cream. So Gloria took her by the hand — the one without the big bandage — and we went to a nearby treat shop called The Gay Parfait. It was indeed a festive place, painted bright red and white and filled with balloons and displays of all sorts of sugar confections.

We ordered ice cream and sat at a small table with Tina Lynn on Gloria's lap, snuggling close as if they were old friends or even mother and daughter. The girl jabbered almost nonstop about her hurt finger, the folding chair, the hospital, the doctor, and the big bandage. She was not the most coherent three-year-old we had ever met, but she was alert, happy, and very beguiling. I could see already that Gloria was charmed. She must have wanted me to feel that way, too, because when our ice cream order was called, she said she would go get it, and she handed Tina Lynn to me. In a flash, the babbling little girl was transformed into a wailing fountain of tears. Her shrieks filled the restaurant. Nothing I did or said would stop the flow, which only mounted in intensity until Gloria hurried back with our ice cream.

That was my clumsy introduction to Tina Lynn Jackson — not exactly a warm and fuzzy moment. But I could tell, just watching Gloria dry those huge tears, that this was the child she already wanted as our second daughter.

We returned her to the state office building and went back home to talk things over, as the caseworker had instructed us to do. From Gloria's perspective, there was little to discuss; this indeed was the daughter she had been hoping for. I agreed that Tina Lynn was a lovable, darling kid. But I wondered how her life would unfold after the cute stage. In development, she appeared to be somewhat behind the normal three-year-old. Would she be able to catch up? What if she couldn't? Gloria and I considered these questions and discussed the possibility that the answers — her fate, in other words — might be determined by those who would become her parents. I was particularly intrigued with that notion, having recently read

Beyond Freedom and Dignity by B. F. Skinner. I was immensely influenced by his words: "We have not yet seen what man can make of man." Maybe, I reasoned, we could provide Tina Lynn Jackson with a loving, nurturing environment that would help her overcome her disadvantaged start in life. Gloria was only too happy to accept that logic. We agreed to proceed.

Compared with our first adoption, which was speedier than most, the second time around was like lightning. We were told that all the remaining steps could be telescoped to whatever extent made us feel comfortable; if we wanted Tina Lynn, the Children's Services Division would place her in our home just as quickly as we could be ready. So about a week after the encounter at the ice cream parlor, we loaded Steve, Lynn, and Mike into our van and headed for Corvallis to rendezvous with Tina Lynn and her caseworker at a city park. While the four children played, we told the woman — whose name we cannot remember today, which indicates just how quickly this adoption went through — we were ready to take Tina Lynn home. And that was just fine with the caseworker. She got into her car, drove away, and returned an hour later with most of the girl's clothes and toys.

Before we left for home, however, Gloria brought up a sensitive matter with the social worker: would it be all right to change Tina Lynn's name? We already had one Lynn in the family. Also, Gloria was having emotional difficulty with the name Tina, which she associated with a girl she hadn't gotten along with in her teens. Somewhat to my surprise, the caseworker said a name change sounded like a good idea — for the child's sake as well as Gloria's. Tina Lynn was young enough that a new name might feel right to her as she joined a new family, the woman told us. And she said it would be foolish to let something like a name, weighted with negative associations, interfere with mother-daughter bonding.

From that day forward, as Gloria and I drove home with our newly enlarged brood, Tina Lynn Jackson was known as Liska Maril Bates. Fortunately, she immediately embraced the new first name, a shortened form of the Russian moniker Eliska, which Gloria had come across in the newspaper. For a long time I felt self-

Steve and Lynn during Lynn's first week as part of the Bates family, June 1970

From the day Liska joined the family in June 1972, Lynn was less than thrilled with having a sister

Grandfather John Bates with the girls at Odell Lake

photos courtesy of the author, except as noted.

Mike and Liska on top of Lynn and
Steve at the beach, July 1972

Gloria and Lynn at the lakeside
cabin

Liska at age five, in a cap knitted
by her great-grandmother,
Grandma Grace

The girl with the perfect 'fro: Lynn on her seventh birthday, February 13, 1973

Ten-year-old Lynn with a sixteen-inch rainbow trout she pulled from the lake

Liska and Lynn on the Matterhorn ride at Disneyland

Above: The Bates kids fooling around in the boat called *Old Yeller,* July 1977

Below left: Lynn and Mike enjoying popcorn at the lake

Below right: Eight-year-old Liska on the dock

Above left: By age twelve, the athletic Liska was accomplished at track, soccer, volleyball, swimming, and basketball. *Right:* The teenage Bates kids in December 1982, during Steve's senior year

Below: Gloria with Liska at her high school commencement, June 16, 1987

The author fishing with Lynn and others on Odell Lake

Gloria and Doug Bates, August 1988

Doug and Gloria with Lynn on her wedding day, August 22, 1992

Kamaria, Steve, and Sofia at the wedding reception

Paula Lincoln

Hours after Lynn's wedding, she and Liska patched up years of differences in an emotional reconciliation.

The author with his grandchildren Sofia, Kamaria, and Terrell

Paula Lincoln

conscious about having tampered with her name, but Liska today puts my conscience at ease. "I'm *glad* you changed it," she says. "I like my name. It stands out. Never in my life have I met another Liska."

Liska's arrival in our family contrasted sharply with Lynn's. Instead of coming to us with a pitiful cardboard box of belongings, Liska had a whole vehicleful of nice clothes, toys, stuffed animals, books, and even her own toothbrush. Her most poignant possession, wrapped around her black doll, was a tiny handmade blanket with an inscription, ADOPTED MEANS I LOVE YOU, a goodbye gift from her foster mother the first time she was placed for adoption.

Despite this bounty, the people around us insisted on showing support in material ways. Our relatives responded with a deluge of gifts, and the Thoeles put on a welcoming party where Liska was showered with even more toys and clothes, including a beautiful green dress designed and sewn by Sandy.

Keenly observing all of the giving and celebrating was six-year-old Lynn. Her growing jealousy of this new little charmer was one of several ripple effects that caught us by complete surprise. We had wanted a sister for Lynn, but that didn't mean Lynn wanted a sister.

"After almost two years in the family, I was really settled and everything was stable and life was perfect," Lynn says today. "I was feeling comfortable, like I was here to stay and this is really good and I had all the attention I wanted. Then all of a sudden Liska came along. I was so angry. I thought, 'Well, maybe they didn't like me enough so they got another one.' The fact that she looked like me baffled me even more. She was real cute and sweet, and I didn't like her. For two years I'd had my own room, and then she came and I had to share it with her. She got into my stuff. I *hated* that. As I got older I accepted her more, and I love Liska, but we never really got along. I turned into a little demon."

Both of our boys became close to Liska, which only made things worse for Lynn. She seemed to resent any affection toward Liska and began competing for attention in a creative variety of annoying ways. Obviously, in the blitzkrieg adoption of Liska, Gloria and I did not adequately deal with Lynn and the troubled feelings we should have known she would experience.

There were other surprises, too, such as Gloria's parents. They had succeeded so well in accepting Lynn that we blithely assumed they would be equally warm and open to Liska. And unlike Lynn, who would always be stiff and resistant to any form of physical affection, Liska loved to cuddle and hug and give kisses. We were confident Merle and Mildred were going to adore this kid. It became painfully apparent, though, on the first day the Burtons saw her, that Gloria and I had miscalculated. They could not hide how they felt, which could be described in one word: heartsick. For weeks, for months, Merle and Mildred acted as if they could hardly stand to be around our family. Every conversation was strained and tense. Merle made a halfhearted attempt at showing some interest in Liska, even holding her on his lap and talking with her, but Mildred responded by tuning out both girls, as if denying they were even in the room. Meanwhile, our boys continued to receive attention and affection. Lynn, always a sharp little scorekeeper, instantly picked up on the inequity and responded in the only way she knew how, demanding her rightful share of grandparent attention by being incredibly loud and obnoxious.

At first Gloria and I felt confused and angry. Her parents' unexpected reaction to Liska's adoption was making the Burton family get-togethers almost unbearable. But the more we thought about the situation, the more it made sense. Our disappointment in Merle and Mildred turned to sympathy as we realized they were still mourning the death of Marilyn. It was possible, we decided, that Gloria's parents could not help resenting our little newcomer, named after their dead daughter. They were not longing for this strange new grandchild, who happened to be darker than Lynn; they were longing for Marilyn. I noticed that the Burtons almost never mentioned Marilyn and seemed uncomfortable whenever Gloria or I did. Far better, it seemed to me, to talk about their sense of loss — to get it out, to get angry, to get even.

"Maybe you ought to sue the doctor," I told them. "Nobody

should die of mono anymore. I think his botched diagnosis deserves a lawsuit."

But the Burtons were offended at my suggestion. They despised litigious people. Better Christians than I, they said the physician needed their forgiveness more than they needed his money. They continued to use his services.

I also suspected that the Burtons were troubled by changes in their surviving daughter. After Marilyn's death, Gloria began looking and behaving increasingly like what her conservative parents would call a hippie. She let her hair grow long and straight, almost to the waist, and began dressing in colorful floral and paisley garments that appalled her mother. And when we painted our new home, Gloria picked out the brightest, most nontraditional colors she could find, painting the kids' rooms Day-Glo green, electric blue, and canary yellow. No longer did Gloria put away her incense burners, peace beads, and antiwar posters when her parents came to visit, and no more did she hide her strong feelings on the subjects of Vietnam, racism, and the Nixon administration. Over and over we unintentionally upset her parents over petty things — for instance, the peace decal that Gloria bought for the rear of our van. The first time Merle spotted it, he gave me a frown that left no doubt he was offended. Also memorable was the time her parents offered to buy draperies for our new home as a housewarming gift and we picked out the gaudiest, most psychedelic pattern in the Sears fabric catalog. Gloria and I can't help smiling every time we think of those ugly drapes today, but her parents were not laughing back then, when they visited us and saw what their money had purchased.

I was part of their problem. Eugene by 1972 had become a mecca for the nation's burgeoning counterculture. The farms and forests surrounding the city had come alive with hippie camps and communes — lured by the community's liberal reputation, by the area's pastoral beauty (and perfect conditions for growing marijuana), and by the presence of such counterculture celebrities as the novelist Ken Kesey, who settled on a farm just outside Eugene with some of his Merry Pranksters. On its front page, the *Wall Street Journal* heralded Eugene as "the last refuge of the terminally hip." All of this was a major story for my newspaper, the *Register-Guard*. Along with my reporter colleague Mike Thoele, I was assigned to cover the phenomenon. So I let my hair grow daringly long over the ears, sprouted a walrus mustache, and exchanged my old horn-rim eyeglasses for a wire-rim model that made me look a little more like some of the people I was interviewing. For three months I was detached from my regular duties to go out to the communes and pot farms and write about what was happening.

Gloria and I certainly were not hippies, but her parents thought we were, and they were alarmed. I guessed that their unresolved grief over Marilyn was heightened by a mistaken notion they were losing their other daughter, too. Instead of feeling proud of Gloria, they viewed her as metamorphosing into an unsavory peacenik who was turning our family into some sort of interracial UNICEF program. They did not understand, as I did, how profoundly her sister's death had affected Gloria, sharpening her sense of the fragility of life. To conquer her sorrow, she needed to celebrate being alive.

After seeing how Mildred and Merle initially reacted to Liska's arrival, I began to worry about my parents. Would they disappoint us, too? After all, they were just as conservative as Gloria's mom and dad. John and Patricia Bates were lifelong Republicans, members of the Elks, leaders of the business community. They, too, had seemed worried about changes Gloria and I were going through in the early seventies. As I watched Merle and Mildred Burton struggle emotionally with our adoption of Liska, I hoped my parents weren't going to have the same kind of feelings.

They did not, as it turned out. Outwardly, at least, John and Patricia accepted Liska about as graciously as they had welcomed Lynn. For this I have always privately credited my brother Tom — a judgment that needs some explanation.

Tom was special. I know my parents loved all five of their children, but Tom was the war baby, the first born, and the chief beneficiary of the gene pool. All five Bates kids were tall — six feet or more — but Tom stood tallest. At six-five he could slam-dunk a basketball (until he wrecked his back while quarterbacking the football team). He was a brilliant student, too, and a hero at our high school — the kind of student-athlete who comes along maybe once in a generation in a town as small as Oakridge. In 1962 a classmate of mine who idolized Tom dubbed him the Duke of Earl, a nickname that stuck. His entire college education was financed by scholarships. Twice he received full-year grants for study in Europe; he collected a dazzling portfolio of such awards and honors on his way toward a doctorate in history from the University of Wisconsin. In our family's eyes, the Duke seemed to do everything right — even marrying a Catholic girl, Eloise, also a fine scholar and French-language teacher.

There was no mistaking my parents' enormous pride in Tom when he and Eloise moved to Athens, Ohio, in 1971 for his first teaching job, at the University of Ohio. Likewise, it was obvious that my parents were badly shaken on May 9, 1972, when Tom and Eloise were put in jail. They and seventy-five others were arrested at the campus ROTC building during a nonviolent sit-in protesting the U.S. Navy's mining of Hai Phong Harbor in North Vietnam. After being locked up for nearly twenty-four hours, Tom and Eloise pleaded no contest to trespass charges. A judge gave them fines and suspended jail sentences. A photograph of Tom, showing a peaceful giant of a man being led away by police, appeared on the front page of the campus newspaper. The university fired him, and he was banned for life from teaching in the state of Ohio.

Fortunately for Tom, he had already decided he disliked academia. In a letter to me he had described Athens as a place where "the buildings are made out of brick, the streets are made out of brick, and the students' heads are made out of brick." Long before his arrest he had made plans to return to the West Coast, where he would embark on a highly successful career as a magazine editor. But his jailing and firing hit my parents like a thunderbolt, forcing them to reexamine many of their long-held values and convictions. If the Duke of Earl, the pride of tiny Oakridge, was willing to sacrifice so much to express his opposition to the war, maybe U.S.

involvement was not such a good thing. Perhaps it was even immoral, as Tom and Eloise claimed. I sensed that the day they spent in jail was the beginning of the end of my parents' lock-step support of the Nixon administration and the war in Vietnam. And as those views began softening and changing, so did their perspective on other issues that had been tearing the generations apart. My parents, after May of 1972, seemed quite at ease about Liska and my interracial family.

Not so relaxed, however, were some of our neighbors in north Eugene. A bedtime comment that summer by our blond, blue-eyed, seven-year-old son Steve helped us realize we had a problem with some of the white families on Rio Vista Street. "You know that new boy down at the end of the block? He asked me why my sisters are niggers." Steve's words were matter-of-fact, but we could sense his hurt feelings and the plea for comfort and discussion. This was not the first time he had reported hearing "nigger" in our overwhelmingly white, blue-collar neighborhood. He certainly understood how ugly and destructive the word was, but how could he explain that to other white kids, who were being programmed to hate?

Steve's remark made me think of something our next-door neighbor had said to me a week or so earlier. He seemed like a nice enough fellow — a Southern Pacific employee who suggested we go together on building a cedar fence along our property line. So we spent a Sunday afternoon sipping beer and pounding nails and trading stories about what we did for a living. As chicken cooked on the barbecue and his kids and mine ran happily around our yards, he told me he hated working for the railroad. "One of these days," he said, "I'm gonna quit and get myself a white man's job." I glared at him a moment, but he did not seem to have any idea how offensive and hurtful his comment had been. When I patiently tried to explain it to him, he clearly didn't grasp what I was talking about. "Hey, I'm not a racist," he said. "There are black guys on my train crew, and we get along fine. But that's what I mean: it's not white man's work."

After Steve's bedtime remark, Gloria and I realized that it was time to talk with all four kids about how they were getting along in the neighborhood. Their answers shocked us. We learned that Lynn's favorite playmate at school, a white girl, was not allowed to come to our house; Lynn could play at the girl's home, under the mother's watchful eye, but our place was off limits. The mother, evidently, assumed Lynn's family was black. Steve and Lynn told us about a family just a few houses away that welcomed both Steve and Mike to play with their children while not allowing Lynn and Liska in the yard. All of our kids told of hearing the "N-word" applied routinely to Lynn and Liska.

Gloria and I were determined not to be elitist or hypersensitive, but we suddenly realized this was not a good neighborhood for our family. For the first time we began to comprehend the rejection Liska's first adoptive mother, the Forest Service wife, encountered in her small mountain community. We considered our options and found ourselves wishing Eugene had at least one racially diverse neighborhood where our family would be welcome and feel comfortable. The city had no such area in those days, so we thought about our second-best alternative: a white-collar neighborhood in south Eugene, near the university, where residents might be expected to be better educated and more racially tolerant. Homes in that part of town, though, were far more expensive than those where we lived. After pricing a few campus-area houses, we became discouraged and gave up the idea for a while.

That summer and fall brought some unforgettable events — the terrorist slaughter of Israeli Olympic athletes, the Watergate break-in, and the landslide reelection of Richard Nixon — but Gloria and I remember that period mostly as the time we found our dream house. Actually, it was Tom who found it. He and Eloise had moved to Eugene that summer and were aware of our futile search for a residence we could afford in south Eugene. One night Tom phoned us, excited about a house he had stumbled upon while going to a yard sale. It was a big, turn-of-the-century, Tudor-style dwelling on a half-acre lot that was reasonably close to the university. But the place was in shambles, being rented out as a hippie crash pad. Several couples shared the place, which looked like a haunted house from the street. Many of its windows were broken;

weeds grew waist-high in the yard. Inside, the plumbing leaked, the hardwood floors were covered with filth, and the walls and ceilings were painted with hideous Army-green paint. In earlier times, though, the house had obviously been charming. Tom suspected that the property had deteriorated so much that it could be acquired for a reasonable sum, and then, with a few thousand dollars and a lot of hard work, it could be restored.

The house was not for sale, but Gloria and I tracked down the owner, a religious man who had rental properties all over town, and we convinced him that God wanted him to sell us that house. He practically gave us the place for $15,000.

Gloria's parents, who probably were still smarting from the Sears bill for our psychedelic drapes, seemed aghast when they got their first look at our new house. If they needed any additional proof that we had lost our minds, this spooky old place was it. "Good God," Merle muttered when I showed him around. "What was wrong with the house you had?" Somewhat defensively, I tried to explain our frustrations with racial prejudice in the other neighborhood, but his facial expression and body language told me he was not impressed. It certainly was a good thing we were not trying to lead our lives to please the Burtons; this latest decision had left them disgusted.

As 1972 came to a close, Gloria groped for a way to pull her parents out of their gloom. I warned her there might not be anything we could do, short of getting our hair cut and giving Lynn and Liska back to the Children's Services Division. "Well," she told me, "even if Mom and Dad are beyond help, *I'm* not going to let our family's holiday season be a downer." It was time, she decided, for the first big gathering in our new house. We would have a Christmas feast.

In the few months since moving in, we had not had time to do much to our new residence beyond replacing broken window panes and cleaning up years of grime. Somehow, though, our twinkling lights and tinsel and nine-foot Christmas tree brought out the house's hidden charm. Even the Army-green interior paint job seemed right, for once, with all the red garlands and bows that we draped throughout. Christmas Eve that year, before we had remodeled the house, probably seemed more enchanting to our children than any other night in their lives. And the next day's gathering brought surprises I still treasure.

Besides Gloria's parents, we invited her only surviving grandparent, Grandma Edwards, and her only aunt and uncle, Joan and Bud Edwards, and their teen-age sons, Kevin and Kelly. That totaled seven guests, all of Gloria's extended family, together for the first time since Marilyn's funeral.

I had worried that the reunion would be a grim ordeal for all of us, but it turned out to be quite the opposite. A big part of the reason was Gloria. She was radiant that day — a beautiful, loving Earth Mother in flowing locks and a colorful holiday gown she had sewn herself. Our children did the rest. They had no reason to be anything but ecstatic. Gloria and I had gone a bit overboard playing Santa, as had Merle and Mildred, so there were more gifts than any four kids should ever have. But they all handled the excitement and extravagance well. I could tell that Gloria's relatives were impressed with how well the little ones played together and showed respect and affection for their elders. *Sesame Street* puppets were the big item that year, and it was amusing to watch Steve, Lynn, Mike, and Liska act out characters who matched their personalities. Steve, earnest and easygoing, got the Bert puppet. Mike, mischievous and always joking, got Ernie. Liska, cute and funny, got Cookie Monster, and Lynn, of course, got Oscar the Grouch and played the part with practiced skill.

Before long, as the aromas of roasting turkey and sweet potatoes wafted through the big house, our children's laughter was mingling with that of the teen-agers and adults. Liska singled out Merle for cuddling throughout the festivities, while Lynn, showing no signs of jealousy on this occasion, attached herself to Mildred. I saw both of the Burtons laugh that day for the first time in months.

Gloria's dinner came together with military precision and artistic success that clearly impressed her mother and grandmother, both masters of the traditional family feast. By pulling two dining tables together, we were able to seat all thirteen of us as if we were posing for Norman Rockwell. Gloria began the meal with a proper Methodist blessing, and I ended it with a proper Catholic toast. Both of her parents, nondrinkers all their lives, had a glass of wine that day.

In the evening, after a dessert featuring outrageously caloric chess pies baked by Gloria's grandmother, Merle stepped out on our back porch for a smoke. I followed him outside, and he offered me a cigarette. Even though I did not smoke, I took one — that's how desperately I wanted to be accepted, to have our whole family and way of life accepted, by my father-in-law. As a thick Willamette Valley fog settled over our yard, making the neighbors' holiday lights look misty and almost magical, Merle exhaled thoughtfully.

"Gloria seems very happy," he said.

"Yeah," I replied. "I think she is."

Merle took another puff on his cigarette and seemed to study the twinkling lights. I wondered what he was thinking. Finally he broke the silence.

"It's been a wonderful day," he said. The words were warm and sincere. I sensed there was more he wanted to say but perhaps did not know how. Instead, he extended his hand to me. "Merry Christmas, Doug."

"Merry Christmas," I said, accepting the handshake.

That was the closest Merle ever came to communicating approval to me, but it was enough to leave me euphoric. I went to bed that night aglow with happy thoughts of his words, the day's festivities, the delighted children, the laughter, the healing, and the love. Life was turning out all right, I told myself. As I lay there in bed, too elated to fall asleep quickly, I allowed my imagination to drift ahead to many other joyous occasions. I could see college graduations, my sons and daughters receiving diplomas in their caps and gowns as Gloria and I and the elder Bateses and Burtons looked on with pride. I envisioned more holidays, reunions, and weddings, too, with our family expanding through marriage to include handsome new faces — some of them black, which seemed natural and right. And that night I had my first vision of someday gathering all of these loved ones for a journey to Africa. My mind swam with images of all of us — sons and daughters, their husbands and wives and beautiful children of all shades of color — walking proudly with Gloria and me through the streets of Nairobi, sightseeing at Victoria Falls, and gazing at the wildlife of Kenya.

As my fantasy soared, I even imagined Merle and Mildred, older and grayer but happy with the way Gloria's life had turned out, joining us to watch the sun set behind the pyramids of Egypt, and Merle turning to me to say, as stars began to twinkle above us like Christmas lights in the desert sky, "It's been a wonderful day."

7

Black Pride

My basic premise, in opposing placement of black children in white homes, is that being black in the United States is a special state of being . . . I question the ability of white parents — no matter how deeply imbued with good will — to grasp the totality of the problem of being black in this society. I question their ability to create what I believe is crucial in these youngsters — a black identity.

Edmond D. Jones, Assistant Director
Family and Children's Services, City of Baltimore
March 1972

IF GLORIA AND I had thought to talk with a few African-Americans before adopting our daughters, we might have spared ourselves an immense shock. It came in 1972, not long after Liska joined our family, when we saw a newspaper article about the National Association of Black Social Workers. The five thousand–member group was taking a strong stand against what we had done. Black children, including those of mixed race, should be placed only with black adoptive families, these social workers said in a new formal position statement. Noting that up to twenty thousand non-white children had been adopted by white parents in the activist 1960s and early 1970s, the black social workers voiced fears of cultural genocide. They said white parents could not help these children form a black identity and learn to cope with racism.

A craving for approval from anyone, black or white, was not among our motives for adopting Lynn and Liska, but the news item left Gloria and me dismayed nevertheless. We suddenly realized we had done something deemed wrong by the very people whose help we were going to need most as we raised our daughters. Throughout the adoption process we had naïvely assumed that our single biggest weakness — our ignorance of the black experience — was something we could overcome by seeking support from the African-American community. We had no black acquaintances, but we looked forward to developing such friendships — a goal we figured would be made easier by the interracial composition of our family.

Instead, we realized after seeing the newspaper article, we were considered wrongdoers by at least part of black society. What would this mean for Lynn and Liska? That was our foremost concern. Were our daughters going to feel the same kind of rejection from the black community as they had already experienced in the hostile white neighborhood that we had fled?

The stand taken by the black social workers came up rather naturally the next time the Thoeles visited our home. They had just adopted their second mixed-race child, an infant son named Caleb. We had a lively conversation in which Sandy Thoele and Gloria raised intriguing questions about the position that all black children, even those of mixed race, should be placed only in black adoptive homes. What about children like the Thoeles' Caleb and Leith? Both were part Native American as well as part African-American and white. The same was probably true of our Liska. Would black parents be better qualified than we were to help these three children develop pride in their American Indian roots to complement their black identities? Or should our kids' Indian ancestry be considered secondary, along with their white European heritage, as the black social workers seemed to be suggesting? And how about Lynn, whose birth parents were white and mixed white-black? Her ancestry was predominantly Caucasian, so just how much of a black identity should she develop?

Despite all we had in common, Gloria and Sandy and Mike and I could not agree on answers to any of those questions that evening. As I recall, though, we reached a rather loose consensus on several points:

— All four of our adopted children had African-American features and probably would be viewed as black by society at large; if for no other reason, therefore, black pride would be crucial to all four kids.

— White couples like us were indeed at a disadvantage in helping these children develop black pride and identity. Thus, adoption by African-American parents might have been the ideal outcome for Lynn, Liska, Leith, and Caleb.

— However, if the black social workers' association had its way, all four of our children would still have been in foster homes — *white* foster homes — waiting who knows how long for the state to find black adoptive parents for them. Lynn and Liska had already waited too long, we all agreed, and any further delay in their adoption would have been unjust, destructive, and downright unconscionable.

That evening Mike Thoele made a number of remarks that I later quoted in a newspaper piece. "I think it would be great," he said, "if the ideal could be attained, where every black kid could have black parents. But I also think every kid has a right to have permanent parents. And if he has to settle for second-best, which is white parents in this case, that's certainly better than growing up in an institution."

Mike was a gentle but intense ex-Marine, volunteer fireman, mountain climber, and highly talented newspaper reporter with a bushy black beard and eyes that blazed when he spoke with any passion, which was often. I regarded him then, and still do today, as a fair-minded and insightful man whose opinions made a lot of sense. Unlike Gloria and me, who were Oregon natives, Mike grew up in southern Illinois and chose Oregon from among the fifty states. After leaving the Marines and graduating from a small Catholic college, Mike married Sandy, a gifted artist, and moved out West with her. In Oregon they found all their requirements — mountains for climbing, an ocean for sailing, deep forests for hiking, a supportive environment for their careers, and a healthful social climate for rearing their children. I admired Mike's independent thinking and his refusal to fit any neat mold — certainly not that of knee-jerk liberal or gung-ho former Marine. And I respected much of what he had to say, including his suggestion that our two families not allow ourselves to be discouraged by "sophisticated bigots, both white and black, who find sophisticated ways to express their distaste for interracial adoption."

Though heartened by Mike's words, I found myself longing for more information about the National Association of Black Social Workers and its stand on the issue. I began researching it at the University of Oregon Library for an article that eventually appeared in the *Register-Guard* in late 1972. In my inquiry I discovered that many social workers had begun using "transracial" as a somewhat more precise adjective than "interracial" for adoptions like ours. I also learned that public-welfare journals were full of debate on the subject, and I found ample evidence of those whom Mike had referred to as "sophisticated bigots." For example, in the March 1972 issue of *Child Welfare,* a black social service administrator in Baltimore rather viciously denounced transracial adoption by whites and labeled as "criminal" the adoption of a black child by the white actor Beau Bridges and his wife. The writer, Edmond D. Jones, branded the adoption a "phony gesture" and ominously stated:

Nothing can yet be determined regarding the adjustment over time for black youngsters thus far placed in white homes. What are the instances of onset of serious character disorder or mental health problems? I don't believe that the average white parent has done such an excellent or satisfying job in the rearing of his own white youngsters, and I hesitate to expect that something marvelous will happen as we transfer this ineptitude to rearing black children as well.

None of the Bates or Thoele children would grow up with any "serious character disorder or mental health problems." But back in 1972 I had no idea what the future would hold, and I felt increasingly troubled as I continued my research. Had Gloria and I made a horrible error? I needed more information — knowledge we clearly should have sought before going through with our two adoptions. To get some historical background on the subject, I looked up Stuart Stimmel, who was the administrator of the Boys and Girls

Aid Society, a Portland-based agency that was crusading for transracial adoption at the time.

"The number of black children needing permanent homes had soared by the late 1950s to staggering levels," Stimmel told me. "The black community had responded to the best of its ability but could not absorb all the children. Thousands of black children were being reared in institutions and foster homes throughout the country. Finally, it was the leaders in the black communities who wanted to know why agencies were discriminating against children with black ancestry. They pointed out that all other children of minority ancestry, such as Asian and Indian, were placed with good adoptive families without any restriction except the capacity of the families to love and care for the children.

"Black children, including those of predominantly white ancestry, were being denied adoption on the grounds that insufficient black families could be found for them," Stimmel said. "Whitney Young and other outstanding champions of the rights of black people strongly supported the development of interracial adoption from its very beginning. Hesitant agencies were pressured to abandon adoption practices which smacked so strongly of segregation."

Now the pendulum was swinging the opposite way, and Stimmel — who was white — suggested I talk with some of those who were behind the new direction. He gave me the names of two black social workers in the Portland office of the Children's Services Division.

When I interviewed the two women, one of them said she respected what Gloria and I were doing but feared that we and others like us were raising a crop of Oreos.

"Cookies?" I replied, upon hearing this expression for the first time.

"No, Oreo *people* — black on the outside, white on the inside, like the cookies," she said.

The other woman posed a question for me. "Turn it around," she said. "How would white society react to white children being placed for adoption in black homes and being raised black?"

I said I had no problem whatsoever with the notion.

"It doesn't happen," she said. "Think about that."

Racial identity, I said, seems like a meaningless concept for children who belong to nobody. "Isn't the important thing," I asked, "getting such children into permanent, loving families just as quickly as possible?"

And thus began a friendly exchange that went on for a couple of hours and opened my eyes to a whole world of race and adoption issues that were new to me. For example, the two social workers told me it was not true that there were too few black parents willing to adopt all the black children who were lingering in foster care. The problem was that white society's system discouraged such African-American parents from applying for adoption. Deeply ingrained in the black American consciousness is a distrust of social agencies, dating all the way back to the end of the Civil War, the women told me. What black family would want to subject itself to the unsympathetic screening approach typically employed by white-controlled adoption agencies? Traditionally, the screening has been an investigatory process, requiring financial probes, criminal-background checks, and home studies — all highly intimidating to black couples who don't fully trust the white power structure and don't enjoy being judged by it.

I had to admit to the two women that I could see their point. Parts of the screening process had indeed seemed intimidating to Gloria and me — so much so that we had come extremely close to dropping out just before the home study. "And we were whites being judged by other whites," I said. "I guess I can see why more black couples aren't clamoring to sign up for that kind of screening. But what's the alternative?"

They described a sympathetic, positive, nonjudgmental approach that would not treat applicants as if they were questionable characters harboring dark secrets that needed to be discovered and exposed. The new method would be less adversarial in tone and less ethnocentric — more sensitive to differences between white and black culture. "Application forms, for instance, are a barrier to many blacks," one of the women said. "A lot of families have felt too much rejection for such things as employment, on the basis of completed application blanks, so there is fear and resistance to adoption forms. I've seen too many good black couples inquire about adoption and fail to follow through once confronted with the forms that were required."

The women also told me the cost of adoption was a problem for many African-American families, and I could certainly appreciate that, too. The answer, they suggested, was for states to subsidize adoption of hard-to-place children by parents who would not otherwise be able to afford it. Such financial help with legal fees, medical expenses, clothing, and so forth would cost no more — and usually less — than long-term foster care.

Finally, they told me state and private agencies needed to try harder to find black adoptive parents. Creative, well-designed, energetic recruiting programs were a must, they said. And money should be allocated for employing competent African-American caseworkers to implement such programs and provide the necessary link to the black community.

I thought the two social workers' comments made sense, and I told them so. But I also said I thought their national association was only half right. White parents like Gloria and me were indeed poorly prepared to help our adopted children develop a black identity and cope with racism. But I said the black social workers were wrong in saying such adoptions should be prohibited. A far more helpful position, I said, would sound something like this: "You white people don't have all the tools you need to raise those kids right, *so please let us help.* Let us reach out to you through a black community resource network to provide volunteer counseling, personal contacts, group discussions, and positive role models to help you overcome your disadvantages as parents of black youngsters. And meanwhile, let us all work together to change this country's adoption practices so more and more black parents will step forward and help provide loving homes for all these children."

Both women smiled indulgently and told me my suggestion had merits but was too idealistic and would never be embraced by the National Association of Black Social Workers. The interview ended on a warm note, though, as both caseworkers wished me well and said they were not overly worried about Lynn and Liska — remarks I gratefully accepted as compliments.

"But don't you raise them to be Oreos, now," one of the women warned me with a smile.

"How about if we raise them to be decent, happy human beings?" I asked. "Would you settle for that?"

They said yes, they would.

Within days of my interview in Portland, transracial adoption made national news on the basis of a scathing denouncement in *Social Work*, a professional journal. An article by Leon Chestang, a University of Chicago professor of sociology, predicted doom for Gloria and me and our children:

> The white family that adopts a black child is no longer a "white family." In the eyes of the community its members become traitors, nigger-lovers, do-gooders, rebels, oddballs, and, most significantly, ruiners of the community. The black child reared in his own community can at least retreat to his own people for solace when the situation demands it. What of the black child who is defined as an alien in the white community and a traitor in the black community? Obviously, such a child would be under inordinate stress and would be likely to crumble under the tension.

Were Lynn and Liska destined to "crumble under the tension" of being raised in our family? I discussed Chestang's prophecy with Gloria, who found the article offensive. If not racist, she said, his remarks were at least divisive and unmindful of the needs of tens of thousands of American children who desperately needed permanent homes. She also saw perilous, slippery-slope logic in the opposition to transracial adoption. If you accept the argument that such adoption is wrong and should be outlawed, she said, then you're inching dangerously close to agreeing that interracial marriage is wrong, too, and should be outlawed for exactly the same reason — that one member of the couple, presumably the white one, is considered incapable of helping their children develop a black identity and cope with racism. Such marriages were still illegal then under miscegenation laws in some of the Southern states. Did the black social workers disagree with civil rights activists who were working to overturn those laws? I thought Gloria raised some good questions.

Although both of us were bristling, the critics of transracial adoption had done us a big favor: they had helped us realize we needed to get off our behinds and pay more attention to our parental obligations on the subject of race. Liska had been with us only a short while, but Lynn had been in our family two years by then, and we knew we had not done enough to nurture her black identity.

It was obvious from the beginning that Lynn needed help. Just as she had come to us not knowing what a toothbrush was, she clearly did not know what a black person was. She had never seen one, as far as we could discern. Nor had she ever been told that she was part black and that society defined her as a person of color.

"I just thought maybe I fell from the sky or something," Lynn says today. "I knew from my skin color and hair that my foster parents were different from me. I felt like I didn't belong to anybody. They made me feel that way. Back then I knew I looked different from all the rest of the foster kids. That made me feel even more like an outcast. I didn't feel like I belonged to anybody but myself."

We could tell that Lynn was confused about why she looked different from members of her new family, too. Common sense and instinct told us to proceed gently. It would be wrong, we felt, to sit her down right away for a discourse on her black ancestry, in effect saying, "Guess what, Lynn — not only are we your new parents, but you're also part African-American." We thought we should take it slow, giving her plenty of time to adjust to her new environment and allowing her to let us know when she was ready to talk about our physical differences. In other words, quite frankly, we muddled forward.

For a while I felt intimidated by the task ahead. Talking with Lynn for the first time about her racial ancestry loomed as if we were being called upon to split a diamond, something we had never been trained to do. It seemed to me we would have just one chance to strike the precious stone. With luck, we would succeed; but if we erred, which seemed highly possible, irreversible damage could result.

It soon became clear, though, that talking with Lynn about race was not at all comparable to splitting a diamond. The task turned out to be more like polishing a jewel. The first rub made no visible difference. Nor did our second, third, or hundredth stroke. Only after years of patient burnishing would this gem begin to shine.

We knew from the start that Lynn was highly inquisitive, and it was only a matter of time — a rather short time, actually — before she began asking about racial differences. Pictures in magazines and books were the catalyst, especially children's books by such authors as Ezra Jack Keats. His beautiful illustrations of children of all shades of color piqued Lynn's curiosity and gave us an easy opening. We let her raise the questions, which we tried to answer simply, honestly, and in the most positive ways, and we tried not to lecture or to drill black pride into her head.

Most of Lynn's questions during her first two years with our family dealt more with her birth and adoption than with race, and we responded with the same basic approach of simplicity and honesty. Not until Lynn was well into her twenties, though, did we tell her about her birth parents' drug use and prison sentences. When she was little, she seemed satisfied to hear just part of the story — that her first mom and dad were very young and had many problems and could not take care of her. We told her that her mother was a pretty white woman and her father was a handsome man who was part white and part African-American. No, we told her, we never met them, but yes, they must have loved her, because we loved her, too, and we could imagine how they felt. Later, when Liska joined our family, we used the same approach, which she also appeared to accept with equanimity.

After being shocked by the black social workers' stand on transracial adoption, Gloria and I stepped up our efforts on racial identity. Liska, only three, seemed to soak it up happily. Lynn was another story, and three things began to come clear: she now understood clearly why she was physically different from us, she was unhappy about it, and the black social workers had been right that we were poorly suited to help her feel otherwise. The more Lynn became attached to us, the more she despaired of being dissimilar. She communicated this to us in many ways but mainly by resisting participation in any conversation — no matter how delicately and sensitively we proceeded — on the subject of African-American heritage.

We could see that meeting our responsibility was going to be far more challenging than we had imagined. Rather suddenly, we realized it mattered little that our home library was full of black literature, history, and social commentary. If we were going to help Lynn accept her black ancestry, it was obvious the best thing we could do was to transform ourselves magically into African-Americans. That not being an option, the next best thing would be to open our home to black people who could help us.

Sometimes today I still cringe when I recall our early attempts to meet African-Americans. Our sincere intentions would have given us all the entrée we needed, had we lived in a multiracial neighborhood. There, we could have formed friendships in the relaxed, casual setting of people who live in close proximity, sharing streets and parks and backyard fences. Eugene had no multiracial neighborhoods in those days, though, and we knew of no black families living near us. Our new friendships were going to require different avenues.

Schools and the workplace were the most obvious ones. We ruled out the former quickly; neither Steve's first-grade classroom nor Lynn's kindergarten had any children from African-American families. So that left my place of work, the *Register-Guard*, a newspaper with about three hundred employees at that time, only one of them black. His name was Greg. He worked in the plate-making department in the building's basement, and I knew he existed only because I occasionally saw him in his gray engraver's apron when we passed each other in the employee entrance. Awkward as it seemed at the time, I went out of my way to get acquainted with Greg. We chatted in the hallways and stairwells a few times, and I rather surreptitiously found out when he took his breaks so I could stroll into the company lunchroom and just happen to find him there.

Over coffee, I found out that Greg — a slender man with a bushy black mustache and a neatly cropped Afro hairdo — was in his mid-thirties, single, and from Texas. Likewise, he learned that I was from Oakridge, married, and the father of two adopted black daughters. When I mentioned our difficulty in making African-American acquaintances in Eugene, Greg laughed. "Tell me about it," he said. "It's hard for *me* to meet anybody here, this place is so white." He described the black community as so dispersed that it didn't feel cohesive. "And there's no social life for single black men in Eugene, I'll tell you that. If it weren't for this job, I wouldn't be here."

The moment seemed right, so I asked if he would come to dinner at our home sometime. He said that sounded good. I explained that my family and I were about to load our van with tents and sleeping bags and take off on a California camping trip, but we would be back in four weeks and would set a date then. Greg seemed pleased as we parted.

A month later, when I returned to work, I went downstairs to the plate-making department to find Greg and was surprised to learn he was gone. He had quit rather abruptly to accept a job in Houston, where he would be near relatives. Our acquaintanceship was over almost before it had begun. It would be a long time before the *Register-Guard* had another African-American employee I could invite over to meet the family.

There were other opportunities, though. One of them came our way through a Eugene group called Open Door Society for Adoptable Children. It was a loosely organized association that held meetings intended especially for prospective parents of "special needs" children awaiting adoption. Our caseworker, Leith Robertson, had recommended Open Door to us as a good way to meet other adoptive couples grappling with the same challenges Gloria and I were beginning to face. We had dutifully attended a couple of Open Door meetings but had found them to be not particularly helpful; the group's leaders seemed more interested in adoption-related political action than in talking about mutual problems in rearing our children. However, when Gloria and I learned that a black sociology professor from the University of Oregon had agreed to meet with Open Door parents, we decided to show up. It seemed like a good way to learn something and possibly make a new friend — or at least get some advice on how we should go about meeting African-Americans.

The Open Door meeting was held in Eugene's Unitarian church, where the university professor and his wife, also black, sat facing Gloria and me and about a dozen other white adoptive parents. From the start the gathering felt strained. The university couple looked uncomfortable being there. They fielded questions politely, choosing their words with care, but they seemed troubled by all these white men and women asking naïve questions about how to raise their black youngsters. The professor and his wife did not have to say what they were thinking; I could tell they did not fully approve of all these adoptions. Realizing this, I felt embarrassed by comments from some of the Open Door parents — particularly an overly exuberant woman who exulted in having "instantly fallen in love" with a black child she described in patronizing terms more appropriate for a puppy or kitten. The woman meant well, but I could see that her gushing remarks offended the professor and his wife. For the first time I began to understand how black social workers, dealing with such blissfully naïve white parents, might conclude that they should not be adopting children of color.

The Open Door dialogue became tense when one of the fathers boasted a little about his and his wife's success in helping their mixed-race daughter accept her biological ancestry. He said she had responded remarkably well to a black doll and to music by black recording artists. The professor frowned at the man's comments. "You can't just hand a child a doll and put some Ray Charles on the stereo and expect her to grow up to be a proud black woman who understands what it means to be a person of color in this country," he said.

Most of the white parents, though, were there to ask a reasonable question, the same one perplexing Gloria and me: How *can* we give our black children that pride? The professor and his wife said they were not optimistic we could succeed, especially living in an overwhelmingly white city. Our children were going to need lots of meaningful contact with people of color, they said — not just with other adopted kids but with "real" blacks.

The professor also told us what we already knew — that meeting African-Americans and forming trusting relationships was not going to be easy. He warned us not to be surprised if some black adults reacted with resentment at being invited into our homes to provide "an instant session on blackness" for our children. Nevertheless, he said, we needed to work at the task by getting involved in community events and activities where we might make African-American friends. He suggested the university's forthcoming "Black Pride Week" as an example of such an event, loaded with opportunities for us and our children.

Gloria and I left the Open Door meeting feeling a little chastened but more resolved than ever to fulfill our responsibilities to Lynn and Liska. I clipped the Black Pride Week schedule out of the campus newspaper, and we underlined several events that looked promising for our family. Sponsored by the university's Black Student Union, the week-long festival opened with a Sunday dinner featuring traditional African fare. Gloria wondered whether our kids — especially Mike, a notoriously finicky eater in his early years — would enjoy the meal. I, however, thought it sounded like a splendid way to introduce all of us to African culture and possibly to some new friends.

The dinner, held in the Wesley Foundation meeting hall on the edge of the campus, turned out to be a memorable occasion for us. Gloria and I and our boys were almost the only whites there — a development I found surprising but also appealing. For all of us, this was a first-in-a-lifetime experience: being in a large gathering where most of the people were black. The only other whites we saw were a few women, who appeared to be there with black men, and one white man who was accompanied by a black woman.

We bought tickets, then went through the food line, where servers dressed in colorful African garb heaped our plates with interesting bean and rice and vegetable dishes that had been prepared by African students. We were told we could sit at any of a number of long tables set up with a view of a stage where students from Kenya, Nigeria, Ghana, Zaire, and other African nations were performing traditional music and dances. Only one table still had room for the six of us, so that's where we sat — alone, feeling a little isolated and hoping others would eventually join us. Throughout the dinner, however, we noticed many more black couples and families arrive, go through the food line, then look around for a table and pass us by in favor of jamming in with other blacks at tables that were already crowded. I didn't take it personally. Many of these people obviously knew each other and wanted to sit together, so why should they dine with us ill-at-ease strangers?

Gloria and I have always enjoyed a variety of ethnic fare, and both of us liked the African dishes, especially a spicy stew with goat meat. Our kids, however, would not touch the food. Even Steve, normally willing to try almost anything, seemed leery of his dinner. I suspected that the exotic entertainment, the sea of black faces around us, and the foreign clothing had all combined to convince our children that the food was from some other planet. Over and over, with little success, Gloria and I urged the four of them to try this and try that. Eventually our coaxing gave way to stern commands that they at least take a bite before deciding they could not eat something. As we struggled with the kids, I noticed two black couples watching us with interest from an adjacent table. Involuntarily I blushed a little.

The dinner was gradually becoming a disaster as a family outing, but I felt determined to salvage something from it. I asked Gloria to excuse me for a few moments, and I walked over to a distant table where I had recognized the professor who had spoken at the Open Door meeting. He was seated with some men; his wife was nearby, talking with a group of women. Uninvited, I pulled up a chair at the men's table, sat myself down, and listened in, waiting for a chance to introduce myself and get acquainted. They were enjoying a lively conversation, punctuated with laughter and more black slang than I could easily follow. The professor spoke not at all as he had talked to us white parents at the Open Door session. I had difficulty making out what he — or anyone around the table — was saying. Obviously, I had blundered into a social situation where I was hopelessly out of place. The men were "talking black," and as I sat there it seemed as if they turned up the tempo for my benefit.

After several minutes of increasingly excruciating awkwardness, I rose to leave the table, hoping somehow to slip away unobtrusively. But everybody suddenly stopped talking and looked at me. Collectively, their facial expressions seemed to say, "Well, you came over here and interrupted the good time we were having, so don't walk away now without saying what it was you wanted."

I met the professor's gaze and said something about appreciating his appearance at the recent Open Door meeting. I told him who I was and said I would like to call him sometime and follow up on a few of his comments.

"I'm in the book," he icily replied. I waited a moment, hoping he would introduce me to the others or even invite me to stay. But it remained silent around the table with all eyes fixed on me. Clearly I was not welcome at these festivities, and neither was my family. Feeling ridiculous and somewhat ambushed by the professor, who had suggested we attend in the first place, I excused myself and hurried away. I could hear them resume talking and laughing, and I could not help imagining myself the object of their mirth.

We left the dinner without having made any new friends. On the way home, we stopped at a drive-in restaurant and bought hamburgers for our ravenous kids. The rest of that week, neither Gloria nor I could muster much enthusiasm for attending any more Black Pride Week activities. I did take Steve and Lynn to an evening panel discussion called "The Black Cultural Revolution," but the presentation turned out to be too complex for the kids and was sprinkled with antiwhite invective. We left early. I never called the university professor who had recommended these events.

Years later, I would have African-American friends, primarily in the newspaper business. And our household would echo with the laughter of many black friends, mostly young people who found the way to our home through Lynn and Liska. My daughters would absolve my feelings of guilt over the inadequacy of my numerous clumsy attempts to introduce them to black society. As it turned out, black society found *them*.

In the intervening years, I was served well by advice from an unexpected source: my Grandma Grace. It came late in the summer of 1972, when Gloria and the kids and I drove to visit her and collect a bounty of homegrown food for our freezer. Even at age eighty, Grace still had a big garden. We loaded our van with sacks of her sweet corn, walnuts, grapes, apples, pears, and plums, and boxes of strawberries, raspberries, and applesauce.

Over the years she sent us home with enormous quantities of delicious produce, but it was a different sort of generosity that endeared her to us most. That summer day she rummaged through her things and came up with an old book for Lynn and Liska. It was Booker T. Washington's *Up from Slavery*. "He was a great American Negro who founded the famous Tuskegee Institute in Alabama," she said. "The girls will want to read this when they get older." We thanked her, and I decided against telling her that Booker T. Washington had been somewhat discredited by modern civil rights leaders. Instead, I told her quite truthfully that the book would be a welcome addition to our expanding home library of black literature. I also mentioned that we were concerned about our ability to help the girls grow up feeling proud of their racial heritage, especially now that the National Association of Black Social Workers had taken a stand against adoptions like ours.

Grandma Grace had not heard about the black social workers. She seemed disturbed by their position and asked several questions, which I gladly answered. After listening until her patience ran out, she squinted through her thick glasses and interrupted me with a pronouncement I will never forget.

"Oh, brother," she said in disgust. "People sure seem to have to look hard these days to find things to fret about. If I were you, I'd let the critics do all the worrying. You and Gloria just take care of raising those kids, and everything will turn out fine."

We followed that advice and learned to shrug off criticism from those who resented the interracial nature of our family. I also used

Grandma Grace's words in my 1972 *Register-Guard* piece on transracial adoption — the only time I ever wrote about the subject during a twenty-five-year newspaper career.

After that summer, adoptions like ours began steadily decreasing throughout the United States. Wary of controversy, agencies grew uneasy about placing children across racial lines, and many public and private organizations began to bar such adoptions altogether. Today they are restricted in thirty-five states while the focus has shifted to the recruitment of more black adoptive families. The National Association of Black Social Workers seeks federal legislation outlawing most black-white transracial adoptions. Meanwhile, as increasing numbers of white parents are seeking to adopt, more than 150,000 African-American children are said to be languishing in foster care while agencies fail, for whatever reason, to find them the black parents our system now insists they must have.

8

Reading, 'Riting, and Racism

Dear Teachers,
   I have decided to be nice to you. I will not be loud in your class. Starting Tuesday I will be good. My mom will check with you on Friday. I hope that you will understand what I'm saying. I hope that you can be nice to me and I will be nice to you.
   Your friend,
      Liska Maril Bates

                                        Note from Liska, age ten

AN UNFORTUNATE EVENT on Lynn's first day of school in the third grade should have compelled Gloria and me to reconsider the community we had chosen for raising our family. Lynn, however, didn't tell us about the incident until many years later. That was typical. At home, she always resisted talking about anything that emphasized the fact that she was different from her white parents and brothers and classmates.

   Her third-grade teacher unwittingly trampled on that sensitive emotional turf on a sunny September morning in 1974 when the school year commenced at Eugene's Ellis Parker Elementary. Gloria remembers how happy Lynn seemed that morning when she hopped out of the car in front of the school. Clutching her new pencils and crayons and paper tablet, she looked adorable in a new red dress and white stockings and black patent-leather shoes. Her crowning touch was a beautiful, perfectly shaped Afro hairdo — a style enjoying its peak popularity that year. It was still the coiffure of choice for most black celebrities, including The Jackson Five, Lynn's favorite recording group at the time. As she waved goodbye to Gloria, Lynn seemed pleased by, even proud of, the way she looked. It was the last time she would feel that way for many years.

Lynn's teacher greeted her pupils with a traditional ice-breaking exercise. "The teacher told everyone to take out their color crayons and draw a picture of somebody other than themselves in the class," Lynn recalls. "She told us all the drawings would be put up on the wall afterward. She said we would get a prize, a little star, if people could tell who it was we had drawn."

Lynn admired the woman. She was pretty and friendly, Lynn thought, so she decided right away she would draw the teacher. Applying her best effort and concentration, Lynn finished the picture just in time as the recess bell sounded. She proudly turned in her work and went out to the playground with the other kids.

Later, upon returning to class, Lynn received a shock. All the crayon pictures were up on the bulletin board, and almost everyone in the room had drawn Lynn. There she was, in nearly twenty different amateurish sketches, all of them highly unflattering to her. Several crude pictures exaggerated her African-American features, caricaturing her with enormous fat lips and a nose that spread the width of her face. Some classmates had drawn her with light brown skin and big black freckles like spots on a leopard. Others had colored her dark chocolate brown or even coal black. Every picture magnified her attractive Afro hairdo into an outlandishly large, frizzy bush. Lynn was deeply hurt.

"When I started crying, the teacher said, 'Well, Lynn, you should feel good that everyone in the class wanted to draw you.' She was really nice and tried to make me feel better, but all I felt was humiliation. The one thing I wanted most was to be accepted, to fit in, but it seemed like everyone was making fun of me — which they were, as a matter of fact."

Never again would Lynn want to wear her hair in an Afro style.

Today, that long-ago incident stands as an example of how ill-prepared most of my daughters' Eugene teachers were — even the best ones — to deal with diversity in the classroom. A teacher experienced in having only one or a few minority-race children in class would probably avoid an art exercise rife with potentially hurtful consequences. Or, faced with that outcome, a more racially sensitive teacher might have handled Lynn's feelings better and would have notified Gloria and me so we could help deal with it at home. I understand why Lynn waited years before mentioning the incident to us; I regret that the teacher never told us about it.

Both Lynn and Liska agree that it was chiefly the racial isolation at school, not Gloria's and my white ancestry, that created problems for them. In fact, parental skin color is somewhat overrated as a factor in adoption screening, both daughters say today. Now in their mid-twenties, Lynn and Liska admit they have had troubled feelings over racial identity, but neither thinks she was psychologically damaged or racially transmuted by the experience.

"I know who I am," Lynn says. "Yes, I did have a big identity crisis in high school, when I had black friends and wanted to be accepted by them. They always categorized me as acting white. Blacks often made fun of me, saying, 'Oh, you just think you're better because of being raised in a white family.' And I would say, 'How could I think I'm better when this is all I know? Just because I don't talk like you do or act or dance like you or know soul food, I'm still black.' If you wanted to be accepted as black, you had to act a certain way or you were out. For a while I wondered, 'Who am I?' But I figured it out as I got older: It doesn't matter, black or white. It's all in the way you were raised and what you're used to. That's all. I'm just myself, and I get along equally well with people of any color. As for adoption, I think it boils down to the home, not race. If it's a good home and it has the love, that's all the adopted kid is asking for."

Lynn laughs at the suggestion that she does not know what it means to be an African-American. When you're black, she says, you are reminded of it every day of your life — at school, in stores, at work, and on the street — and whites who judge you by the color of your skin make no allowances for the race of the parents who raised you. Lynn says she has known white rejection as far back as she can remember, "and I've never heard any employer say, 'Oh? You were brought up in a white home? Wonderful! You're hired.'"

Liska has several black friends who were adopted and raised by white parents. She suggests that the "black experience" is actually multifaceted and that she and her adopted friends possess their own variety of it, which is no less real than that of African-Americans raised by blacks.

"I don't mind being adopted into a white family," Liska says. "To tell you the truth, I'd rather be in a white family than have no family at all. There are some black people who wonder why my parents didn't adopt white. I don't listen to them. Some black friends have commented that I wasn't really black because of my background. They said being adopted by whites, my feelings couldn't be black feelings. They're wrong. I see myself as black. I know what it is like to be black. I know what it is like to be discriminated against."

I think I understand what my daughters are talking about. I have seen more than twenty years of it — in literally hundreds of subtle incidents, such as the white sales clerk tailing Liska around a swanky resort-hotel gift shop, obviously presuming she is a shoplifter, while Gloria and I are free to browse, and in far more blatant ways, such as the little white girl in the shoe store moving to another seat when six-year-old Lynn sits down next to her, saying to her parent, "Ugh, a *Negro* girl, Mommy!" Today, like every other black adult in America, Lynn and Liska can recite a litany of insults. They have had no choice but to learn to cope with racism. And Gloria and I have had to deal with it, too. We concede that many black parents could have done a better job, but we tried hard, learned a lot, and somehow managed to raise two daughters who say they know who they are and seem comfortable with it.

Next to the racial isolation that resulted, our second-biggest drawback as their mother and father, both daughters say, was still not our whiteness. It was that we arrived very late in their lives and that we were not their biological parents — twin facts that have always enflamed their insecurities about love and their doubts about identity. Negative experiences prior to being adopted, combined with our residing in an overwhelmingly white community, were at the root of much of the turmoil Lynn and Liska encountered as young women, they say today.

I agree with their analysis, although I suspect it is somewhat too kind to Gloria and me. We know we made mistakes. One of them, quite clearly, was that we decided to stay in Eugene.

"I don't think people who adopt black children should live where there are only whites," Lynn says. "You have that choice. The kids need to have black friends and black teachers. It would be a lot easier on the children. They should live in a racially mixed atmosphere. That way they won't be confused and feel like outcasts."

Liska concurs. "The only hard part that I really had [being raised by white parents] was when kids at school made fun of me or called me racial names. I could tell my mom and dad about it, but all they could really say to me was not to worry about it. If they had been black parents, they could have given me different ways to handle it. They couldn't really understand, not being black themselves."

She is right that we were unable to comprehend what it is like to be the target of antiblack bias. I can only guess that the feeling is much more painful and frustrating than most whites imagine, if it's anything like being the target of religious prejudice, which I *have* experienced. There weren't many Catholics in my hometown, but I didn't realize I was part of an Oakridge minority until Ash Wednesday when I was in the sixth grade. I did not go to mass that morning, but a classmate named Penny did, and she came to school with the traditional smudge of ash on her forehead. Fellow students taunted her so savagely at recess that she ran home in tears. The teacher responded by holding a special discussion on religious beliefs and attitudes. First, he asked members of the class why they had made fun of Penny. Some of the answers astonished me: "Catholics worship statues," "They look up to Mary more than Jesus," and "They do devil rituals, like smearing ashes on their faces." Then the teacher went around the room and had all of us identify our religious faiths. Out of about twenty kids, I was the only Catholic besides Penny, who had not returned from home; everyone else was a Protestant of one denomination or another. My ears burned as I told my classmates they didn't know what they were talking about. I'll never forget their stares or the way I felt. But at least I had a rescuer. The teacher disclosed that he was a Jew and that I was right: my classmates were poorly informed about Catholicism — and woefully intolerant.

Neither Lynn nor Liska ever had an African-American teacher. No authority figure at school could identify with their feelings and come to their rescue as the Jewish teacher had done for me. Worse, perhaps, throughout the lower grades and in most of their high school years, the two girls were the only blacks in their classrooms. Of 344 seniors who graduated from South Eugene High School in 1984, Lynn was one of only three blacks. When Liska graduated from Eugene's Sheldon High in 1987, she was the only black among 241 seniors. Gloria and I are proud of the way our daughters dealt with being racial loners all those years, but we feel regret and guilt today that we allowed it to happen.

Not that we didn't consider options. I was doing well at the paper in the early seventies and became, at age twenty-six, the youngest member of management in the newsroom. I felt fairly confident I could find a good reporting or editing position in any city we wanted to live in. And it was an exciting time to be in journalism and looking at career options. The Watergate scandal and the fall of the Nixon administration had suddenly made the news business far more prestigious than it had ever been, and I thought about joining a paper that excelled in national reporting. The glamorous jobs were in the biggest cities, of course, but Gloria and I could not imagine being happy there. A smaller Pacific Northwest metropolis — probably Seattle or Portland — appealed to us more. For a while in the mid-seventies, we discussed making such a move and rearing our children in a racially mixed environment. Those conversations began after we learned that our new white-collar neighborhood in south Eugene had many of the same problems we thought we had left behind in working-class north Eugene. Our children began coming home from Ellis Parker Elementary with reports of racial incidents.

First there was Lynn, who was obviously troubled by something going on at school. She refused to talk about it. Steve shed a little light on the problem, saying a group of tough girls had been picking on Lynn, calling her names and teasing her about her skin color and her Afro hairstyle. Earlier, she had grudgingly told us about her embarrassment in a folk-dancing program. "There were boys who didn't want to touch a black person, so they would put their sleeve out, and instead of holding my hand, they made me hold their sleeve," she said. I gently told Lynn I could remember naughty boys pulling the same kind of stunt when I was little, and all the girls had been white, so Lynn's race might not have had anything to do with it. She corrected me, though. "These boys said they didn't want to get African cooties," she told us.

Then came news about our Mike, a second-grader, fighting with a classmate who had been making offensive comments to Liska, who was in the first grade. "The guy kept calling me a nigger," she recalls. "Mike overheard it and he came and beat up the other boy. Mike told him not to ever call his sister that again."

Liska was obviously proud of her protector when she breathlessly told us about the incident after school. We, too, were glad Mike would stand up against such behavior — a trait he has carried into manhood — but we had to admonish him against fighting for any reason other than personal defense. We assured all the kids there were ways to combat racism without resorting to violence, and I demonstrated it the next day by calling the elementary school principal to report the name-calling and ask that steps be taken to see that it did not continue.

How naïve I was. The principal told me his staff was instructed to react vigorously to incidents of that kind, but he added that teachers had little control over offensive behavior and language that pupils were learning at home. I bristled a bit and suggested that with a little more imagination he might think of some things that could be done in the classroom. "When kids learn poor grammar at home, you try to correct it at school. What's any different about poor racial attitudes being taught at home?" He replied rather defensively that appreciation of racial and cultural diversity *was* part of the curriculum, copies of which were on file for me or anyone else to inspect. And he concluded our telephone conversation with a mild lecture. "All children experience razzing at some point in their lives," he said, "whether it's for being fat or skinny or having freckles or curly hair." He cautioned me about the inclination of some of us, "particularly our minority parents," to be overly sensitive to this common childhood behavior.

"I'm white," I told him. His surprise was evident in the moment of silence that ensued. Then I gave *him* a little lecture. "Kids need to learn early in life to respect differences, not attack them," I said, sounding perhaps a bit more moralistic than I meant to. "If some forms of cruel needling are taken lightly as 'common childhood behavior,' you're just opening the door to racial tormenting, and that's a disastrous form of harassment that can't be tolerated in America in 1975." I told him I had a fairly thick skin, being a newspaperman, but the school would do well to avoid getting Gloria upset. "Any more race-related problems," I said, "and you'll get to meet my wife. She makes me seem like a mild-mannered reporter, which is what I am, actually."

I was right about Gloria. Soon afterward, she received a second-hand report, through a friend who was the mother of one of Lynn's classmates, about a group of white girls who had been terrorizing Lynn in the school lavatory. The exact nature of what was going on was vague, and Lynn refused to talk to us about it at the time, but it was enough to mobilize Gloria. Today, Lynn fills in some of the details she wouldn't discuss then.

"I was being harassed in school a lot when I was in the fourth grade," she says. "I was the only black person in the whole school, and I got threatened that I would get beat up if I didn't use what the others called the 'black' toilet in the girls' lavatory. It had one toilet with a black seat and the rest were white. Every time I went in there during recess and between classes, these other girls followed me in and warned me that if I didn't sit on the 'black' toilet they would beat me up, so I always had to use that one. Then these girls would crawl up on the adjacent stalls and look down at me and start laughing and making fun of the black girl on the 'black' toilet.

"It was just me and this other little pudgy Indian girl; she had to do the same thing. We were the only two that had to do it. She was a Native American girl who lasted only two or three months at that school. I'd always get on the other kids about making fun of her because she was really heavy-set. In P.E. all the other girls would crouch under the trampoline to see if it would touch the floor when she was jumping on it. They really ridiculed her, and the teacher wouldn't do anything about it. I'd say, 'That's not very nice' and get on everybody. She'd run off to the back crying and I would go back there with her.

"I actually don't remember being called any names," Lynn says. "Maybe it happened behind my back, but not to my face — never. But they humiliated me in other ways, especially about my hair. They would run up to me and make fun of it. My hair was a lot different from theirs. I wore an Afro. They'd grab it and squeeze it and ask if they could use it to mop the lavatory.

"Whenever I could, I sneaked in there and used the 'white' toilets, just to get even with those girls. I was always afraid to turn them in. It was like me against all of them. I didn't tell anybody about it because I feared it would get back to those girls, and I wanted so much for them to accept me that getting them into trouble was the last thing I wanted to do. Then I definitely wouldn't have had any friends."

Gloria and her pal, Dottie Hardy, not knowing the half of what Lynn and the Indian girl were enduring, marched into the school the next day, unannounced. The principal and school staff were stunned to see the two mothers posted inside the girls' lavatory and out in the hallway. The tactic was rather flamboyant, but it worked. Lynn was no longer systematically harassed by the gang of girls, and Gloria and Dottie continued monitoring the lavatory daily until the principal agreed to guarantee that the persecution would not resume.

As things began settling down at Ellis Parker, Gloria and I considered the wisdom of staying in Eugene. We felt frustrated that after we had moved all the way across town, into a supposedly more tolerant neighborhood, our children were still encountering racial hate. The only difference was that now the perpetrators were the offspring of merchants and lawyers rather than the children of truckdrivers and millworkers. We still thought, however, that a more diverse neighborhood and school would be a healthier environment for all four of our kids.

So why didn't we relocate? We rationalized, dredging up a lot of reasons for staying that sounded better then than they do today. We weighed the fact that almost all of our friends and relatives lived in the Eugene area. Why move hundreds of miles away from the people you care about? Gloria and our children were the only surviving kin of Merle and Mildred Burton. How could we desert them? Also, we could not afford private schools for four kids, and the Eugene schools — rated among the best public education systems in the nation — provided us with an attractive alternative. Why trade it for an urban school that would almost certainly offer lower quality along with the racial diversity we desired?

Meanwhile, our town was basking in positive attention in 1975 as the result of a national survey rating Eugene as the "most livable" city in the United States. Besides great public schools, Eugene was touted for its mild climate, clean air and water, low crime rate, progressive local government, vibrant arts community, excellent state university, enlightened land-use planning, and resistance to uncontrolled growth. Gloria and I shared in the sense of community pride that resonated in Eugene after the Kansas researchers' "most livable" ratings made national news. We loved our city's libraries, swimming pools, parks, bike paths, and jogging trails. We boasted about the fact that I could drive from home to work in less than ten minutes, at any time of the day. We could not imagine living anywhere else.

Our final excuse for remaining in Eugene was a cleverly biased poll of our kids. The results — surprise! — were unanimous: no, they did not want to move away and have to make new friends.

So we stayed, and Gloria got more involved than ever at school. She and Dottie Hardy became active in the PTA and emerged as constructive critics of the Ellis Parker administration. Both of them also served as "room helpers" — volunteers assisting teachers in the classrooms, on the playground, and at holiday room parties. Despite the two mothers' positive effect on pupil behavior at the school, our family continued to have problems. One surfaced later that school year, when Dottie found out something else Lynn had not confided at home: a music teacher had lost patience with Lynn and slapped her in the face — in front of the whole class, including Dottie's daughter, Debbie. As a result of our complaint about the incident, the teacher was reprimanded, placed on probation, and required to apologize formally to Gloria and me.

Lynn, it turned out, had been socializing too much in the classroom. She did indeed goof around and talk a lot in class throughout her school years, probably as part of her incessant search for acceptance, but she was never known to be disrespectful toward a teacher. Gloria and I could understand how Lynn might earn a disciplinary visit to the principal's office — but a slap in the face? We could only guess what would make a teacher lose control with a nine-year-old girl enough to strike her in anger. Was it her race?

Lynn thinks so. Throughout school, some teachers seemed friendly to her and some did not. It is normal to have both kinds, of course; Lynn understood that and holds no ill feelings toward teachers who were not particularly warm or helpful. Her white friends and brothers were in the same situation, she realized. In Lynn's case, though, she says there was a third group of teachers — those who loathed her. The music teacher who slapped her was part of that very small group, the handful who detested Lynn for her color.

"Believe me, you *know*," she says. "It's there. You learn to recognize it in countless ways. There's a certain tension right when you enter the teacher's room. You see it in unguarded first glances. You feel it. You can also sense when somebody is being phony about the whole thing — when they really are prejudiced against you but they're playing it off like they're not. You can tell when they're for real about it and when they're not."

After the slapping incident, Gloria and I reconsidered the idea of leaving Eugene but once again rationalized staying put. We relied on our previous list of reasons, bolstered by a pair of new ones: I thoroughly liked my editor role at the Eugene paper and felt committed to staying, and Gloria wanted to accept a job at our kids' school. Through her volunteer work she had won the staff's respect, and when a position opened for an instructional aide, faculty members urged her to apply. She did and was offered the job.

Thus, instead of going back to complete her college degree as she had once planned, Gloria embarked on a career as a noncertified teacher's aide. She worked at various Eugene elementary schools for the next fifteen years, most of that time in special education, helping learning-disabled children learn to read.

Although staying in Eugene was probably not the best decision for Lynn and Liska, there was a bright side: both girls received an excellent public school education that probably surpassed the quality of what they would have had in another city. Eugene's well-financed school system enjoyed the highest per-pupil expenditure of all public districts in Oregon. The Eugene schools were loaded with outstanding teachers and a rich array of programs for gifted students and for the disadvantaged as well. Liska, in particular, benefited from year after year of special tutoring.

"School was sometimes hard for me," Liska says today. "Math and history were very hard. Reading was easier, and so was writing. I liked them the best, and making reports. In high school I really enjoyed child development classes and home economics, too.

"I think one of the best qualities that I have is the fact that living with my parents and going to school in Eugene made me better educated than many of the other black people I know today. I don't mean I'm any better than them, but I did have a better education."

Lynn was an above-average student who did best in language arts, like Liska. Partly on the basis of good grades, Lynn made the rally squad in junior high and spent the eighth grade as the only black cheerleader in the Eugene school system, which had about twenty thousand students. "I always did the homework, and I got a lot of help at home. Whenever Mom didn't know something, I would ask Dad. If any of us kids got a bad grade, we knew we would get into trouble — unless the subject was too hard for us. Then we'd work something out. There was always help from home when it came to that."

Lynn's marks dropped dramatically in high school. She attributes it to her attempts to be accepted by a handful of other black students who made her feel that by doing homework, going to class, and studying for exams, she was "trying to be white." In Lynn's mind at that time, she could be charged with no worse crime. "I know it sounds weird," she says, "but there was a point in my life where I was confused by accusations like that. Should I go ahead and act as if I was tough and hated school because I was around people like that? Or was that really me? It's hard to explain, but eventually I figured out that if you just be yourself you will be more accepted than trying to act like others want you to act."

Both Lynn and Liska exhibited one form of school behavior that could not be characterized as either "black" or "white": each tried her best to be the class comedian.

"Basically, I stayed to myself at school, because making friends was pretty hard," Lynn says. "I would clown around all the time in class to get attention. I thought that if I was funny, people would say, 'Oh, she's not that bad a person,' and then they would become friends with me. Each year it got better. Towards my senior year I had a lot of friends and quit goofing off so much. But in the early years I was in trouble all the time for acting up at school, thinking that's how I could be accepted. I'm sure it was a self-esteem thing."

Whatever it was, Liska had the same malady in elementary school. "I was a real terror," she says. "I'd try to outdo everyone and show off. I wanted to be liked, so I was a class clown. Lots of people laughed, but sometimes I did stunts that got me in trouble."

For two black girls who wanted so badly to be accepted at over-whelmingly white schools, one of the worst times came in the final week of January in 1977. That's when many Americans — up to eighty million of them — were riveted to the television miniseries *Roots*, adapted from the best-selling novel by Alex Haley. Every episode was required watching in our household, and Lynn and Liska grew increasingly uncomfortable as the week progressed.

"I kept getting up to go to the bathroom every time the slaves got whipped," Lynn recalls. "I couldn't watch it. It really bothered me. And every day at school that week, my teachers wanted to discuss *Roots* with the class, and everybody kept staring at me. That bothered me even more than watching the show. It was like that all through my school years. Whenever Africa or slavery or blacks were talked about in class, everybody would turn and look at me. It made me feel uncomfortable."

Liska tells of exactly the same ordeal. "In high school, if the topic was black history, the teachers would emphasize the word 'black' and a lot of the students would turn and look at me to see my reaction. That bothered me."

Being the only black girl in school wasn't always a dreadful experience, though. There were times when Lynn and Liska received favored treatment, apparently for no other reason than the color of their skin. "Coaches, for example, would seem to say, 'Oh, a black girl! Let's get her into sports!'" Liska says. "Every sport you can name, I was recruited into it — softball, soccer, volleyball, basketball, gymnastics, swimming, track. I got a lot of individual coaching and attention, which I enjoyed. Sports kept my mind off doing drugs and all that kind of stuff. I liked to win and do the best I could. I really did get deep into sports and I'm glad."

There are some mirthful memories, too. One of them occurred on Halloween in 1973, when seven-year-old Lynn discovered that one thing worse than having brown skin at her school was having *green* skin. She was fascinated by the televised movie version of *The Wizard of Oz*, a film so scary to Lynn that she had to leave the room at times, especially when the cackling Wicked Witch of the East appeared on the scene. Not too surprisingly, Lynn decided she wanted to dress up for her school Halloween party that year as her favorite witch. So Gloria sewed her a black witch's dress, made her a pointed black hat, and crafted a wicked-looking broom for her. As Lynn dressed for school on October 31, she was a great little witch even before Gloria applied the final touch, a facial coating of green greasepaint.

An hour or so after Gloria drove the kids to school, she received a phone call from the principal's office. A secretary was making a routine report that Lynn was absent. Instantly alarmed, Gloria replied that she had dropped Lynn off at school at the usual time and that Lynn, wearing her witch costume, had been excited about the Halloween party. She *had* to be somewhere in the school building, Gloria insisted. The secretary, urging Gloria not to worry, said she'd take a look around and call right back.

Sure enough, a few minutes later the woman telephoned Gloria again. Our little Wicked Witch of the East had been found hiding in the girls' lavatory. The secretary said Lynn had somehow got her facts wrong about the Halloween festivities. Children were supposed to bring costumes to school but not put them on until the party, which was to be at the end of the day. Upon arriving at school that morning, Lynn had been mortified to discover she was the only costumed kid at Ellis Parker Elementary. Fellow pupils reacted to her black-robed, green-tinged countenance with howls of derision. Too humiliated to go to class, Lynn did exactly what any normal second-grader would do: she hid in a toilet stall, waiting for the horrible school day to end.

Gloria drove back to the school and rescued Lynn. They hurried home, scrubbed Lynn's face, changed her clothes, and stuffed the costume into a shopping bag, which Lynn took back to school with her. She refused to have anything more to do with the green greasepaint.

Liska topped Lynn's Halloween tale a few years later. Just as Lynn had been captivated by the witch from Oz, Liska was enchanted by Casper the Ghost, and that's who she wanted to be on October 31, 1977. Gloria, who has always thrown herself passionately into holidays and special occasions, got out her sewing machine and some old sheets and obligingly made Liska a ghost outfit. Liska, though, was disappointed in Gloria's initial effort. Casper the Ghost had a white hood, Liska insisted, and she produced storybook pictures to prove her point.

So Gloria went back to work and sewed a pointed hood to top off our high-spirited little ghost. That afternoon, when Liska tried on the finished product, Gloria and I laughed until tears came to our eyes. Wearing her white sheets and the pointed hood with eye holes cut out so she could see, Liska looked nothing like a ghost; she resembled a diminutive member of the Ku Klux Klan. Liska was hilarious, but no way were we going to take her trick-or-treating like that. The hood, we said, had to go.

Anyone who knows Liska could have predicted her reaction to that. She loved the hood and thought it made her look exactly like Casper the Ghost. In tears, she insisted we had to let her wear it. And besides, she had never heard of the Ku Klux Klan.

That night, as I took the kids around our neighborhood with their trick-or-treat bags, I grew increasingly touchy about the surprised looks Liska was receiving from parents answering the door. Steve was dressed as a mummy, Lynn as a witch, Mike as a devil, and Liska, from all outward appearances, as a Klansman. "Liska is Casper the Ghost," I explained over and over in my embarrassment.

After the trick-or-treating, our whole family went to a Halloween party at the nearby home of Blaine and Joanna Newnham. They were good friends who had generously allowed Liska to attend Joanna's private preschool in 1973 on a "scholarship" after learning that Gloria and I could not afford the tuition. A few years later, the Newnhams, too, adopted a special-needs child — a three-year-old white son named Deejay. That evening in 1977 was Deejay's first Halloween party with the Bates children. Blaine Newnham, who was my newspaper's sports editor, greeted us at the door and chuckled when he saw Liska in her white hood.

"Looks like you brought the Grand Dragon along with you tonight," he said. It was a harmless wisecrack, but it finally pushed me over the edge.

"She's a *ghost,* dammit," I snapped.

The annual Halloween parties at the Bates and Newnham homes were wildly creative extravaganzas that most of our children remember as a high point of the year. There were always treats galore, but to get at them the kids first had to maneuver through a cleverly spooky haunted house that Blaine and I and other friends would work for hours creating in one of our garages. Each year our friend and co-worker Brian Lanker, the Pulitzer-winning photographer, performed the role of Mogo, a monster inside an enormous cardboard box. The children had to reach through holes in Mogo's box to receive treats — or unpleasant surprises like shaving cream or cold squid. We invented a lot of zany party games for the kids and lavished the winners and losers with funny prizes. And always, our parties were noted for elaborate, sometimes ingenious costumes.

The year Liska went as Casper the Klansman, it was quite warm at the Newnhams' house, and much to my relief, all of the excited, sweaty Bates kids soon took off their masks — or hood, in Liska's case. I saw where she put it. Later, when she looked for it, the pointy thing was nowhere to be found. Too bad. Maybe Mogo took it.

❦ 9 ❦

Hair

Mom & Dad,

   . . . Work is going great. I'm building my clientele up faster and faster. For example, I usually do at least two curls a day, plus nails, so that's a good $120, and in between I help do the owner's chemicals because he's so busy. My speed is picking up better and better. I'm not used to doing black hair, but I have to be motivated to learn to take that first step or I'll be losing money, and you know I need it!

   Take care. Love,
      Lynn

Letter from Lynn, age twenty-four
Seattle, Washington
May 1990

NO ONE WHO KNEW LYNN as a girl was surprised that she grew up to become a hair stylist. Throughout adolescence Lynn was obsessed with her roots, and not just the kind Alex Haley wrote about. Hair has occupied an important part of her consciousness since the day in 1970 when she first saw Gloria in the Eugene pet store.

"The first thing I remember about my adoptive mom was her long hair," Lynn says. "I'd never seen hair like that, parted in the middle and hanging very long and straight. Both of my new parents were a lot younger and hipper than my foster parents. They had seemed so old, like a grandma and grandpa. My new mom was unlike anyone I'd ever seen. She wore short dresses back then — *really* short dresses — but it was her hair that fascinated me. I thought it was beautiful."

At school or at summer camp, whenever Lynn was assigned to

draw a picture of herself, she portrayed a little girl with long, luxurious hair just like Gloria's. Lynn herself had lovely hair when it was fixed in suitable African-American styles, but she was never able to wear it long the way her white girlfriends and her mother and even her adopted sister could. For Lynn, the subject was a source of alienation at school, strained relations with Gloria, and envy of Liska.

"I was extremely self-conscious about my hair as I was growing up," Lynn recalls. "Mine was so different from everyone else I knew. Liska's hair was a lot softer than mine and had a whole different texture. She never really had to worry about it. My hair was very kinky and curly and nappy. I always had problems with it, and Mom wasn't much help. She didn't know what to do. But she learned how to relax and straighten Liska's hair, and it would go clear down her back. I was always envious of that. Mine was just there, in an Afro."

Throughout the early and mid-seventies, while the style was still in fashion, Lynn could wear a perfect 'fro of any size. The look was quite becoming for her, but that made no difference; she wanted to wear her hair long and wavy and feathered back, as most of her schoolmates did. At times Lynn's inability to conform seemed to tinge her childhood with sadness. Hair became a fixation. She rejected her first black doll, which had a short Afro, but cherished her second one, which had long, straight, silky black hair. Her favorite television show for years was *Charlie's Angels*. She would sit on the floor in front of the TV set, with a T-shirt pulled sphinx-like over the back of her head, and flip her cotton coiffure along with Farrah Fawcett. Many other times Lynn was seen prancing around the house with braided nylon pantyhose pinned to her hair and hanging long down her back. Sometimes she would stand before a bathroom mirror, with the business end of a mop on her head, tossing and flipping the strands as if she were preening for a shampoo commercial.

Acknowledging Lynn's obsession with hair in no way trivializes the story of her adoption. For our family, her tonsorial frustrations have always been a symbol of the problems and challenges involved in transracial adoptions like ours. And in fairness, it must be said that our entire family and American society as well have been consumed by the subject of hair as far back as Gloria and I can remember.

As I entered my teens, my parents would not allow me or my two brothers to wear a greasy pompadour like James Dean's or Elvis Presley's. We docilely submitted to military-style close-cuts performed by my father with his home barber shears. Gloria, meanwhile, was even more severely restrained by her parents, who would not allow her to wear a ponytail when that was in fashion, or even to attend an Elvis Presley movie when *Jailhouse Rock* was making teen-age girls swoon. Long hair was equated with rebellion in the Bates and Burton households long before the Beatles came along.

By the late sixties, when Gloria and I were married and on our own, flowing locks had become an important antiestablishment statement in America. Politicians were ridiculing college students with long hair. Families were feuding over it. Hippies were getting beat up over it. Workers were being fired over it. Rock stars were singing about it. Broadway was even producing a musical about it. I doubt whether anyone born after that era can fully grasp the depth of emotion that Americans attached to hair in those days.

Throughout the late sixties and the seventies, Gloria's long, auburn hair was a barometer of personal conviction and family harmony. She began letting it grow out in 1968 after Robert Kennedy was assassinated and Richard Nixon defeated Hubert Humphrey for president. By the time we adopted Lynn two years later, Gloria's hair drooped far below her shoulders. It was halfway down her back by 1972, when Liska arrived. Gloria's parents despised her long hair. Merle especially seemed distressed and often said so. All that did was increase Gloria's resolve to let it grow.

Off and on she trimmed the loose ends, but her hair reached waist level in 1973, at just about the time the Arab oil embargo began destroying her father's automobile business. Merle was an exceedingly depressed and fearful man in those days, after the disgruntled

Middle East oil-producing nations shut off the flow of petroleum to the West, protesting America's support of Israel. For Merle, the timing could not have been worse. The embargo reached full force in the fall, just as General Motors was unveiling its big, new car models for 1974. In an instant, his Chevrolet dealership was devastated. After a decade of considerable prosperity, he suddenly discovered nobody in Oakridge wanted to buy gas-guzzling Impalas and Corvettes from him anymore. As fuel prices soared and panicky American motorists jockeyed for position in long lines at service stations, Merle bitterly speculated that the domestic fuel shortage was an opportunistic conspiracy by the oil companies. And he blamed the news media — including me and my newspaper — for abetting the alleged plot and for fanning public hysteria.

"Whose decision was it to run this picture?" Merle asked me on a dark, dank Thanksgiving day at his home. He angrily waved the front page of the *Register-Guard*, dominated that morning by a large photo of cars lined up for blocks at a gas station.

"That was the news editor's decision," I rather lamely replied.

"Aren't *you* the news editor?" he demanded.

"Yep."

"Thanks a lot," he said, his words heavy with scorn. "Every time you guys print a picture like this, it just causes more panic. Do you think anybody's going to buy a new car tomorrow after seeing this in today's paper?"

"I'm sorry," I said. "That's my job."

Merle was plainly disgusted with me, my line of work, and even my wife — his daughter — whom he had decided was a peacenik, environmentalist, and long-haired hippie. Merle's world was falling apart, and I could not help feeling sorry for him. Even six months later, after the Arabs lifted the oil embargo, fuel prices remained high and the automobile business was irrevocably changed. Customers did not flock back to Burton Chevrolet; they began shopping out of town for energy-efficient little Datsuns and Volkswagens. Meanwhile, his president, Richard Nixon, was sinking ever deeper into the mire of the Watergate scandal, and Vice President Spiro Agnew resigned after agreeing not to contest a charge of income tax evasion. By late 1974, when Nixon quit in disgrace, Merle Burton seemed sad and disillusioned. But despite my editing role with one of his enemies, the newspaper, he seemed somewhat closer to me than to his own daughter. I guessed it had something to do with hair and symbolism.

"That's a good haircut," he once said to me, not long after I had gone in for a trim. Gradually, as I had become more involved in management, I had gotten rid of the John Lennon glasses and mustache and mutton-chop sideburns. "I'll bet the top bosses take you more seriously now," Merle told me. He said I was smart. Gloria, with a laugh, said I was selling out.

"Gloria, you used to look really good with short hair," Merle told her. "I sure wish we could talk you into getting it cut again."

No chance. She kept letting those tresses grow right on through 1974, as Gerald Ford became president and pardoned Nixon, and through 1975, as the United States pulled out of Vietnam and Saigon fell to the Communists. Merle's personal misery reached a crescendo that year; the energy crisis mounted, the American automobile industry continued its tailspin, and he was diagnosed with lymphatic cancer. The illness forced him to sell his big house and what was left of his car dealership.

By the end of 1976, after Jimmy Carter defeated Ford for the presidency, my wife's long mane was beginning to rival Rapunzel's. Gloria's resistance to cutting her hair was not founded in antiwar, antiestablishment, or even antiparent sentiment, as her morose, ailing father assumed. Her reasons were more complicated and personal. As many of her friends began styling their hair in short, perky, career-woman cuts, Gloria told me that getting her own hair cut short would make her feel as if she were shedding the idealistic values of our earlier era. "I don't want us to change," she said. "I'm *afraid* of us changing."

In 1977, when Gloria finally talked about having her locks shorn, it was not because Elvis Presley had just died or because the disco age had arrived. She offered to do it for Lynn's sake.

Lynn was having a personal crisis over her hair by then. She was entering junior high school, the Afro style that was attractive on her was quickly going out of fashion, and she was suffering deep despair over being unable to wear her hair long and layered. Gloria, too, was feeling desperation over her repeated failures to help Lynn deal with the problem. For years, Gloria had tried to do Lynn's hair at home because the professional beauticians in our community — all of them white when Lynn was young — had no experience with black hair.

"I remember the first haircut Lynn got," Gloria says. "I took her to a salon where I'm sure she was the first black girl the beautician had ever worked on. The woman tried to comb through Lynn's hair with a regular comb. Of course, that didn't work too well. The woman became very frustrated. I suggested picking it out with a hair pick, and she didn't know what I was talking about."

Despite the best of intentions, though, Gloria's home hair operations were no answer for Lynn, either. "Her hair was certainly a challenge," Gloria says. "Some of it was almost straight. It had a nice wave to it. But the other part was tight curls, very frizzy. I would try to get both types of hair looking the same, but I was never too successful. If I curled Lynn's hair, the straight part wouldn't curl enough, and the frizzy part would curl so much I couldn't even comb through it. When I tried to relax her hair, I would have to leave the solution on for quite a long time. Sometimes her hair turned bright orange and I would have to put a color on to cover it up. I usually bought a light brown hair color, but it often turned out black because Lynn's hair was so porous.

"The more I worked on Lynn's hair, the more frustrated she and I became. Her hair never seemed to turn out how she had hoped it would. It certainly never looked like the pictures on the boxes of hair perm."

By the late seventies, black hair products finally began showing up at one Eugene drugstore near the university campus. Gloria and Lynn became regular customers. "I found an over-the-counter perm called 'Dark and Lovely' that worked much better for Lynn than perms made for white people's hair," Gloria recalls. "Lynn's hair would look pretty good for about a week after I did it. Then the new growth would start showing and kink everything up again. The older growth would become dry and brittle and start breaking off. But even if that hadn't happened, Lynn still wouldn't have been happy with her hair because she wanted it to look just like all her white friends' hair, loose and feathered back."

For Lynn, the subject was nothing but heartaches. "At school," she recalls, "I was always made fun of because of my hair. It was so different. I couldn't feather my hair no matter how hard I or Mom tried. That really upset me a lot. I didn't understand how come I had to have hair like that when everyone else had good hair.

"Mom did my hair most of the time and really did try to help. But for years she used Caucasian perms. She just rolled it like Caucasian hair. Today, I know that with black hair you need to break it down straight first and then put the rollers in and the curl solution. Mom didn't know that. She just slapped on the Toni perm. That's how she did *her* hair."

By the time Lynn was eleven or twelve, Eugene's first black-operated beauty shop opened. "Mom took me there one Saturday and we were sure they would be able to solve all my problems," Lynn recalls. "I was really excited and had high expectations. But it took seven hours to get my hair done that day, and it didn't end up looking any different than when Mom did it."

Lynn's unhappiness with her hair became almost legendary in our extended family. Bates relatives all over the state of Oregon sympathized with Lynn and equated her dejection, quite correctly, with her difficulty in embracing her black identity. Several members of my family tried hard to help.

My sister Jill, a talented artist, gave us one of her oil paintings, depicting black musicians all wearing their hair in Afro styles. We displayed the picture prominently in our home.

My mother, after inviting Lynn to stay at her home for a week, took her to a black beauty shop in Portland, where experienced professionals gave her an updated cut and curl — which Lynn did not truly like. Her hair still wasn't anything like that of her white classmates.

My brother Dan, Lynn's favorite uncle, took her to a photography studio to pose. It was an act of kindness by Dan, who took the photographs himself. He thought of the photo session as a way to help Lynn believe that black indeed was beautiful and so was she. After seven years of selling Cadillacs and Oldsmobiles, Dan had left the car business. His marriage had broken up, and the energy crisis and foreign-automobile competition were destroying his livelihood, so he became a newspaper photographer. With a generous assist from our mutual friend Brian Lanker, Dan began his new career at the *Register-Guard,* and soon, through his own hard work, intelligence, and impressive creativity, he became one of the Pacific Northwest's more respected news photographers. His studio photographs of Lynn, suitable for a modeling portfolio, are family treasures today. Lynn says that despite her love for her uncle and her appreciation of his efforts to help her feel black pride, she hated her pictures.

Brian Lanker always took a deep interest in our girls. (Looking back, I realize Brian's generosity and interest in Lynn and Liska foreshadowed the 1989 publication of his critically acclaimed book, *I Dream a World: Portraits of Black Women Who Changed America.*) Once, trying to help, he gave Lynn a Supremes record album with a gorgeous cover photo of Diana Ross, Mary Wilson, and Cindy Birdsong. Unfortunately, all three black singing stars were photographed with their hair straightened, in essentially Caucasian styles that Lynn could not duplicate. She loved the Supremes' music, but her hair-related disappointment only mushroomed.

Ebony magazines and other potential sources of help found their way into our home, to little avail. Lynn did not want to wear her hair like Barbara Jordan or Angela Davis or even the glamorous Cicely Tyson.

"I didn't mind being black," Lynn says. "I just wanted my hair like Charlie's Angels. They could flip their long hair. I wanted to be able to do that. It was so beautiful to me. I couldn't even move my hair. At fairs, I envied people on the carnival rides. The wind would fling their hair in their faces. That's why I pinned old mops on my head at home, to help me fantasize what it would be like."

In the meantime, Lynn could not help noticing how easy it was for her sibling rival, Liska, to wear her hair any way she pleased. Liska's hair was much darker — almost jet black — but it could easily be curled or straightened. She could go to school as Maya Angelou one day and Oprah Winfrey the next. For fall soccer Liska would fix her hair like any white girl; then she'd switch to pigtails for winter gymnastics and beads and corn rows for spring track.

"Liska's hair was not tightly kinked like Lynn's," Gloria says. "I relaxed Liska's hair and it was very manageable. Not only could she style it many ways, but it would also grow longer than Lynn's hair without breaking off."

Liska was acutely aware of the matter. "People would always tell me my hair was good and looked so nice," she says. "No one ever said that about Lynn's hair. I could always tell by the look on Lynn's face she didn't like that. I knew that it upset her, and I felt sorry for her."

All of Lynn's grade school and junior high pictures show her with short hair — most often in a variation of the conventional 'fro but sometimes straight, and always with barrettes or combs holding it flat on top. She hated having her hair stand up on top; none of her schoolmates' hair did that, and it was one small way in which Lynn could impose control. Even during basketball season, when Lynn was a starter on the girls' team, she refused to take those barrettes out of her hair, even though they caused excruciating pain whenever she caught an elbow on the crown of her head.

I tried to help in various ineffective ways; then, in 1978, I was struck with a grand idea. A short time before, my newspaper had hired a young black woman as a clerk-receptionist for the newsroom. Cheryl was her name. She was a highly intelligent, beautiful lady who could have stepped right out of TV's Cosby family. The daughter of a Portland physician, Cheryl was a University of Oregon graduate, married to a former star player on the football team. I told Cheryl about my daughter's grooming frustrations and asked if she would mind coming to our home sometime to give Lynn and

Gloria some hair-care advice. Cheryl kindly agreed to help out in any way she could. One evening she came to our home and spent several hours with Lynn.

"She was black, with a small Afro, and really beautiful," Lynn recalls. "I remember she tried to show me how to work with my hair. How to use a pick. It did help. The lady had me fix it in a perfect Afro with sheen and had it perfectly round."

I thought Lynn had never looked better. At work the next morning I thanked Cheryl profusely and assured her she had single-handedly solved one of my family's oldest and most vexing problems. Back at our home, though, just before Lynn hurried off to school that morning, Gloria accidentally walked in on her in the bathroom and was astounded by what she found. Lynn had combed out her new Afro on top and was flattening it down with braids and barrettes.

"I didn't want the round look," Lynn recalls today. "There was no way in the world I wanted it that way. I would have been made more fun of at school.

"I remember Dad and Mom telling me that my hair was unique and special, that I should want to be different from everyone else. They'd say, 'Well, everyone doesn't have to have the same hair.' Mom would say she wished she had my hair. She couldn't get her hair to curl. 'Lots of people go out and pay money to have a perm to make their hair curl,' she'd tell me. She'd say I was lucky because I already had curly hair. That didn't help at all."

As Lynn's frustrations mounted, Gloria eventually suggested cutting her own flowing mane and getting a short perm. That, at least, might help Lynn relate more to her and ease the tension between them over hair. Lynn, however, hated that idea. Mom clipping her locks? That seemed blasphemous. Lynn talked her out of it.

A minor miracle occurred when Lynn was a senior in high school. She found out about Brenda, a newly arrived black woman in town. Brenda did hair at her home, and she was wonderful. "Lynn's hair turned out really pretty," Gloria recalls. "Brenda seemed to know what she was doing, and Lynn liked the results a lot. She looked like a fashion model in her high school graduation photos."

Lynn's grandmother — my mom, Patricia — tried for years to help Lynn feel proud of being black and having black hair. "Grandma always wanted me to become a news person on TV," Lynn says. "She always wanted me to cut my hair really short, to just wear it natural. She said it was beautiful that way. She'd cut out little pictures of black models who had very short hair and give them to me. Grandma said I talked well and liked talking and there weren't many black, female news people. She thought I could do it. And Mom, she thought I should be an airline pilot, or a flight attendant. But I didn't want to be a journalist or a pilot. My mind kept going back to hair. Could I cut people's hair on the plane? Could I do perms at the news station? I didn't want to be a TV news anchorwoman; I wanted to do the anchorwoman's hair.

"I guess that's why I became a beautician. It was thrilling to be able to use curling irons and do things to other people's hair that I couldn't do to mine. That's how it was in the beginning, but then I started working in black shops. Then I really started feeling good about *my* hair. I love helping people who have hair like mine but just don't like it. I can fix it for them. I know how to do it — finally."

So what did our family learn from Lynn's long ordeal? For starters, we now know that any white parents who adopt black children should lose no time finding their own Brenda. As a licensed hair stylist in Seattle, Lynn is aware today that many African-American people don't know the right way to handle certain types of black hair. White parents, as a group, are far more uninformed, of course. She says, and we concur, there is no substitute for highly skilled professional help.

That was our pragmatic lesson. I think we also learned something more spiritual while groping with hair problems as our daughters grew up. This occurred to me after an evening in 1978 when I came home from work and found Lynn moping in the family room.

"What's wrong?" I asked.

"It's Mom," she said.

"What happened?"

"You'll see. She's in the kitchen."

I went in and found Gloria fixing dinner. The sight was a shock. She'd had ten years of hair lopped off just below the ears.

"Good God!" I blurted out. "Why did you do it?"

Gloria did not reply right away, and when she did, her voice was subdued. "It was just hair," she said. "Dead cells, actually." She did not look up at me or offer any explanation for having it cut after all those years.

Our kids — or three of them — didn't seem to understand their mom's drastic haircut but probably didn't spend much time wondering about it. Lynn, though, seemed briefly troubled. As much as she had envied Gloria's long tresses, she had not imagined her mother without them. I sensed that Lynn mistakenly interpreted the haircut as a mother's misguided effort to make her daughter feel a little better about her own short hair. Privately, however, I had a different theory.

The following day Gloria visited her cancer-stricken father at the hospital. Her new look pleased him, and he complimented her in an extraordinarily emotional moment. Merle Burton had worried for years that Gloria had become some sort of estranged, long-haired hippie he could not communicate with. After Marilyn's death, the widening ideological gap between father and surviving daughter had seemed huge and irreconcilable. Now, though, we look back at those differences and realize they were dwarfed by similarities. Essentially, the things Merle had wanted out of life were much the same as the hopes and dreams of Gloria and me, and of our white sons and black daughters. It is a cliché but true: we are all more alike than we are different. Most of what separates us from our fathers and our other fellow human beings, we have learned, is magnified by ungraceful communication and a clutter of symbolism, too often focusing on meaningless physical attributes, such as skin color. Or hair.

There would be no trip to Africa with Gloria's father. A few days after that hospital visit, at about six in the morning, three weeks before Christmas, Merle's life ended. He was fifty-eight. He had lost his beloved daughter Mouse, his health, his automobile business, and his big house on the hill. Gloria, though, had done what she could, through a symbolic gesture that struck me as sweet and generous, to make sure he left us knowing he had never lost his other daughter, the free spirit, the one he had never understood.

❧ 10 ❧

Brothers and Sisters

Dear Mom & Dad,

   . . . Sorry I haven't written sooner. I'm usually so tired after work that I just crash out. I do enjoy carpentry. I just wish I had more free time to play music or write letters . . . I've gotten together with Mike and Liska a few times this month. We met once at Liska's for dinner. She makes some great chili. Speaking of Liska, it'll be nice when she gets out of that tiny apartment. That area she lives in has been plagued with shootings, fights, and other assorted felonies. I worry about her a lot.

Letter from Steve, age twenty-five
Eugene, Oregon
October 26, 1990

Dad & Mom,

   I've got a lot to be thankful for: a large family that cares about each other and that is still together, and parents who believe enough in their own dreams that they are not afraid to take chances and follow them. It is for that reason I can feel confident enough in my own personal dreams to make a couple of sacrifices and follow them. I am living the start of a long-awaited dream to be a deep-sea diver. Thank you for being my role models. Thanks for my life. Thank God.

Card from Mike, age twenty-three
Coronado, California
Thanksgiving Day, 1991

FOR THE MOST PART, watching relationships blossom and mature among our sons and daughters has been a tremendously rewarding aspect of our interracial family. Gloria and I have felt blessed as we've seen deep and lasting feelings develop between Steve and Lynn, Lynn and Mike, Mike and Steve, Steve and Liska, and Liska and Mike. Our memories are crowded with images of sibling affinity: Mike and Lynn getting up before sunrise on summer mornings to go fishing together; Lynn spending all her baby-sitting money on a birthday gift for Steve; Liska tearfully applying a cold compress to Steve's face after a baseball injury; Steve, many years later, buying diapers for Liska's baby and helping her move to a safer apartment; Mike, after becoming a Navy diver, telephoning from the Persian Gulf to cheer up his lonely sister Liska even as Patriot missiles were being rushed in to defend against SCUD attacks by Saddam Hussein.

We have known only one disappointment over our children's interrelationships: the girls were not close. As much as Lynn and Liska have always showered their adoptive brothers with words of love and admiration, neither daughter was disposed to show that kind of affection for her sister. Their chilliness toward each other surprised and perplexed both Gloria and me while causing sadness for all of us in the family. We always knew there was love between Lynn and Liska. Both of them concede it today. So why was it so difficult for them to show it all those years? And why, conversely, did our two black daughters always have such an easy time expressing love for their white brothers?

What has resulted from these interracial sibling relationships? How have they affected the lives of Steve, Lynn, Mike, and Liska? The answers, it seems to me, are complex and best provided by our children themselves.

LISKA ON STEVE:

"My oldest brother, Steve, is about six foot two and has blond hair and blue eyes. He has a nice build and looks like a California beach kind of guy. He is very good looking but doesn't feel that he is. Steve is shy and doesn't have a lot of self-confidence. That is the only thing he is really lacking.

"Growing up with Steve was great. He was adventurous and fun to be with. When he was little he would always play with his chemistry set or build model cars. He was always building things, so I guess it's natural that he builds houses now. He is also very talented musically. He can play any kind of instrument.

"Like Mike, Steve is very funny, but his sense of humor is more serious than Mike's. Steve has a great heart. He cares. Because I'm his little sister, he looks after me. He plays the big brother role and likes to lecture me a lot. I know that it is coming from his heart, so I don't mind. I've always hated lectures, but I listen to him and take heed to what he says. Sometimes it's about managing my money or handling the kids. Sometimes it's about guys. I know Steve loves me. I can feel it. I love him a lot, too."

LYNN ON STEVE:
"I mainly remember Steve as being kind of quiet and shy as we were growing up. We weren't super close, but he always was really nice. He always tried to make me laugh. We joked around a lot. When my feelings were hurt, he was always there to try to make me feel better. He said that everything would be okay.

"I was always impressed with Steve's ability to build things. And I always thought it was cool to have a brother in a band. I didn't really care for his friends, though. I never got along with one of his buddies in the band. We fought, verbally, all the time. Steve didn't know whether to stick up for his friend or for his sister. That was kind of a bad situation.

"I love my brother Steve, of course. I feel he loves me, too. He cares. But in school I hardly ever saw him. For some reason I felt like I was an embarrassment to Steve. We were only a year apart. He'd pass me in the hall and kind of look away. I saw him in the halls a lot but we never communicated with each other. He would sometimes say 'Hi' and then turn away and never really connect with me. Everybody knew that we were brother and sister, but maybe he felt kind of uneasy about it — especially when girls were around. But when he liked someone I was hanging out with, then he'd want me to invite her over to the house. That's when I noticed him being around me more often. But that's a typical brother-sister thing, I think."

MIKE ON STEVE:

"My brother is a tall, good-looking man with a blond beard and a good complexion. He's thin but larger than me. Steve is extremely sincere and hard-working. He is a dreamer but yet very practical. He has an open ear; he listens. He is fun to be with, open to new ideas, and good at giving advice. He's also really bright and good at remembering things. I admire him for being musically gifted. The artistic part of the Bates family went his way. He would be a great architect or engineer. Above all, he is a great brother and a true friend."

STEVE ON LYNN:

"My sister Lynn is attractive, shy, self-conscious, and the shortest person in our family, maybe five foot two. She is very perceptive — smarter than she gives herself credit for.

"I didn't have a close relationship with Lynn as we were growing up, but I have always felt like she was my sister. In the old days I thought she was pretty nutty. Lynn could always make me laugh. Sometimes she would fidget. Other people intimidated her, possibly.

"It seemed like I didn't see Lynn that much in high school, even though she was only a year behind me. She had her own friends and was always gone with them. Or I was doing something on my own or working. In high school, people would often ask if it was really true that Lynn was my sister. I'd say 'Yes,' and they would say that she was beautiful. That always made me feel proud of Lynn. I was never embarrassed of her, but I can remember seeing her at school only a couple of times. I felt we got along well, but it wasn't as close as with Mike or Liska."

LISKA ON LYNN:

"Lynn always said that she was not a very attractive person, but I think she can be pretty if she dresses herself up right and takes care of herself. Lynn is really insecure. I don't think that she has enough faith in herself. She can't look you in the eye. She can't express herself emotionally. She probably has a lot of unanswered questions. Maybe she doesn't feel loved.

"When we were growing up, my sister, Lynn, used to be really fun to hang out with. She had a neat sense of humor. I always thought Lynn was intelligent, but she's really not mature for her age. I always felt more mature than her, even though she was three years older.

"Lynn is not a real emotional person. It is hard for her to express love. She can't say 'I love you' to anybody. I think it's because she had a rough early childhood, in the foster home. I think she might have more emotional problems about that experience than I do.

"Lynn is a good sister. But I wish that we would have had a better relationship as we were growing up. I love her and hope we will become closer now."

MIKE ON LYNN:
"I would say Lynn is intelligent, funny, very attractive, short, and thin. She is a very light-skinned lady who has had some funky hairdos. She has a great sense of humor and always knows when I'm kidding, which is much of the time.

"I was only two when she was adopted, so I can't remember life without Lynn. She's always been my sister. Period. So has Liska. I can't even remember when it was I learned they were adopted — not that it ever mattered.

"Lynn never seemed to have a problem with identity. I thought she knew who she was. To me, she didn't seem insecure. Liska sometimes did, maybe. When Lynn and I got together she didn't have as many buttons to push as Liska. Lynn and I could just joke about things and laugh, and nobody took it personally. We'd kid around all the time, about anything. I could be sarcastic to her, and instead of Lynn crying or getting mad and hitting me, she'd just say something back, more sarcastic than me. Then we'd just go on laughing and carrying on.

"I haven't seen Lynn very much in the past few years, and I regret that. I miss her a lot."

LYNN ON LISKA:

"I love Liska, but we were rivals growing up. Even the happiest times, like going to Disneyland, were a pain because I had to go on rides with Liska. We didn't like touching each other. I don't know what it really was. You'd think that we should have been the closest, both being adopted and both being black. But we were just so opposite from each other. I held in my emotions, and Liska spilled them out. I didn't cry very often, for example. If I *did* cry, which was hardly ever, it would be someplace where nobody would be around to see it. But Liska cried easily. Every time the two of us had a fight, I would always get the bad end of it because she would shed a tear or give a sob story, and Mom and Dad would feel sorry for her. I would be the big bad wolf.

"There were times when we got along really well — usually when we both got into trouble. Then we could sit and talk for a while, because we had that common bond. But it never lasted very long."

STEVE ON LISKA:

"Liska is an extremely loving, warm-hearted sister — a true 'people person.' She loves everybody and cares deeply about everyone in her family. She's also funny and pretty outspoken on what she believes.

"In her high school years, she was more aware of being black than Lynn was. Liska had more friends who were black. School was hard, socially and academically, for Liska. She seemed to seek out her black identity. I can remember Mike and me making fun of her because she would try to speak black slang or jive, sounding like the typical white person trying to talk black. It was pretty hilarious at first, but she got better at it after she had more friends who were black.

"I was probably closer to Liska than Mike was. They would get into more arguments. I think I grew up closer to Liska than to Lynn. That's probably because Lynn was off with her friends a lot of the time. Liska and Lynn had a stormy relationship. Sometimes they would get along, but usually they didn't. Maybe that's partly why each of them grew up so close to both Mike and me."

MIKE ON LISKA:

"Liska and I are very close today, but we had a lot of tension growing up. It was never racial. It was just personality conflict. And attitude problems. In junior high school, Liska seemed real angry. She would lash a lot of that anger out at me. She thought I was the family pet. In return, her accusations would make me angry. I'd get really sarcastic with her. We'd fight back and forth verbally. But it was probably just a teen-age thing we went through.

"Later, in high school, we became closer. She seemed really proud to have a white brother. She'd come running down the hallway and throw her arms around me and hug me.

"I remember that Liska would come to me a lot during high school to talk about some of her relationships with people. After I started going out with [a girlfriend], Liska and I started growing a little closer. I think she respected me in a sense because I was seeing someone on a regular basis and I had all these new emotions. Liska loved to hear about them, and she wanted to pour out some of her own feelings.

"I would describe Liska today as about five foot four, very pretty and athletic. Liska is a sweet person — very kind, with a big, *big* heart. She is always there to lend a hand, even though she has her own problems. She is a good listener. She has always been there for me, especially in the past few years."

LISKA ON MIKE:

"Mike is just like my mom. He is fun-loving and active — *really* active. He wants to experience everything and is trying new things all the time. He is tall, over six feet, and has curly brown hair and light hazel eyes. Mike has a great smile. He is very, very nice looking and could get any girl he wants. He is very adventurous and likes to live dangerously — skiing, wind-surfing, bicycle racing, scuba diving, whatever. I wasn't surprised he became a Navy diver. He is a real hard worker and dedicated in anything he does. I'm just as proud of him as I am of Steve.

"Mike has always been really fun to be with. We haven't ever had any serious fights. Little quarrels maybe, but we always made up.

"Today we are really close as brother and sister. He is real protective of me. He tells me there is nothing to worry about, and he makes me laugh. When I'm sad, he can make me feel happy. Like Steve, he's a really good big brother. I love him very much and I know that he loves me."

STEVE ON MIKE:

"Mike is a goal-setter. He has a strong sense of himself and what he wants to achieve. He is a dedicated, athletic, outdoorsy person. He is physically fit — in a lot better condition than I am in. We both do physical jobs, but he is leaner and really well-defined, from a muscular standpoint. I remember that when he was younger he was self-conscious about being skinny, and he didn't want to go out for high school sports.

"Mike had a great imagination and still does. He was a creative, impressionable little kid. For instance, the summer when we saw the movie *Jaws*, Mike couldn't sleep at night. He was afraid the shark would somehow come through the floor and get him, unless I let him have my top bunk on our bunk beds. And for a long time afterward he was afraid to go in the ocean. The fact that he *works* under the sea today strikes me as pretty funny.

"I think Mike and I were closer than most brothers that are three years apart. Maybe it was because Mike and I like the same things. Or because he realizes he has such a cool older brother.

"Just kidding, of course."

LYNN ON MIKE:

"I'm not sure why, but Mike is the only person who could ever tease me about my hair without upsetting me. Mike and I could joke all the time, about anything, and nobody's feelings would get hurt. I don't know why. For me, it's a special relationship I have never had with anyone else in the world.

"Mike and I were fishing pals when we were kids. At the lake, we would set the alarm for five in the morning and go out in the boat and have a heyday, talking and laughing and teasing each other. We both had the same sort of weird sense of humor. And somehow we always came back with fish.

"At home we were always pulling adolescent pranks our parents never knew about. We weren't bad; we just had a lot of fun that Mom and Dad wouldn't have approved.

"Once we were in high school, Mike and I started drifting apart a little, doing our own thing. But even today I love Mike and I feel he loves me. I hope we can go fishing together again."

MIKE REVISITED:

"I think having two sisters who are black has made me more open-minded than I might have been otherwise. If all the people around me had been white, I might have grown up having racial biases. But my family had black in it. Black people were not complete strangers. I learned they aren't so much different from us.

"The Navy is very integrated. No slurs or harassment are allowed. That goes both ways. It's not just a white thing. At the Great Lakes Naval Training Center near Chicago, I saw more black hatred toward whites than the other way around. It was obvious. Some black sailors were harassing whites and other minorities, like my Asian roommate. A lot of it was verbal. They called us trash right in our faces. There was a gang of four or five in our training school. They were loud and obnoxious. The group of them, if they caught you alone in a hallway or latrine, would run into you and push you to the side. I felt their behavior was uncalled for. I considered it discrimination. The Navy found out about it a couple of times while I was there, and serious action was taken. Some white sailors hated the blacks. That's maybe how I'm a little different, having Lynn and Liska for sisters. I don't lose perspective; the gang was just five or so out of fifty blacks at our training school. Most of them were great. I had a lot of black friends.

"Growing up with black sisters was never a problem, except when school friends would make racial jokes. Usually I would say something like, 'Hey, I don't think that's funny,' or 'Where do you get off saying that?' Then the next time they'd begin to tell such a joke, they'd notice my presence and stop, apologizing and saying, 'I didn't know you were here.' To that I would always reply, 'Should it matter that I'm here?' In the military it was exactly the same way. I hope I opened a few minds.

"Scott Davis, my best friend in Navy dive school, was from the South. He had a lot of difficulty learning to watch his language and respect my feelings about race, especially after I showed him pictures of my sisters. Scott was born and raised in Florida, in a very small town near Fort Meyers. We grew up the same way, but with different values. I think being friends changed him more than it did me.

"He described his hometown as very narrow-minded and prejudiced — cowboy boots and blue jeans, whites only. At dive school in San Diego, Scott was totally blown away seeing mixed white and black couples walking around in the shopping malls, downtown, near campus, everywhere. He couldn't believe it and said you don't see that sort of thing where he came from. I don't even notice mixed couples, but Scott pointed them out to me all the time. Scott used the word 'nigger' a lot when I first got to know him. When I went on leave with him to visit his relatives at home, they were the nicest, sweetest people I've ever met, but they all used the N-word like it was second nature. By the time Scott and I graduated from dive school, after eighteen months together, 'nigger' was no longer a word in his vocabulary. He referred to blacks as 'blacks,' with respect. His relationship with me was the reason for the change.

"I'll never forget something that happened right before we graduated. Scott and I were in the divers' locker room, and in came this group of young white students who were just entering the program. Behind them were two black students washing their faces in the sinks. One of the younger white guys made a racial joke and started talking about 'niggers' and this and that, and Scott went over there and hit the guy. Then, as the guy was picking himself up, Scott said, 'Man, you're the dumbest, cruelest son-of-a-bitch I've met in a long time. You're a piece of shit.' Scott liked those two black guys. They were friends. It was probably the first time in his life that he stood up for a black. I was pretty proud of him."

STEVE REVISITED:

"Sometimes in high school my same friends who would ask me about my sister and say Lynn was beautiful and nice, they would turn around and tell racist jokes, right in front of me. It really bothered me and made me uncomfortable. They were insensitive, and I didn't know how to handle it. At the time, I didn't speak up and tell them I didn't appreciate that. Now, I would say something to a friend, but back then I didn't have enough confidence.

"Today I sometimes have the same problem at work. I hear a lot of racist talk on construction jobs — so-called jokes like, 'Why did the black man wear a tuxedo for his vasectomy? Well, he figured if you want to *be* impotent you have to *look* impo'tant.' Very funny.

"People using the word 'nigger' bothers me more than the bad jokes. It seems more hateful. But at work I still walk away from offensive people rather than say something. It builds up inside and bothers me. I wish that I was more of a hard ass sometimes, but I'm too concerned with other people's feelings. I'm too sensitive, or so I've been told. It drives me crazy. Just once I wish I could tell someone, 'You are so simple-minded, you're a moron, fuck off.'

"But I think I'm still probably a better person than I would have been if I hadn't been Lynn and Liska's brother. I care about my sisters. I can see through color.

"I really liked most of Lynn and Liska's black friends who came over to our home all the time. I think it's easier for me to interact with minority people than it is for my peers who haven't had such exposure. I don't think I would be as aware of racism if I hadn't had black sisters."

LYNN REVISITED:

"Liska has always been very moody. I never knew if she was going to wake up in a good mood and act goofy with me or wake up in a foul mood and tell me off. In recent years she has shown such anger toward me. She's always been very judgmental of me — *very*. Everything I did was a mistake in Liska's opinion. I've never really understood. All my life she's been so domineering. It's almost as if *she* was the older sister and I was the younger one.

"Liska is very sensitive, very emotional. She's always protective of her ego. She's blunt, right to the point, despite your feelings. If you do something she doesn't like, she is very direct about letting you know. She's loving, though. She loves just about everybody. But does she love me? I honestly don't know."

LISKA REVISITED:
"I always liked going to school with my brothers and seeing people react. It was fun to tell them that there was my brother. They would reply, 'No way is that your brother!' I'd really confuse people. It was fun. As long as my brothers are comfortable about it, then I am, too.

"When there is a man in my life, he has to respect the fact that most of my family is white. If he can't do that, then I don't want to have anything to do with him. I look at my family as anyone else thinks about theirs. They are my family. My brothers just happen to be white. So what? I don't love them less. As long as they can accept that their sister is black, then that makes me love them even more.

"Nobody could ask for better brothers. I thank God for them.

"Lynn and I got along sometimes, but we fought a lot as we were growing up. We could never be friends. She was jealous of me because my hair looked better than hers, and I was jealous of her because she was a cheerleader and got the boys first. There were times that we would try to be friends, but we could never be together for more than three or four days without arguing.

"It's silly that something like hair had to be so important and ruin a relationship. I feel that I got robbed out of a sister while I was growing up.

"I'll love Lynn forever, but I don't know if we'll ever be as close as we are with our brothers."

❧ 11 ❧

Fishing and Religion

Dearest Dad,

My birth father may have left me, but please never let *you*
leave me. You're the best dad any color of a child could have.
We may not look alike but we both have something no one
else will have and that's each other's love. There's a saying
that the son does all kinds of things with his father. Well, I
hate that saying, because I have always just wanted to be
with you. So Dad, let's you and me go fishing together,
okay? Stay as sweet as candy. I love you.

Liska Maril Bates

Note from Liska, age fifteen
Father's Day, 1984

MY DAUGHTERS' PRICKLY RELATIONSHIP always seemed
to take a holiday at Odell Lake. Every summer, when we drove up
to the high country for family reunions at the Bates cabin, the two
girls' mutual dislike evaporated into the crisp, fragrant mountain
air. For all sixteen of my parents' grandchildren, the cabin at the
lake was a treasured part of growing up. For Lynn and Liska,
though, the place was more than that. It was practically holy ground
— the one location on earth where the two of them, for at least a
few days, could become totally unconscious of race, blood ties, and
sibling rivalry.

"It's hard to explain," Lynn says, "but Odell Lake was the only
place where there were no black people or white people, no adopted
kids or biological kids, just family. I always felt totally, unconditionally accepted there by all my cousins, aunts and uncles, Grandma
and Grandpa, everybody. It was a feeling of security I never had at
home in Eugene, where we were always dealing with racial stuff and

other problems of school and the outside world. Up at the lake, there *wasn't* any outside world."

Liska once told me that going to the lake, for her, was almost a religious experience, "like going to church." Her remark reminded me of *A River Runs Through It,* Norman Maclean's poignant auto-biographical masterpiece about the relationship between two brothers in Montana. In his family, Maclean wrote, there was never much of a distinction between fishing and religion. The same could have been said about the Bates family of Oakridge, Oregon. Other families went to church on Sunday; John and Patricia Bates and their five kids more often went fishing. The tradition had substantial practical value, considering that my mother was Catholic and my father was Methodist. I have always thought their resolution to that conflict ingenious: Mom got to raise the children in her faith, while Dad got to decide what we'd do on Sunday, his only day off from work. Throughout fishing season, from late April through October, we seldom went to mass; we went to the mountains.

The Cascades surrounding Oakridge are dotted with beautiful lakes, and we pulled fish out of them all. One lake especially captured my parents' hearts. That was Odell, a deep, cold pool of glacial runoff stretching six miles along the Willamette Pass at nearly a mile above sea level. The lake's majestic setting, framed by towering peaks, evokes comparisons to the Black Forest lakes of Germany and some of the lochs of Scotland.

Odell is fed by many pristine creeks — Princess, Rosary, Antler, Orphan, Crystal, and perhaps a dozen others, some of them developed with public campgrounds. My parents' favorite was Trapper Creek, a beaver-friendly torrent of snow-melt rushing off the flanks of 8,700-foot Diamond Peak. For many summers my family pitched camp on the banks of Trapper near its confluence with the lake. My dad bought a little yellow fishing boat and set about becoming an expert at pursuing Odell's kokanee and Mackinaw trout.

Late in the sixties, after my brothers and I had grown up and left home, Dad and Mom bought a rustic cabin at the west end of the lake, in a placid cove near Trapper Creek. The cabin was not big or fancy, but it was charming, secluded, and blessed with a breathtaking view of the lake. Even though there was electricity, my parents eschewed telephones and television. The "outside world," as Lynn calls it, definitely was not invited to Odell Lake, a once remote gem that went unseen by white explorers until three months after the Civil War ended in 1865. The lake was named for a surveyor who plotted a military wagon road over the Cascade summit, not far from where the Bates cabin is nestled today amid ancient alpine spruce and fir.

The cabin was already part of our family experience by the time Lynn and Liska joined us. Neither can remember a summer without visits to the lake while they were growing up. My parents were remarkably generous with the place, inviting all of their children and grandchildren to descend on them at their summer home every Fourth of July or Labor Day weekend, or both, for more than two decades. Today, Lynn and Liska insist they always blended right in with their white adoptive relatives as they picked huckleberries, swam off the dock, went on hikes, caught crawdads and periwinkles, and told stories around the campfire at night. As both of my daughters have often said, racial differences were meaningless among children in that setting. I cannot recall any mention of race over twenty-five years at the lake, except the time my mother discreetly put away an old Aunt Jemima cookie jar after learning how some African-Americans feel about such symbolic artifacts in the possession of whites.

The lake was a place of special discovery for our children. All of them except Lynn, who hated to be seen with her hair wet, learned to water-ski at Odell. They also mastered the arts of building a campfire, driving a motorboat, diving off the dock, and playing pinochle, Sabotage, Oh Heck, Spite and Malice, Crazy Eights, and many other card games that were family favorites at the cabin. Above all, the kids learned how to catch and clean fish.

Odell has always been home to many popular trout species — rainbow, German browns, cutthroat, Dolly Varden, and Mackinaw, especially — and Bates kids reeled in all of them over the years. The most prized catch was the beautiful kokanee, a species of landlocked salmon. Those who enjoy dining on salmon tend to prefer kokanee once they've tasted its more delicate pink meat. Unfortunately — or perhaps luckily, in the view of my family — kokanee are harder to catch than Odell's other species. Hooking them is difficult enough, especially later in the season, and getting them into the boat is even more challenging. Kokanee have extremely soft mouths and easily come off the hook. Once they hit, the angler has to exercise considerable restraint and finesse to reel them in successfully.

My father, a man of impressive patience with kids, taught Steve, Lynn, Mike, and Liska and most of their cousins to be skilled kokanee fishermen. In Dad's view there was only one correct way to go about it: trolling from a boat, using simple red lures trailing three feet of monofilament attached to leaded, calibrated, twenty-pound line. We would often see tourists landing kokanee in May and June, when fish were schooling near the surface, but in July through September, when the kokanee fed deep, my parents were among a handful of Odell veterans who knew where to find them, what time of day to go out, how deep to fish, and what direction and speed to troll, based on wind and weather. Even when most boats were coming back skunked, John and Patricia usually had fish.

The most amazing thing about them, though, was their tolerance and trust in their grandchildren. The kids were not allowed to take out Grandpa's big powerboat, which could speed us several miles to the east end of Odell if that was where the fish were biting. But any of the young ones, once they had passed their grandfather's boating exam, were welcome to go out on the lake in Old Yeller. That was our name for my parents' other fishing boat, the little yellow four-teen-footer. Powered by a perky six-horse outboard, Old Yeller was a safe and sturdy vessel that endured twenty-five years of adolescent learning experiences. I never saw my father even so much as grit his teeth as our children navigated Old Yeller back to the cabin with broken props, lost oars, missing fishing tackle, and lines tangled in the motor. Coming in off the lake, they'd usually bang Old Yeller against the dock in their excitement before leaping out to show off their catch. My parents always expressed effusive admiration for the fish, made sure the kids cleaned them right away, and admonished them only in matters of safety: life jackets and a fire extinguisher were a must; no speeding or reckless driving allowed; no staying out on the lake after dark.

I think our sons and daughters learned some things out on that lake, lessons in responsibility, environmental sensitivity, self-reliance, safety, and a sense that it really doesn't take much to make a person happy — maybe just an old fishing boat, a rod and reel, and a quarter of a tank of gas. As they were growing up our daughters participated in Campfire Girls, attended summer camp, went river rafting, and took private lessons in dance, swimming, and riding, and all four of the kids accompanied Gloria and me on camping and resort vacation trips throughout Oregon and other Western states. Not one of those memories, however, measures up to how our children feel about their visits to my parents' cabin.

"My happiest times were at the lake," Lynn says today. "A lot of kids didn't get to experience the things we did at Odell. It was always my favorite spot. Grandpa Bates was so kind, teaching us to fish. And Grandma Bates was good to us. She was a great cook. I always liked to watch her in the cabin kitchen. Grandma was a real morale booster, too. She was always encouraging me, trying to get me to be my best. She said that if anyone makes something of themselves, it would be Lynn. She told me this many times. She said I had a lot of motivation and I could do whatever I wanted."

Like Lynn, Liska has glowing memories, slightly tinged with regret. "I will always remember our big family get-togethers at Odell," Liska says. "I loved the cabin a lot. It was a place to get away from everything that was bothering you. I loved the bonfire, roasting marshmallows, singing, listening to Grandpa's stories. I had a lot of fun with him. He took me fishing. Playing cards against him was the most fun, the way he'd joke around with me all the time. Grandma Bates was stricter than Grandpa, but she also could be funny. I remember her being a good cook and giving me a lot of hugs and kisses. In more recent years we've had our ups and downs. We're not as close as when I was little. Grandma had things she hoped Lynn and I would do, or be, and I felt we disappointed her.

"I feel my grandparents are not proud of me, but I still love them.

I also love every one of my cousins and all my aunts and uncles. I wouldn't trade them for any family in the world.

"That even includes my uncle Tom. I didn't have a close relationship with him. He always seemed so serious, hard to talk to. He reminded me a little of my dad. But I love Tom a lot. He could be funny at times. He was really tall and gave me big bear hugs. We always called him King of the Dock. He liked to throw us off, and nobody in the family could throw him off because he was so big. Tom helped me learn to water ski, which I appreciated a lot.

"I was a lot closer to my uncle Dan. He was always very quiet, real sweet, maybe a little shy around Tom and my dad. I could relate to Uncle Dan.

"My aunt Jamie has always seemed very warm and caring, but I never got to know her too well, because she and Uncle Michael moved to Florida when I was little. But I've always, *always* been really close to my aunt Jill. Our relationship began growing a long time ago, when Lynn and I took the Greyhound bus to Portland and stayed a week or so with Jill after she and Uncle Dave were divorced. Aunt Jill relates to a lot of the same problems I have had. She's open and I can talk about just about anything with her.

"When I'm around Tom, Dan, or Jamie, I feel loved by them but uncomfortable, like I'm under some kind of test. But it's different around Aunt Jill. She's easy to talk to. She's fun. She has black friends. She goes to church with me sometimes. She's like the big sister that I always wanted, the big aunt-sister."

Jill, whose twin daughters, Caitlin and Deirdre, have remained close to Liska today even as young adults, thinks her twins benefited from all those experiences at the lake and other frequent encounters with their black cousins. "Even as far back as grade school, Deirdre and Caitlin respected diversity," Jill says. "They were always good to the kids who were different. When they would hear snide racial remarks, they would make reference to Lynn and Liska, and they would stick up for them.

"My early memories of Lynn are all loving, but I never felt as close to her as I have Liska. Lynn doesn't let anyone get too close.

There is a polite barrier of some kind that has always been there. Up at the lake, even when she was a high school girl, I would try to put my arm around her and try to talk with her about what was going on in her life. Lynn would always stiffen up and use very short answers. She had a wonderful laugh, though, which I remember vividly. Lynn is a beauty, a real doll.

"By contrast, I could talk to Liska from the time she was little. Liska would bubble over with honest feelings. Later, as an adult, Liska would phone me a lot and write once in a while. In Eugene she lived close by, so we saw each other a lot. Sometimes we had chaotic experiences and got on each other's nerves, but then we'd go out to lunch and smooth it over. We just grew closer and closer. We were family, but we also became good friends."

My younger brother, Dan, in his own way echoes Jill's remarks. "I'm just a white, middle-class, ignorant, blissfully dumb guy," he says, "but I think the adoption of Lynn and Liska had a positive effect on me and my own kids. It has helped make all of us better citizens, in terms of our views about other people. I'm sure that my kids are not as quick to draw stereotypical, negative conclusions about people of other races, especially black, because of their love for Lynn and Liska.

"When I lived in Eugene years ago and those girls came over and stayed with us, I didn't even think about the fact that they were black, except maybe the first time we took them out to a restaurant. I remember us all sitting at a table, laughing and talking, my kids and Lynn and Liska and Steve and Mike, just having a good time, and I felt a strange thing in the air. I looked around and noticed that people were looking at our family. And then I figured it out. They were staring at us because we were different, a racially mixed family. People were trying to figure out what was going on. They were looking at us like, 'Let's see, where did they get these two black kids?' It didn't embarrass me or slow me down any, but it bugged me a little bit. That was the first time I realized what it must feel like to be a black person in a white environment."

Our family tradition at Odell Lake began changing in the eighties as a couple of unforeseen trends emerged. Around the dawn of the new decade, out-of-state tourists started discovering our mountain paradise and changing its character. In sheer numbers, Californians seemed to lead the invasion. They began jamming Odell's public and private campgrounds with their motor homes and fifth-wheelers, bristling with CB antennas and TV satellite dishes and noisy electrical generators. Many of the invaders brought along that odious symbol of eighties self-centeredness: the personal stereo boom box, scourge of the forest. Worse, our lake became home to screaming jet skis and speedboats that shattered Odell's serenity, churned up the cove, and sent mini–oil slicks lapping at the mouth of sacred Trapper Creek.

As if their noxious toys were not enough, Odell Lake's new arrivals also introduced a high-tech form of fishing deemed repugnant by my father. Their boats all seemed to have electronic fishfinders — sonar apparatus — that quickly and legally located the elusive schools of kokanee. These anglers would anchor their boats over the fish, drop lines to the precise depth indicated on their electronic gear, and begin "jigging" — basically just raising and lowering their lures in the school of fish until they would strike.

My father considered sonar equipment and jigging to be unsportsmanlike and contemptible. All of us grew to resent gazing out across the lake and seeing vast fleets of sonar-equipped boats anchored for jigging over the kokanee schools, hauling in the precious fish like commercial tuna harvesters and blocking access by traditional trollers. Dad would not condone jigging from his boats. Gloria and I admired his flinty stand on the subject and privately entertained the notion that he also despised jigging for the etymology of the word. We considered it to be a euphemism for "nigger fishing," derived from the racial epithet "jiggaboo." Indeed, Lynn's dreaded outside world had finally intruded on our utopian hideaway.

The eighties' second new trend at Odell was even harder for many of us to accept. The era of the big Bates reunions at the lake was coming to an end. The family was getting too large, and my parents were becoming worn out. A generation earlier, there had been only ten or twelve Bateses at the annual cabin bashes. But by the time

Dad and Mom retired in the middle of the decade, there were well over thirty of us, through marriage and the birth and adoption of children. The little fishing cabin, creaky Old Yeller, and the grandparents' energy level were no longer adequate. My brothers and sisters and I and our spouses began forming plans to shift the universe a little, moving its center to different lakes or mountain ranches or seaside retreats for the next generations.

The transition was jolting to some of my parents' grandchildren, especially Lynn and Liska. Any change in family habits and traditions has always rattled their fragile armor of security. For them, the end of reunions at Odell was like knocking away one of life's underpinnings.

As the gatherings at Odell Lake diminished in the eighties, I did not think it was a coincidence that my two daughters began turning elsewhere for spiritual experience. Both Lynn and Liska, with no nudge from home, finally found their way to church.

The Eugene area had two small black congregations in 1983, the year Liska discovered formal religion at age fourteen. One of her first African-American schoolmates, Lisa Carmichael, introduced her to the smaller of the two churches, Saint Mark's Christian-Methodist-Episcopal.

"I started going to Saint Mark's in the eighth grade, and I immediately liked it," Liska says. "The church was small, but it really didn't matter. I made a lot of African-American friends. I liked to go on church retreats with them. Some were young and others were older. They liked to have a good time. Some of them were not saved. They partied on weekends, gossiped about other people, then went to church on Sundays. I didn't like that. But I liked the minister. I could understand what he talked about. He was a good man who got the church fixed up and painted. He tried to do the best he could for a congregation that didn't have a lot of money."

After Liska joined the church, Gloria and I wrote her a modest check each week to put on the collection plate. Liska incessantly begged us to go with her. Gloria went a few times and enjoyed it, but I resisted. "I'm a Catholic, a very *lapsed* Catholic," I told Liska. "I wouldn't be allowed at your church," I lied.

After two or three years of unrelenting pressure from Liska, I finally gave in and went along with her and Gloria one Easter. Saint Mark's faithful gathered in a wood-frame house converted to a church in one of Eugene's light-industrial areas. I had been by the place many times, dropping Liska off and picking her up, but I had never been inside. That Easter I found the building crammed with fifty or sixty worshipers, almost all of them black. A pianist, a soloist, a panel of clergymen, and two choirs in splendid robes were all somehow squeezed into that little church. We arrived just in time to find seats together; those who streamed in after us had to stand along the walls. It was hot in Saint Mark's. My white dress shirt and the armpits of my dark pinstripe suit were sweaty by the time the service began. Then, for two hours, every image of African-American religious fervor I had ever seen in films or on television was fused that day into a raucous, pounding, soul-shaking, shirt-soaking experience that showed me why Liska always seemed to come home from church emotionally drained.

I remember being extraordinarily impressed, deeply moved, and occasionally uncomfortable. Especially when the whole congregation joined with the choir in singing, swaying, clapping, and shouting praise, I felt way out of my element. Liska smiled at me a few times and urged me to "loosen up," and I tried, but the last thing I wanted to look like was a ridiculous white politician trying to get it on with black voters in their church on Sunday. Few things have ever struck me as more laughable than the sight of white people trying to be black. Instead, I just relaxed and somehow got through the service without embarrassing Liska or myself.

Toward the end, as people throughout the church were wiping perspiration from their faces, the minister invited members of the congregation to introduce their Easter guests. Several black adults took turns standing up and presenting their visiting relatives, each time to polite applause. Finally Liska rose. With a huge smile she proudly introduced her mom and dad. As we stood, Liska gave each of us a hug, and applause rocked the little church. Never had I felt such warmth and acceptance from total strangers. As the minister welcomed us, I looked around and saw a sea of friendly, smiling faces turned our way. The emotion of the moment was so powerful and unexpected that I still remember how relieved I was that we visitors were not being asked to speak; I would not have been able to find my voice.

Later, Liska was sorry Gloria and I did not join her congregation and keep going with her, but she seemed only mildly disappointed. The warm glow of that Easter service lasted many years for all three of us.

Lynn eventually went to Liska's church off and on for a while. Somewhat caustically, Liska says her sister was less interested in finding God than in meeting boys. Lynn, however, says the boys at church — and some of the men — actually drove her away.

"Liska talked me into going to the church with her, and for a period of time I did, but it really turned me off," Lynn says. "I'm sorry to say that, but some of those people who were praising the Lord inside the church were doing bad things out behind it — drinking alcohol and smoking weed. I thought, 'What kind of church is this?' Some guys in the choir — married men — were always trying to hit on me. So did a visiting minister. I was only sixteen or seventeen. It was all phony to me. That's why I quit and never went back."

But church was different for Liska, who still attends regularly today. "Religion became really important to me," she says. "I feel that without God I wouldn't be as strong as I am. He's helped me through a lot of problems and mistakes."

Liska's interest in religion helped draw her closer to my Southern-born grandmother, Grandma Grace, a devout Methodist. She always took a deep and sincere interest in both girls, just as she cared about all her grandchildren and great-grandchildren. Grace wrote letters to Lynn and Liska, displayed their photographs prominently in her little living room, and never overlooked either of their birthdays. She was fond of Lynn but came to have a special relationship with Liska, a result of their mutual spirituality and feelings about Christianity. And when Grace heard Liska reveal that her black congregation was part Methodist, the old woman actually had to fight back tears.

"I loved Grandma Grace a lot," Liska says. "She and I always talked about going to church together. She wanted me to visit her church. But we didn't see her much — not as much as I think we should have. The times we did were always pretty special. She was so thoughtful, always giving us walnuts for Christmas, jams and jellies, digging in her freezer for food to send home with us. You couldn't even come in her house until you got your hug and kiss. We'd all kind of line up for it on her porch. She'd always tell each one of us how tall we were getting and how we were growing up so fast. Then we'd go inside her house and she'd tell great stories. *Long* stories."

Grandma Grace could hold forth on a vast array of subjects, and few seemed to impassion her more than religion. Her point of view was more that of historian than zealot. She told us tales, for instance, of Negro religious revivals she had witnessed as a girl in Tennessee, and she talked about her own spiritual journey into Methodism. Her discourse on the evangelistic teachings of John and Charles Wesley was sometimes enough to make the eyes glaze over, but I recall once being jolted to attention by her surprising confession that she believed in reincarnation. Grandma Grace, a closet Shirley MacLaine? It was true. Grandma even gave us a book on the subject.

For several years we talked about driving Liska to McMinnville some Sunday morning so she could go to church with her great-grandmother. We knew the idea had nothing to do with flaunting, although Grandma Grace was certainly proud of Liska. Instead, going to church together was to be a form of spiritual union — sharing and bonding between an elderly white woman and a young black girl of the same faith.

Today, I can hardly believe how fast those years slipped away. We kept procrastinating, and by 1987, after Liska had been going to Saint Mark's for nearly five years, it was too late for her to go to church with Grandma Grace. At age ninety-five, though still mentally sharp, she was too frail to attend church or stay in her house by the swale, where my parents had been caring for her. It was time for a nursing home.

Grandma Grace was unhappy in her new surroundings but pleased to hear from us that Liska remained devout and continued to attend church regularly. Church, in fact, is why Liska stayed in Eugene on Easter Sunday of 1987 when the rest of our family drove to McMinnville to visit Grace in the nursing home. Though she had been lonely and was delighted to see all of us, she brushed off our apologies about Liska staying home. "I'd rather have her go to Easter services than come and see an old woman like me," she said.

Four days later, Grandma Grace died during a nap. Nobody had expected her to go so soon or so peacefully. But Liska was devastated she had not joined us for the Easter visit that had turned out to be our final goodbye. For a few days Liska's depression was so severe I feared we were going to have to take her to a doctor or a counselor for help. But after sobbing through the funeral she seemed to come out of it.

"I know Grandma Grace forgave me for not saying goodbye," Liska told us on the drive back to Eugene. "But I'm not going to forgive myself. Not ever."

12

Black and White and Read All Over

Dear Dad,
Thanks for the nice stuff you gave me. I really appreciate it. I know you sometimes have a hard day at work. Thank you for spending your time at work to make money. I feel I am very lucky.

Note from Lynn, age eleven
February 1977

MY TEMPLES THROBBED one evening early in 1992 in the newsroom of the newly merged *San Diego Union-Tribune*. The headache, no doubt, was a byproduct of my work habits: I had not taken a full day off in over a month while assisting in the merger, which meant eliminating 125 news-editorial jobs to help shore up the publisher's sagging profits. That evening, as I watched surviving employees of the *Union* and the *Tribune* trying to work together in the chaos of the hurriedly planned new organization, my head pounded so painfully it made my eyes squint. Noticing my distress, a fellow editor kindly offered some aspirin.

"You know why they're white, don't you?" he asked as he handed me his bottle of pills.

"What?"

"You *do* know why aspirin are white, don't you?" he repeated, smiling slyly.

"No," I replied as I gratefully took a pair of tablets from his bottle. "Why are aspirin white?"

"Well," he said, "you want them to *work*, don't you?"

Great, I thought. A racial joke. I frowned at him in disbelief. He thought from my reaction that I didn't understand his punch line.

"Get it? Aspirins are white. So they work."

My colleague, who was white, had worked with me for nearly two years at the San Diego paper but did not know about my daughters or my feelings about race. He never would have risked making such a wisecrack openly in the newsroom, for fear of racial harassment complaints from our handful of African-American employees, but he assumed the comment was safe between the two of us. In my lightly starched white shirts and striped neckties, I looked just as Republican as he did. Both of us were assistant managing editors, part of senior management on a newspaper notorious for the ultraconservative views of the publisher, Helen Copley. Her vice president for news was Herbert Klein, who had served as Richard Nixon's director of communications. Her editor was Gerald Warren, who had been Nixon's deputy press secretary. Just as racially offensive remarks had been a well-documented part of the culture of the Nixon White House, such talk was occasionally heard in private conversations among white males in the San Diego newsroom's inner sanctum. In that corporate climate, my fellow senior editor blundered badly in presuming I would appreciate his attempt at levity.

"Thanks for the aspirin," I told him, "but the joke was out of line. The idea that black people don't work is a vicious racial stereotype. Frankly, it's repugnant."

I did not try to explain my reaction by telling him my daughters were African-American — a fact that I shared with very few people at the *Union-Tribune*. I didn't think Lynn and Liska had anything to do with my taking umbrage at the guy's bad gag line. It should have been deplorable to anyone.

My acrimonious response surprised and embarrassed the other

editor. To his credit, he mumbled an apology, but I was still stewing inside — and still enduring the headache — when I went home that night and mentioned the incident to Gloria. Both of us felt depressed. Here it was, 1992 — twenty-two years since we had adopted Lynn — and both of us were hearing more disgusting racial remarks than we had heard two decades earlier. What was happening to the country? Where was the leadership we needed to put a lid on such unacceptable behavior? The fact that the aspirin joke was told at my place of work, in an encounter with a fellow lieutenant of an institution that society depends on for enlightenment and direction, made me even more despondent. It also reminded me of a troubling undercurrent in my relationship with my two daughters.

As they were growing up, Lynn and Liska constantly struggled to believe the story of their adoption. Our explanations strained their credulity. Sometimes when their sense of security was ebbing perilously low, they could not help wondering whether it was true, as a few of their African-American acquaintances had suggested to them, that we adopted them to further my newspaper career.

For years, like little district attorneys, they repeatedly asked Gloria and me to go back over our story one more time. Our replies never seemed totally convincing to them; our motives for adopting them remained suspect. "But *why* did you want a daughter?" "Why didn't you just have another baby?" "Why did you pick *me*?" "Why not adopt a *white* girl?"

Our testimony never strayed from the truth. We had wanted a daughter. By way of adoption. An older child. Preferably healthy. Race didn't matter. And later we wanted a second daughter. By way of adoption. Et cetera, et cetera.

But no matter how many times the girls put us back on the witness stand to recite the facts as we knew them, Lynn and Liska never appeared completely satisfied. They just knew, as some of their friends had tried to convince them, that we were guilty of onerous charges: adoption for impure reasons. Our daughters seemed determined to trip us up and expose inconsistencies in our story. Perhaps then they could cry out with gratification and glee: "A-*ha*! We knew it all along! You adopted us to *draw attention to yourselves!*"

Our girls were no different from most other children adopted at older ages. Many of them spend years — whole lifetimes, even — wondering whether they are truly loved by their adoptive parents. More than most people, such children have great difficulty believing that a parent can really love someone else's child.

"That was always a mystery in my mind," Liska says today. "Why did Doug and Gloria adopt me? There must have been other little kids. White kids. So why did they pick me out of the whole batch? Why was I the fortunate one? Was it for publicity? Did they want people to notice them more? Was it to help my dad's career? It was always a big question to me. A lot of my friends asked that question, too. But whatever the answer was, I felt glad. I was very grateful."

The first time I heard the jab about my career-boosting intentions, I did not know whether to feel hurt or amused. I had always fancied that my modest achievements in the newspaper profession had resulted from ability and hard work, not from office political skill, family connections, religious favoritism, or the color of my skin or my children's skin. I do feel that the adoption of Lynn and Liska made me a better newspaper editor — perhaps more racially sensitive than many of my white counterparts — and I never sensed that the interracial composition of my family held me back professionally in any significant way. On the other hand, being the white father of black daughters never endeared me to my employers. In fact, unbeknownst to my daughters and through no fault of their own, their blackness often caused conflicts and awkwardness for me in the overwhelmingly white, conservative world of newspaper publishing.

Eugene's minority community was growing in the early 1980s as Lynn and Liska became teen-agers. Both girls began meeting other young African-Americans through church, school, Campfire Girls, and athletic competition. With a few of their new friends, our daughters, like typical teen-agers, developed love-hate relationships.

They would be best pals one day and bitter adversaries the next, impassioned by youthful feelings of envy and resentment, often involving boys or status in their loose circle of friends. There was always one sure-fire way for an adolescent rival to even the score with Lynn or Liska: hit her in her most vulnerable spot — her anxiety about parental love. Thus our daughters, most often Liska, endured mean suggestions that Gloria and I adopted them not out of love but to advance my newspaper career.

In responding to those charges, I tried to be logical. I said they were based on false assumptions. One, obviously, was the notion that it's difficult, if not impossible, to love another person's child. The truth, I said, is that the only parents who could not possess unconditional love for an adopted child are those unable to have unconditional love for their biological offspring. When such love for the genetic progeny comes easily, it comes easily for the adopted children, too, I said. Love is not something an adoptive parent has to work at and fight to achieve; rather, I said, love is the most powerful of all human emotions. There's no stopping it. In fact, I went on, there are too many unhappy, self-doubting people who question their own capacity for love even as they give and receive it. In fact the love is there, I said, and everybody ought to just relax and enjoy it.

The second false assumption, I said, was that Gloria and I adopted Lynn and Liska in a utopian community that rewards people for acts of racial goodwill and fellowship. Oregon, after all, had a glowing national reputation as an environmentally conscious, socially progressive state. And our town, Eugene, was known as the most liberal-minded city in Oregon, so what better place for a young newspaper editor to impress his employers by taking in a couple of needy black kids?

In truth, our state and our city have a long, sad history of hate and racism. The Ku Klux Klan once flourished in Oregon and Eugene, and the state once had many racist laws, including one curbing property rights of nonwhite citizens — an old statute that remained on the books until voters repealed it in 1970. Sundown laws that denied blacks freedom of movement after sunset were enforced well into the 1950s and 1960s in some Oregon communities.

For twelve years, from 1921 through 1933, Oregon was a hotbed of Ku Klux Klan activity. "Konvocations" were held in cities across the state, enlisting thousands of members who were required to be white, non-Jewish, non-Catholic, non-Communist, and born in the United States. In white Klan regalia, throngs of men and women marched to public worship in Protestant churches and became a powerful political force in Oregon. At the peak of the Klan's influence, it fanned anti-Catholic passions throughout the state and helped win voter approval of a measure outlawing parochial schools — an act later ruled unconstitutional by the U.S. Supreme Court. The Klan burned crosses on top of Mount Tabor in Portland and at other landmarks in Medford, Bend, Hood River, and Eugene.

Even today a forty-eight-foot, electrically lighted concrete cross blazes in the night sky atop Skinner Butte in the heart of Eugene, on city-owned property where the Klan once torched wooden crucifixes. Back in 1964 a band of midnight Christians erected the controversial cross, which survived a lengthy legal battle when a friendly Oregon Supreme Court ruled the symbol to be a constitutionally acceptable "war memorial" that could remain on public land. Today, when the cross is lighted on Christian holidays, the sight is galling to the community's Jews and disturbing to the handful of African-Americans and Catholics who are aware of Eugene's fiery Klan era.

The bleakest time in Eugene's racial history, however, came seventeen years after the Klan in Oregon had collapsed of internal political disunion. By the end of World War II, several black families had settled in tin-roof squatters' shacks near Eugene's rendering works and garbage dump. The slummy district, on the banks of the scenic Willamette River, became the city's first black neighborhood. Civic leaders broke it up in 1949 in a most heavy-handed way. They decided the riverfront area where the African-American families lived should be cleared for the approach to a new bridge. The county sheriff stood by as bulldozers moved in and frantic residents scurried to remove their possessions. The twenty-two black families were relocated to a swampy, low-lying area of decrepit houses and shanties outside the city limits. That winter the settlement flooded. A handful of longtime Eugene residents, outraged by the civic leaders' actions in 1949, still tell stories of seeing black parents carrying their children on their backs through the rain as they waded in and out of their marshy new surroundings. Eventually, even that neighborhood lost its identity as whites developed the property and the black families scattered, some leaving town. Today, Eugene officials have to be careful not to boast about the city's absence of racially segregated neighborhoods. Old-timers know it has less to do with racial harmony than with civic bullying.

I also perceived a third shaky premise in suggestions that adopting Lynn and Liska somehow advanced my career: the assumption that newspapers are bastions of tolerant, broad-minded, liberal values. That is a myth. In reality, the newspaper industry ranks among the most conservative, change-resistant, and bias-prone institutions in the United States. Empirical evidence abounds, and none is more damning than the newspaper industry's record at hiring people of color for jobs in American newsrooms. Industry surveys show that over half of the nation's daily papers employ no minority journalists at all. At papers that *do* have nonwhites in their newsrooms, the figures are universally low — far below the percentages they should be to reflect fair representation of the general populace. A lot of excuse-making and finger-pointing occurs each year when the minority-hiring survey results are released, but I don't think there is any escaping the institutional racism at the root of the problem.

Meanwhile, other virulent strains of prejudice run rampant in newsrooms across the nation. Newspapers continue to follow archaic, racially destructive news policies. Much content in today's papers is racially insensitive and divisive, contributing to our society's wrenching problems. Minority staff members at American newspapers complain of being isolated, harassed, and professionally obstructed. Publishers cling to biased, hostile management practices. Racial tension pervades the newsroom. A few editors even whisper moronic aspirin jokes. No, the newsroom is not always a friendly environment for the parent of black children.

I had no way of knowing it at the time, but my problems with racial bias in the workplace were foreshadowed in my teen-age days, when I was editor of the *Ridge Hi-Breeze* at Oakridge High School. Technically, the faculty adviser for the school paper, a kind Native American teacher named Benjamin Twitchell, was supposed to check all copy before publication each week. He trusted me, though, and allowed me the freedom to edit the paper as I saw fit. The only rules, he said, were that I exercise good judgment and keep him from getting fired. That policy worked fine for months, but eventually I got both of us in trouble over a matter of race.

In interviewing a graduating senior who was bound for medical school, I asked him a rather sophomoric question about his predictions for the future of the world. He thought a minute, then said whites and blacks would intermarry in such great numbers that in another two thousand years everyone would be brown. I quoted him and went to press.

Someone on the Oakridge School Board found the published remark about interracial marriage to be in poor taste, and Benjamin Twitchell and I were summoned to the school principal's office. Protecting me, Mr. Twitchell said he had approved the quotation before publication and saw nothing wrong with it. The principal, however, said many people in our community considered miscegenation to be an offensive topic, inappropriate for a school newspaper. I received a verbal warning; Mr. Twitchell got a formal reprimand.

Later, in rehashing the matter with him, I apologized for the flap and said I was mystified by it. "What," I asked, "is so horrible about saying everybody will be brown someday?"

Mr. Twitchell, a full Aleut whose skin was already brown, laughed at my ingenuousness. He said the race-mixing prediction I had quoted was a widely held anthropological theory, one that he happened to embrace himself. He told me not to apologize; he would have approved my article just the way I wrote it. "Next time you handle anything like this, though, let's talk about it before we print it," he said. "Nothing can stir up a hornets' nest faster than a story involving race."

A heart attack killed Benjamin Twitchell shortly after I graduated from high school. His advice about hornets' nests and race, though, came roaring back to me time after time throughout a twenty-five-year newspaper career. A number of times I got stung.

Right out of college in 1968, my first reporting job was at a newspaper that adhered strictly to several news policies that were clearly hostile to African-Americans. The *Daily Chronicle* in Spokane, Washington, would not publish pictures of racially mixed couples or permit the word "black" as a synonym for "Negro." Even Muhammad Ali, who had converted to the Muslim faith and had changed his name three years earlier, was still Cassius Clay in *Chronicle* boxing stories. The entire news staff was white.

A year later, when I went to the *Register-Guard* in Eugene, I was joining another all-white newsroom, but it seemed more racially enlightened. Ali, at least, was no longer Cassius Clay, and the word "black" was preferred over "Negro," which had become politically incorrect everywhere in America except in many parts of the South and in conservative enclaves like Spokane. I had no work-related problems with racial topics before adopting Lynn and Liska. Afterward, however, I found my objectivity as a journalist to be in question forevermore.

The first instance of it left me stunned. It happened in 1973 after I had moved from the Eugene paper's reporting staff to the news desk, where I was entrusted on weekends with front-page decisions. One Friday evening that summer, the black political activist Angela Davis came to Eugene and gave a speech attended by several thousand people on the university campus. She talked about her imprisonment and acquittal on charges related to California's 1970 Soledad Brothers shooting, and she reflected on her firing at UCLA on the basis of her Communist Party membership. Little else was going on locally in the news that day, and I gave front-page play to Angela Davis's Eugene appearance. Our story and photograph ran on "the fold," in the center of the page, secondary to a national story full of ominous predictions of an oil shortage.

The following day, I was astonished when my boss, the news editor, took me aside and sharply criticized my decision to play the Angela Davis story "out front," on page one. He told me the publisher had raised hell about the story play and had decreed that he didn't want to see any more "glorification of black radicals and anarchists" on the front page of his newspaper.

There was no defensiveness in my initial reaction to this upbraiding. I was sincerely amazed and said so. My decision on Davis had seemed like an easy call at the time. The story had been well handled and, quite simply, it was news. I said I disagreed with the publisher's judgment but would try to respect his wishes in the future. I did not become angry until a few days later when an assistant news editor told me, without directly mentioning Lynn and Liska, that I needed to tread carefully; my objectivity on matters of race, he said, was now viewed as suspect by the boss.

A few years later, when I was the paper's regional editor, my daughters' race caused an entirely different kind of worry for me at the paper: fear for my family's safety. Toward the end of 1975 I began doing some investigative work on a white supremacist group called Posse Comitatus — a sort of latter-day Ku Klux Klan whose members fervently believed, among other things, that an American race war was imminent. Loosely translated, the Latin words *posse comitatus* mean "the power of the male community." Its members, calling themselves "patriots," insisted that the still-extant congressional Posse Comitatus Act of frontier days gave men in every American county the right to call themselves together in a posse for self-defense — as legal vigilantes, in other words.

The "national commander" of Posse Comitatus lived in Portland. Most of the activity, though, appeared to be centered in the Eugene area. I made contact with the county's posse "chairman," Dean Kennedy, who lived far out of town on an isolated country estate, and arranged for an interview. He did not want me on his property but agreed to meet me on "neutral ground," at the county courthouse.

I found Kennedy to be a frightening man with steely blue-gray eyes, burning feverishly out of a chiseled visage bearing a surprising resemblance to Adolf Hitler. Kennedy declared himself a racist and an admirer of Hitler's *Mein Kampf,* and he said he believed the Jews had plotted an international banking conspiracy. He also predicted a violent "Negro uprising" that required posse members to protect their guns and get ready to die for their country. "I really don't know what's going to happen," he told me, "but I do know there's going to be bloodshed."

As I interviewed Kennedy, I must have done a magnificent job of hiding my revulsion; the man clearly liked me. He made repeated complimentary references to my blond hair, blue eyes, and "Aryan features," as if to let me know his group was looking out for the personal interests of people exactly like me. His flattery was bizarre and unsettling. Obviously, he hoped to use me, through my newspaper, to spread the word about Posse Comitatus. Maybe he even thought he could convert me. I was indeed a rapt listener.

Kennedy invited me to a posse meeting, featuring an appearance by Mike Beach, the "national commander" from Portland. I attended the gathering at a Eugene home, where paranoid-behaving armed men were posted at the doors. Kennedy saw to it that I was allowed in. He introduced me, and I was physically searched by one of the guards. Then Beach, flanked by American and Nazi flags, gave a brief report in which he claimed that four hundred thousand men in forty-eight states had formed posse chapters. "Thousands and thousands of men in the country want to get in, and we're going to organize in every state," he said. "We suggest they stay out of trouble — do things right, through the courts, in every way they can — but then, damn well do everything necessary to preserve the republic."

One of the posse's main strategies, Kennedy said, was mass refusal to file IRS returns in what he called "one hell of a burgeoning tax rebellion by patriotic people who aren't filing because they feel their money is being used for immoral purposes, such as handouts for Negroes who don't want to work."

I pursued the story for several weeks, ultimately establishing that Beach's membership claims were ludicrously inflated. I did, however, compile a list of forty-five Eugene-area posse members and published some of their leaders' names in an in-depth story that quoted both Beach and Kennedy and exposed their bigotry and far-right buffoonery. Surprisingly, both men seemed to love the piece. Perhaps my writing was too straightforward and objective. Or maybe they were too obtuse to comprehend that they had been pilloried. For whatever reason, they seemed to regard me as a convert, or at least as a journalistic sympathizer. They told me "hundreds of patriots" had come forward to join the posse as a result of my reporting. The next thing I knew, they had invited me to what they described as a clandestine, off-the-record posse strategy session at Kennedy's country estate. Warily, I agreed to attend. I wanted to see where all this would lead.

About a week before the posse gathering, I unexpectedly encountered Kennedy at a Eugene supermarket. He seemed excited to see me and buttonholed me in the cereal aisle, jabbering at length about how news media ownership was dominated by "Jewish interests." The federal government, he claimed, was in turn controlled by the media and "Jewish bankers and financiers" in an international conspiracy seeking dominion over the whole world. He wanted me to be aware of my unwitting little role in this monstrous plot.

My four kids were with me in the store. The longer Kennedy pontificated, the more restless they became. Liska, six years old at the time and sitting in my grocery cart, kept interrupting. "Dad," she said over and over, "can we get Cap'n Crunch? Please, Dad? Let's get Cap'n Crunch!" After she had called me Dad a dozen times or so, Kennedy finally stopped talking and gaped at the impatient little black girl in my cart.

"Are these your children?" he asked.

I introduced them and waited for his reaction. Kennedy looked at them, then at me, and then abruptly excused himself and hurried away.

A few days later, when I phoned him to get directions to his home, he told me coldly that the posse conclave had been called off. I never heard from Dean Kennedy again. Evidently, despite my

"Aryan features," I was no longer considered a likely convert to Posse Comitatus. How could a man with black children help prepare for the bloodshed that Kennedy's patriots saw coming?

His eagerly anticipated race war did not materialize, and the posse eventually evaporated, much as the Klan had dried up four decades earlier. For months afterward, though, I was a little jumpy about my estranged relationship with Posse Comitatus. My notes and files were loaded with names and information that could have been useful to Internal Revenue Service agents. I never would have shared my notes with authorities, but the neo-Nazis didn't know that. Every time I saw or heard a strange car on our neighborhood street at night, my pulse rate accelerated and I hoped members of the posse weren't riding out for revenge.

Throughout the seventies I must have done a fairly good job of keeping my racial biases to myself, because the paper in 1981 entrusted me to become news editor, in charge of the selection, editing, and play of stories. I relished the job and threw myself into it with a zeal that led me, for the first time, to begin putting career ahead of family. I knew it was happening to me, but I rationalized that it was the right thing to do. Because Gloria and I had married young and had four children by the time we were twenty-five, we had very little money in the bank — and certainly no college fund for four kids. The responsible course, I figured, was to begin climbing the career ladder, seeking fatter paychecks that would enable me to help put Steve, Lynn, Mike, and Liska through college when the time came.

I was well prepared for the news editor's role and won respect for my work. Eventually, though, the old bugaboo of race emerged once again and put me in conflict in the newsroom. By 1983, after Ronald Reagan and George Bush had been in the White House a couple of years, I had become concerned about a proliferation of gratuitous references to race in news reports — not just in the *Register-Guard* but in newspapers everywhere. Police reporters, in particular, had embraced a trendy pattern of carelessly identifying the race of criminal suspects in stories where such references were inappropriate.

At a news-desk staff meeting, I showed our copy editors a story we had recently published. A transient man had been arrested on charges of attempting to sexually assault a young girl in a home he had broken into in one of Eugene's more exclusive neighborhoods. The story did not mention that the girl was white — any reader could safely assume that she was — but we did identify the suspect as black. I pointed out that race was not an apparent factor in the assault and should not have been reported. Such gratuitous references, I said, served no purpose except arousing racial passions in the community and making life unnecessarily uncomfortable for decent, law-abiding minority residents. In a crime story, I said, we should identify race only if it was germane to the story or if a suspect was at large and police provided a detailed, clearly helpful physical description that benefited the cause of public safety.

Most staff members seemed to accept my guidelines as reasonable. One woman on the copy desk vehemently dissented, though, and I realized in an instant that I had created a problem for myself. Not only had this woman edited the sexual-assault story that I had criticized; she was married to my boss, the paper's managing editor, and had a reputation for reminding colleagues of her marital relationship at every opportunity.

After the staff meeting the woman approached me and spoke in patronizing tones. "I know you have black children," she began, "but I really disagree with your new policy. Readers *want* to know whether criminals are black or white or Hispanic or whatever. My husband feels that way, too."

"Sorry," I replied, "but we're not going to identify race except when it's relevant. To do otherwise is racist and terribly damaging. The policy stands."

She left my office in a snit, after telling me she had endured a "bad experience" with blacks when she had been editor of the campus daily at the University of Washington. She had published something that offended black students on the Seattle campus, and a group of their leaders angrily marched to her office to complain. She said the blacks had made her feel threatened, and she feared for her physical safety. "Personally," she told me, "I thought they were far too sensitive, and that's how I feel about this new policy of yours."

The woman's influence on her editor husband was reputed to be so strong that staff members, behind her back, called her Lady Macbeth. So much for climbing the career ladder in Eugene, I dismally thought. Shortly afterward, I accepted an offer to become the general news editor of the *Seattle Times.*

In Seattle I finally found myself working in a newsroom with some real diversity. The staff was still predominantly white, but for the first time in my career I had colleagues who happened to be black, Indian, Hispanic, and Asian. The *Times* was an excellent newspaper with a staff that I considered to be superb, in part because of its relatively healthy racial and ethnic composition. During my tenure at Seattle I formed a number of friendships that survive to this day, even though I left after a year and returned to Eugene, where I became managing editor despite my political problems with Lady Macbeth.

Back in Eugene, as my responsibilities mounted, I submerged myself to an ever-greater degree in work. My parental involvement, compared with the days when Steve and Lynn were in high school, atrophied to a point where I had very little idea what was going on with Mike and Liska. I let Gloria take over for me as I became increasingly absorbed in the career, always rationalizing that it was really for the good of the kids. Today, when Liska describes her memories of me during that period, it gives me a melancholy chill.

"My dad, Doug, was a serious man — so serious that I felt it was hard for him to express love, because he was always wanting to do work," she says. "It always seemed work was first. He was a great dad, and I knew he worked hard because he had a family to support, but I wished he would stop taking life so serious and start doing the things he liked to do. He used to play the piano. I wished he would forget work just once and sit down at the piano. Also, it was hard to talk to him about my problems then, because he was so busy and had such high expectations. But one good thing that I did enjoy about my dad then was that he taught us girls, like, how to mow the lawn and do the things that are often expected of men, like outside yard work. We learned to do it because he had to work."

After becoming the Eugene paper's managing editor, responsible for the entire news product, I discovered that my most vocal critic lived under the same roof with me. Liska, outspoken by nature, began maturing as a newspaper reader, glancing through each day's edition and finding plenty of things to question — particularly involving race.

"Why is it," she once asked me, "that every time black people get their pictures in the paper, they're either in trouble with the law, or they're athletes or celebrities? You run lots of pictures of ordinary white people, so why not ordinary black people?"

Liska thought she detected racial bias in the paper — in the selection of photographs, in the play of certain stories, in the choice of news receiving coverage, in the labeling of people by race, and even in the wording of headlines. Although she struggled in school and had to work harder at her studies than our other children, I thought she was extremely perceptive in seeing that her father put out a daily news product that was edited by white people for white readers.

"Most white people aren't like you and Mom," she once complained to me. "They don't know any blacks. In Eugene, they hardly ever even *see* any blacks. All they know about black people is what they see in your newspaper and on TV. No wonder they're afraid of us and hate us."

Every other week at the *Register-Guard* I invited someone from the community — a newsmaker, a professor, a merchant, sometimes an opinionated subscriber — to attend our nightly news meeting and give our editors a brief critique of that day's product. One week I asked Liska to come in and do it.

"I remember being very nervous," she says. "But I also felt proud because my dad was there and I was standing up expressing my feelings about the newspaper. It was a good experience. I felt happy because some important people were listening to me as a young adult."

Liska's no-nonsense presentation, using tear sheets from that morning's edition, was a smashing success. She found several complimentary things to say about the paper, but she also pointed out some weaknesses that had not been obvious to the assembled editors. Every story on the front page was a doom-and-gloom "downer," a state budget piece on the front page made "absolutely no sense at all," too many stories were overly long and jumped from page to page, not enough stories appealed to younger readers, and every story involving black people in the paper's lead section was negative in one way or another. She noted that the only black people who had pictures in that day's paper were the pop star Michael Jackson (whom she called "weird"), dead villagers in South Africa (whose corpses she said were too gruesome to look at), and a lot of athletes in the sports section (which she said stereotyped blacks). She asked for more news coverage and photographs of "ordinary" black people.

Afterward, many of the front-line editors heaped praise on Liska's critique and said she had done a great job of sensitizing our all-white management team to matters of race. Partly as a result of Liska's impressive performance, I was able to marshal staff support for launching the paper's first intern program for minority journalists. Our efforts to recruit experienced black reporters and editors to Eugene had repeatedly sputtered and failed; through internships, my strategy was to "grow our own" and help young people of color get started in newspaper journalism.

For months after Liska's visit to the newsroom I sensed a wave of staff support for improving the paper's performance in affirmative-action hiring and in covering news of minority affairs. Eventually, though, as my old high school teacher Benjamin Twitchell might have predicted, another hornets' nest landed in my lap.

I was aware we had a story in the works on police concerns about first-ever evidence of gang activity in Eugene. Despite little voices in my head, though, I decided not to ask to read the piece before publication. Ever since Liska's visit I had become extremely sensitive about my reputation as the managing editor with black daughters. When I had asked to see another race-related story prior to publication, I had detected resentment from the editor who was handling it, and later I was told of snide remarks about *Register-Guard* editors needing to be careful not to offend the boss's outspoken black daughter. So I let the gang story go without previewing it, reassuring myself that it was being handled by one of our finest reporters and one of our sharpest editors.

Big mistake. The moment I picked up the Sunday morning paper and saw what we had done, I knew we were in trouble. The story reported that Eugene had "a growing street gang problem" but provided no supporting evidence beyond graffiti in downtown alleys and the alarming statements of one detective, who said Southern California–style street gangs were moving in. He named three Eugene "gangs" — one black, one Hispanic, and one white — but admitted he couldn't say whether they were committing crimes. Our article provided no rebuttal, or any balancing comment whatsoever, from Eugene's minority community.

A firestorm of complaints erupted the following day, when minority leaders demanded and received an apology and retraction from the Eugene Police Department. "We regret that the information we provided the newspaper was not accurate," a deputy chief said in a formal statement.

Next, a group of black, Hispanic, and white leaders descended on the newspaper. I met with them in a conference room and asked several editors to join me. The angry visitors told us our reporting had damaged race relations in Eugene. They said our "gang" story contributed to a negative racial climate in which nonwhite young men were subject to increased suspicion and hostility — especially when they associated in groups, but even when they walked down the street alone. The visitors said they were just as opposed as police to the notion of street gangs getting started in Eugene, and they told us they wanted the newspaper to report the problem if it really happened. However, our Sunday article had served only to inflame racial hostility while failing to substantiate the claim that a gang problem was here, they said.

My management staff was stunned to hear me agree with our

critics. Normally, the managing editor is expected to stand behind the staff when controversy flares and community factions seek to tilt news coverage one way or another. I had performed that role many times, putting my job at risk, particularly when the powerful timber industry had howled about our coverage of the spotted owl and related issues. This time, though, I did not tell our critics to buzz off. I defended the paper's motives as honorable and the gang question as a valid issue meriting news coverage, but I said I was sorry for the way we had handled the story. Then I followed up with a written apology in my next Sunday column on the op-ed page. It began like this:

> We were wrong.
> Sometimes it takes courage and humility to say those words. Eugene police displayed both traits this past week when they publicly apologized [for the gang report] . . .
> For a police department, it was an extraordinary statement. *Register-Guard* editors can't recall a previous apology of that nature. Something tells me it's time for this newspaper to show a similar dash of courage and humility. If the police are willing to admit they blew it, so should we. Our article was flawed.

Eugene's black leaders were astounded. The *Register-Guard* had never run such an apology. Their response to my column was warm and heartening, and it unleashed an unprecedented dialogue between the paper's editors and the minority community.

To his credit the reporter who wrote the gang story accepted my response with professional grace, and we remain friends today. However, I had damaged my relationship with others on the news staff. Some colleagues vigorously supported what I had done, but among others I soon became aware of an undercurrent of resentment and distrust. It did not matter that I had previously stood up for staff members against strenuous criticism from timber interests, from the business community, from the city administration, and even from Eugene's loosely defined social and civic elite, with whom our publisher closely associated. What mattered was that I had refused to back a top reporter and his editor when their work came under attack from a hostile force in the community. Once again, a trusted colleague told me, there was behind-the-back muttering about the danger of doing anything to offend the managing editor's black daughter. The whole fuss blew over in a few weeks and caused me no lasting difficulty. Thereafter, though, whenever I had to guide our news coverage on matters of race, I felt as if I were walking on eggs.

At home, I never told Liska about my troubles at work, and she never told me how she felt about her editor father. Both of us should have talked to each other more.

"I was proud of my dad," Liska says today. "He was a good man. What he did, he believed in. When he found something he wanted to do, he went for it. He was very intelligent and knew lots of things. I just wished he would have taken more time out to participate, like go to some of my track meets. He went to my church once. I was glad he did. He told me he enjoyed it. But I don't recall ever seeing him at any of my sports events. That kind of made me feel bad. I love my dad and I thank God for him, but he was always busy working."

Actually, I did make it to one of Liska's track meets. It was the district competition at the end of her senior year. I got there late but just in time to watch her win ribbons in the four-hundred and two-hundred-meter sprints and the hundred-meter hurdles. She also ran the anchor leg of the girls' winning four-by-four-hundred relay team. She was very athletic, very fast. I never felt more proud of Liska, although I don't think she saw me beaming in the stands. Between events, she was completely absorbed in flirtatious conversation with admiring boys from high school teams throughout the district. I waved and tried to catch her eye, but eventually I had to give up and hurry back to the newsroom.

No, having Lynn and Liska for daughters never scored points for me in the newspaper business. And way back when the girls came into my life, I never imagined that anyone would cruelly seek to convince them that their adoptions somehow boosted my professional prospects.

Frankly, I'd trade most of that career away today for an opportunity to go back, just one more time, to see Liska run. If life ever magically allows me such an impossible second chance, I will make very sure she spots me in the crowd this time, overcome with feelings, as I watch her soaring over the hurdles, her strides long and graceful and confident, her beaded braids flying in the wind, her smile dazzling at the finish line.

☙ 13 ❧

Hormones

Dear Mom,

... Please? This is my first dance that I know will be fun because there will be more black people and most of the white boys do not want to dance with me. If I can go, I will promise that I will be very good and I will do my paper route on time and be home before dinner every night, and I will stop talking back and being a bitch. (Sorry about that word, but it's how Dad said I was acting.)

Love,

Liska Maril Bates

Note from Liska, age thirteen
October 1982

LATE ONE NOVEMBER AFTERNOON in 1986, as I was convening my daily news meeting with *Register-Guard* editors, a secretary cracked open the conference room door and motioned for me to step outside.

"It's your wife on the phone," the woman whispered. "She said it's an emergency."

I rushed to my office and took the call there.

"I just got home from work," Gloria said, sounding almost hysterical. "Somebody broke into the house. It's a mess. Everything is all—"

"Get out!" I yelled, cutting her off. "Get out of the house!"

"All my grandmother's jewelry is gone," she said, sobbing.

"Just *go*! Now!" I shouted. "They might still be in the house. Go next door while I call the police. Run!"

I had worked in newsrooms for enough years to know the extreme danger awaiting people who walk into their homes and surprise burglars in the act. An intruder could be hiding somewhere in our house at that moment.

Gloria slammed the receiver down. I notified the police, ran out to the parking lot, and raced home at a speed that should have got me arrested. When I reached our driveway and screeched to a halt beside Gloria's car, I was not surprised to see I had beaten the cops to the scene. Eugene's overburdened, understaffed police department was struggling with a budget crisis. Home burglaries, which were epidemic in our town at the time, were being assigned a low priority for response. No officers would show up at our house for another forty-five minutes.

Apparently I had succeeded on the phone in impressing Gloria with her potential peril. She had left the front door wide open when she dashed out of the house. I peeked inside and called out Liska's name, just to make sure she had not come home. She was a high school senior then and our only child still living at home. My shouts drew no response in the darkened house. I felt enormous relief as I remembered that Liska had flag-football practice that afternoon.

I found my badly shaken spouse at the home of an elderly neighbor. We waited there together on her porch, keeping an eye out for Liska and becoming increasingly frustrated with each passing minute. Anybody hiding in our house would have had plenty of time to slip away before Eugene police got around to responding.

The two officers who finally showed up found no one in the house. Gloria and I followed them in and looked around in dismay. A side door had been burst open with a splitting maul that I had kept — unwisely, the police said — beside a stack of firewood on our cedar deck. The wooden door and its jamb were destroyed, with splinters and pieces of the deadbolt lock scattered all over the carpet inside.

Every room of the house except Liska's had been ransacked. Cupboard doors were open. Mattresses were askew. Drawers had been emptied, the contents tossed everywhere. In a walk-in closet in the master bedroom, police found a half-emptied liquor bottle from our kitchen cabinet. In a disturbingly eerie twist, bras and panties from Gloria's lingerie drawer were found strewn on the floor all the way out into the living room.

Almost all of my camera equipment, collected during decades of amateur and newspaper photography, was missing. It was replaceable, fortunately, but Gloria's heirloom jewelry was not. Diamond earrings passed down from her grandmother were taken along with all of Gloria's gold jewelry and several precious keepsakes, including her gold baby ring and bracelet.

The officers took fingerprints from the liquor bottle and other surfaces that the burglar apparently touched, but I knew they were just going through the motions for our benefit. The only thing Eugene police were really doing at break-ins like ours was fooling the victims into thinking the law would help them. Proof of the charade lay in the officers' failure to take fingerprints of Gloria, Liska, and me to compare with any others that turned up in their investigation. They did, however, offer one bit of analysis that I found helpful — and alarming. Both said they suspected the burglar was someone who knew that I kept a splitting maul near the side door, who was familiar with the hours when all of us were away at work and school, and who had previously been inside our home.

Shortly after the police left, Liska came home from football practice and broke into tears when she saw what had happened. She was obviously sickened with the same sense of shock, revulsion, and violation that Gloria and I were feeling. Liska became defensive, though, when I gingerly asked if she had any idea who might have broken in. "You think one of my black friends did it, don't you?" she asked, clearly affronted by my insinuation.

I knew we were on treacherous emotional ground, and I quickly dropped the subject. Most of Liska's friends that year were African-American, and all of the friends who had been to our home in the weeks before the break-in were boys. That sprang from one of our longstanding family rules: if any of our kids wanted to date someone, we wanted to meet the boy or girl first. Over the years Gloria and I discovered a seemingly endless succession of nervous teenagers — mostly males — sitting in our living room waiting to be introduced to Mom and Dad. Throughout high school Liska brought a white boy home only once. The rest were black — young men from her school, from church, from Portland, from the university campus. Privately I told Gloria our residence had been visited during Liska's senior year by the entire defensive backfield of the University of Oregon football team. It was a joke — a gross exaggeration, actually — but she *did* have a lot of young male suitors that year.

After dark that evening of the break-in, I probably should have remained home with Gloria and Liska. They were distraught and frightened, wondering whether the intruder might come back. The police seriously doubted that possibility, though, so I secured the broken door, went back to the newspaper, and worked several more hours. It was an election night, and I felt duty-bound to be in the newsroom, supervising the *Register-Guard*'s coverage.

As it turned out, I might as well have stayed home. The burglary had left me totally distracted. Involuntarily I kept running through a mental inventory of Liska's many boyfriends, trying to figure out which one had done it. I had little doubt that one of those guys, while pleased to accept my hospitality and date my daughter, was also only too happy to come back and desecrate my home.

It was so obvious to me. Our house could not easily be cased from the street. We were fairly private people. Only someone who knew Gloria and me — or Liska — would be familiar with our comings and goings. Only someone who had stood on our cedar deck would know I had unwittingly positioned a perfect burglar's tool there for criminal convenience. Only someone who had already been in Liska's bedroom would know there was no point in ransacking that part of the house.

An uncharacteristic anger boiled within me that evening. I snapped at subordinates and knocked over a full cup of hot coffee in my office. Sour feelings spread inside me like the dark, steaming liquid that was being sopped up by the papers on my desk. I fought those unpleasant emotions, but by the time I went home I felt only resentment toward the whole lot of young black males whom Liska had paraded through our home, one by one, since school began in

September. Among all the visitors I could recall being under our roof during that period, her boyfriends were the only ones who were not close, trusted, longtime acquaintances. In my mind I stood those boys in a lineup, narrowing the field to one young African-American whom I suspected of being capable of the outrage against our home.

I got off work at eleven and found Gloria and Liska waiting up for me, still scared and upset. No one slept much that night in the Bates household. All three of us were struggling with the whole spectrum of ugly emotions known only to the victims of such crimes. I thrashed around in bed for a while, then got up and tried reading. That didn't work, either, so I began cleaning house, as if that would somehow rid the place of our intruder's earlier foul presence. I could not stop reflecting on the ways our lives had been changed — mostly for the worse — since Lynn and Liska had become infatuated with boys. Many parents, I realized, face similar trials when their children become teen-agers. For Gloria and me, however, our daughters' adolescence seemed more challenging than normal. The raging of hormones was complicated by the racial dynamics of our family, the insecurities of our adopted daughters, and the resulting complexities in the rites of dating.

Time casts a wonderful mellow amber tint over some of our memories, of course, but I can't help looking back at the seventies as a golden decade for our family. All of our best times together seem to have been stacked up during those years of our children's prepubescence. Gloria and I were brimming then, almost to the point of arrogance, with faith in the future and confidence in our ability to breeze over any obstacles placed in our path. We were too young and idealistic to care about material things we did not have, and too naïve to see the problems that awaited us.

For us, the eighties roared in with the May 1980 eruption of Mount Saint Helens and a jumble of other forces more powerful, in ways, than the volcano: puberty for our children, acceleration for our careers, disarray for our family, more racial diversity for our community, Reaganomics for our country. Hitting us all at once, those pressures rocked our lives like the sonic reverberations that rattled our windows when the mountaintop disintegrated 120 miles away. What a way to begin a decade that brought us junk bonds, skinheads, and AIDS.

In the weeks after the mountain blew its top, I was cleaning volcanic ash from a new in-ground swimming pool and hot tub in our back yard. I had been rising in the *Register-Guard*'s management ranks; Gloria had become a full-time instructional aide in the schools, helping teach learning-disabled children to read. Our dual careers had suddenly made us feel prosperous for the first time in our marriage. We had bought a new home in one of Eugene's most desirable neighborhoods and invested in the aquatic facilities with hopes of inducing our four teen-agers to hang out at home rather than at the mall. The idea worked beyond expectations. Throughout much of the eighties, our place was a sort of Club Med for our kids and their friends.

The experience was pleasant, for the most part. Our home became a lively, multicultural place where black and white and Asian youngsters streamed in and out from morning until night while stereo speakers pulsated with the sounds of rock, soul, funk, disco, and rhythm and blues. It was not always a party atmosphere, though. I remember lots of long, hot summer days when our kids and their friends quietly visited for hours around the pool, and plenty of cold winter nights when they soaked in the spa, talking over the problems of their world. At the time I often wished there was less socializing and more attention to school work, but I was pleased that our children and their friends felt welcome at our home and that there was virtually no place in their lives for drugs and alcohol.

"My black friends were envious when they came over," Lynn says. "They always thought that I had cool parents. It made me feel proud of my family. When I would bring black friends home, the first thing they would say was, 'Will your parents be prejudiced against me?' I always thought that was funny. Almost every one of them asked that. I'd say, 'My parents adopted *me*. How could they be prejudiced over you?' They would say, 'Because we are darker.' It never made sense to me. Then, when they would first meet Mom and Dad, these friends would always think they had to act real proper — act white. After a while, though, they would always loosen up."

Today, we still enjoy retelling family stories from that era: Mike learning to scuba dive with one of Lynn's black boyfriends, Steve going out with one of Lynn's black girlfriends, Liska bringing home delightful kids from her church, Lynn throwing a pool party for her Vietnamese friends from high school. We all still laugh about the time Lynn found out that University of Oregon basketball star Fred Cofield was going to drop by our home. The night before his visit, she locked herself in a bathroom and sat for over an hour in front of a sunlamp, thinking she might be more appealing to Cofield if her skin were darker, like his. Instead, of course, her long session with the lamp left her face and chest blistered and peeling. Poor Lynn looked frightful by the time our celebrity guest arrived.

For all such funny memories, though, the eighties had a deleterious side for us. The relative tranquility of our home in the seventies was replaced by a frenzy of activity and emotion that often threatened the stability of our family.

"We were all too busy," Gloria says. "I began working full-time. Doug was into management at the paper. We became more socially active with our adult friends. All the kids had sports and jobs at all hours. Baby-sitting. Paper routes. Social functions. Steve had his band going, always coming and going with practices and gigs. We could never have meals all together anymore. Someone was always rushing off to do something. The whole household was chaos."

At the heart of that tumult was a change in our girls — a transformation fueled by hormones and inflamed by racial and adoption-related anxieties. Lynn and Liska became boy-crazy fools, in our view, while they thought Gloria and I were paranoid tyrants who favored our sons. There probably was some truth in both points of view.

The malady hit Lynn first, naturally, as she was three years older than Liska. The symptoms were self-absorption, furtiveness, acute insolence, and chronic sullenness. Today, Lynn describes her old self bluntly: "I was a hard child to raise — angry, temperamental, and unable to show any other kinds of emotion. I knew everything I did was right and everything Mom and Dad did was wrong. A lot of it had to do with freedom. Most of my friends' parents didn't really care what they did. I had curfews. I didn't understand why my friends got to stay out late and I couldn't. Also, I wondered why Steve got to do things I couldn't do, and I was only a year younger. I couldn't understand the reasons. I thought it was because I was adopted. That was always the easy way out of things. I thought, 'Well, I'm black and I'm adopted and that's the reason why my parents won't let me do something.' That was an escape from the real reasons. I think all girls at that age really trip out. You want to be older than you are. You want to grow up quick and dive into life all on your own without any rules or regulations."

Once Lynn passed puberty and boys became attracted to her, the cultivation of that attention became the most important thing in her life. Here, abruptly, was a source of self-esteem she was determined to pursue with every ounce of energy. Mom and Dad were mean-spirited obstacles to her happiness. Steve could stay out until one or two in the morning playing at bars with his pals in their rock and roll band, so why couldn't Lynn stay out that late with her girl-friends, cruising in cars and looking for guys? Lynn could see no difference. And curfews were not really the issue. Gloria and I were not so much concerned with the lateness of the hour as we were with making sure she was safe, knowing whom she was with, knowing her whereabouts, and ensuring her school attendance. All of our parental meddling only proved to her that we hated her. And she responded with an anger so ferocious that Gloria and I had to battle our emotions to keep from behaving exactly that way: as if we hated Lynn.

One chilly Sunday evening in midwinter, for example, Gloria and I had a cozy blaze going in the fireplace as we idled over a jigsaw puzzle and a glass of wine while waiting for Lynn to get off the telephone with a boy. She had been huddled with the phone in hushed conversation most of the day, off and on, and her latest call had droned on for nearly an hour. Meanwhile, I needed to reach somebody at work. Despite my increasingly impatient requests, Lynn ignored me, refusing to cut it off. This went on far too long, in my view, so after one final warning I got up, walked over to Lynn, took the receiver from her, and told the boy their conversation was over. Then I disconnected the call and began dialing the newsroom. In a fury, with one swipe of her hand, Lynn scattered our half-assembled jigsaw puzzle, pieces flying across the room. I hung up the phone, grabbed Lynn, carried her out onto the patio, and tossed her into the swimming pool, frigid in the dead of winter.

"You needed to cool off," I told her as she climbed out, soaked and sputtering.

"Shithead," she said.

I felt sickened by my action and shivered almost as much as Lynn did. That was the closest I ever came to physical child abuse. Today, still remorseful about losing my composure that day, I think I deserved the label Lynn applied to me, and she says she deserved to be doused in the icy pool.

"I feel real guilty," she says. "I wish I could just go back and be a little nicer. I needed to cool off, and I *did* have a phone problem. I was on that phone *all* the time. Now I can't stand the telephone. I hate it. But I remember that call. Mustafa was on the line. He broke up with me. I can't remember the reason. We were back together the next day. All I remember is that I was so angry."

Lynn had many boyfriends as a teen-ager but none more important than Mustafa Isfahan. They met in junior high school when Lynn began volunteering as an English-language tutor for Vietnamese immigrants.

"Mustafa didn't speak any English when I first met him," she recalls. "It was very hard to communicate. We didn't do much talking the first month. We started working together as part of a group, then one on one. Mustafa and I would just sit there. We wouldn't say anything. I felt kind of stupid for a while."

Mustafa was part of a wave of Southeast Asian families who settled in Eugene under church sponsorship in the late seventies after Saigon fell to the Communists. His mother was Vietnamese.

His father was a Malaysian fisherman who had been allied to the U.S.-backed regime. The Isfahan family had to flee for their lives and made a harrowing voyage before ending up in refugee camps and, eventually, in the United States.

The Isfahan children were exceptionally bright and motivated, and all of them — most notably Mustafa — learned English with astonishing speed. Mustafa and his parents and sisters were fine human beings, but at South Eugene High School many students derisively called them boat people.

"Mustafa was an outsider, and that's probably why I felt comfortable with him," Lynn says. "I knew there was no way he could be prejudiced toward me, because there was so much prejudice toward him. A lot of the students ridiculed Mustafa and the other Asians. I felt we had something in common, and I basically stuck with Mustafa all the way through high school. Everyone knew we were together, even though it was on again, off again. We would break up and go out with others and then get back together all the time.

"In high school, my worst times with prejudice were not with whites. It was with the blacks. I know that must sound kind of weird, but it was true. Throughout high school I was basically the only black. Then two more moved in. They were tough. [One of them] would always try to pick fights with me. She would call me names. They didn't like me at all. I was going out with an Asian and they ridiculed me about that, all the time. I think that's what really bonded me to Mustafa. We were both outcasts, to the whites and to the blacks. So we stuck together most of the time."

It was a stormy teen-age relationship, however, often breaking apart when Lynn went out with young black men from other schools and when Mustafa dated Asian or white girls. Lynn and Mustafa were continually feuding or reconciling, and their ever-swirling youthful passions made our moody daughter a difficult person to live with. Gloria caught the brunt of it while I found myself increasingly buried in my newspaper career.

"I felt sorry for Mom. I really did," Lynn says. "I felt so bad about the way I treated her back then, but I kept on doing it. I know I did things that hurt her feelings, but I almost would do it on purpose. I don't know the reasons why. I acted the way I did just to get her upset, and then I'd feel sad. It was anger — a lot of testing. I'd try to be bad just to see if Mom and Dad would give me back [to state authorities]. I was pretty sure that if I kept on saying, 'I don't want to be here,' really getting down and dirty, they would send me away.

"I didn't feel that Mom loved me. There were times that I did, and times that I didn't. That's only natural, because of discipline and things that the boys could do that we couldn't. Steve could go out later. I understand it now, but back then, I would always say, 'Well, you don't love me because I'm adopted and I'm black and I'm not your real child.' Mom probably heard that hundreds and hundreds of times. That was my only weapon that I could use to hurt her. I was real angry. I was angry about the fact that I was put up for adoption. I was angry at the world. I took that out on Mom. Now I know that she loved me. I was just confused."

Lynn sneaked out of the house late at night a number of times and broke plenty of other rules, but she did nothing radically different from what millions of other American teen-agers did, including our sons, Steve and Mike. What set Lynn apart, though, was her temper — as manifested in the demolished jigsaw puzzle — and her wrathful tongue.

"Lynn would complain that Mike and I never got in trouble while she and Liska always did," Steve says. "I would just tell her that we knew how to stay out of trouble. And when we *did* get caught, we didn't lip off to Mom and Dad. We knew when not to talk, while Lynn didn't know when to shut it off."

Liska developed the same trait, and therein lay part of the basis for the girls' oft-repeated accusation that the boys enjoyed favored status. Gloria and I felt tormented and defenseless in dealing with such charges because we knew they had merit.

"Yes, I admit it, we certainly favored the boys during those days," Gloria says. "I always loved Lynn and Liska, but I couldn't stand their disrespect in the teen-age years. We were just a bother to them. They treated us horribly. They were rude and didn't want to hear us suggest anything to them. They talked back, sometimes using foul words. Of course I preferred talking with the boys. They treated us with respect and love. I could not sit down with the girls during that time and talk lightly about different things. Most of the time I was dealing with their obnoxious behavior."

Leith Robertson, our adoption caseworker, had warned us years earlier to expect defiant behavior from the girls after puberty. She said children adopted past infancy typically engage in a lot of parental testing, which usually intensifies during the turbulent teens. "No matter how many times they challenge you and threaten to run away and accuse you of failing to love them," Leith said, "always respond that you *do* love them and they're stuck with you, that running away is not permitted and there's no going back to the foster home. That's really what they will be wanting to hear you say, because they will be acting out their fear of abandonment."

No sweat, we said. Gloria and I listened to Leith's words of caution and felt prepared to deal with whatever troubled feelings our new daughters might have. Besides, we thought, how could such darling little girls grow up to be the kind of teen-age brats Leith was describing?

Boy, were we naïve. Both daughters — especially Lynn — began testing our love within weeks of joining the family and kept it up until they reached adulthood. Today, Gloria and I do not feel we were adequately prepared for dealing with the girls' emotional needs. The two of us would have benefited immensely from post-adoption counseling, which is something we didn't even know about until it no longer mattered.

The early phase of testing was not pleasant, but neither was it overwhelming. Right after adoption each daughter went through a time of apparent tranquility. The smoothness was superficial, though, because the girls had not yet attached to their new family. Inevitably, as Lynn and Liska began to feel stirrings of caring and longing, those feelings stimulated the unresolved pain and loss they had known in their earlier relationships with adults. Lynn in particular began fighting her new attachment, showing hostility and negativity, and she entered a thirteen-year period of testing to demonstrate that Gloria and I, just like her birth parents and her foster parents, would not be keeping her. Anticipating rejection and loss, Lynn kept trying to precipitate what she considered inevitable in order to deal with her anxiety and feelings of helplessness. Liska possessed the same emotions but played them out in a different way, carefully watching her older sister and allowing her to be the troublemaker. While Lynn shouldered the heavy-duty testing, Liska could sit back and observe and enjoy the rewards of being sweet. Later, though, as soon as Liska reached puberty at age ten, she joined the attack with Lynn, and Gloria and I rather suddenly found ourselves buffeted by gale-force testing from both daughters at once. The four of us were locked in a destructive syndrome of escalating mutual anxiety. Gloria and I knew why it was happening; we just did not know how to stop it.

I blame it all on hormones; they are what began the cycle for both daughters. Once Lynn and Liska reached childbearing age and began channeling their testing into the pursuit of attention from the opposite sex, Gloria and I could not help responding fearfully. We knew better than that but were powerless to block our own emotions. As Lynn and Liska, at ages twelve and ten, respectively, began demanding a level of freedom that we felt would endanger them, we could not resist demonstrating the very rejecting behavior that they were trying to provoke. A negative interaction with one of our daughters would trigger our anxiety, which in turn would stimulate our daughter's old fears of being sent away. Those fears would then compel her to act even more provocatively, thus amplifying the negative interaction.

In a book on adoption I once read the answer for parents like Gloria and me: we needed to learn "to communicate love while setting appropriate limits for behavior." That glib platitude struck me as completely unhelpful. There was not a word of specific advice on how an adoptive parent might accomplish simultaneous love-communicating and limit-setting.

So, with little help from books and no counseling whatsoever, Gloria and I muddled through. Luckily, the experience did not destroy our marriage. We knew other Eugene-area couples who ended up divorced after adopting children. If we ever came close to a family meltdown ourselves, though, it began in 1983 when my newspaper switched from evening to morning publication. The publisher's decision was a shrewd business move, highly popular with advertisers, but it turned the lives of many employees upside down. Editors like me, accustomed for years to going to work before dawn, now had to work late into the night to put out the morning edition.

I tried to accept the change as a professional and never complained about the schedule, but it wrecked life at home. Suddenly I was at home alone all morning and then had to show up in the newsroom between one and two o'clock in the afternoon — well before Gloria got off work and our kids came home from school — and could not break away until eleven at night or even later. My children's memories of my obsessive work habits are heavily influenced by the late-night hours I had to work throughout much of the eighties.

That left Gloria to deal alone with the full load of our child-related problems throughout the week. She had her own full-time job with learning-disabled kids in the schools. How could she cope with our household chaos now? It only grew worse. Steve, a senior in high school by then, was working nights as a supermarket box boy and weekends as lead guitarist for The Nomads. Lynn worked part-time at a pizza joint. Mike put in long hours after school and on weekends at an ice cream parlor. Liska had a paper route and was in heavy demand as a baby-sitter. Both girls had private dance lessons and often needed a ride from Gloria. One of Steve's band members lived with us that entire school year after his parents moved away. All of the kids' schedules were so unpredictable that sit-down dinners died as an evening ritual in our home. Meanwhile, as if Gloria did not have enough challenges to deal with, Liska met Reggie.

"Reggie was my first boyfriend," Liska says. "He was a senior at Churchill High School. I was in eighth grade at Roosevelt Junior High. I was young. Real young."

Liska was thirteen when they met at her church. Reggie was at least eighteen and probably nineteen; he had not graduated with the kids his age. At first Gloria and I had nothing against Reggie except his age. He was already a man. Emotionally, Liska was still a girl, in a woman's body. Lynn had gone out with Reggie's brother, who described him as a streetwise lady's man who claimed to have bedded a startling number of Eugene-area girls. We did not feel comfortable with Liska's infatuation with Reggie. She accused us of disliking him because he was black.

We told Liska she was too young to date and have a steady boyfriend. Like any of her friends, though, Reggie was welcome to come to our home and visit. Throughout the first half of 1983, after Liska had turned fourteen, Reggie was a frequent guest at our house, and we had no trouble beyond his and Liska's inability to keep their hands off each other. His welcome wore out late one night, however, when police banged on our door and arrested Reggie on charges of stealing the expensive new bicycle he had ridden over to our house that evening. Before taking him away, one of the officers told Gloria that Reggie had an extensive police record. Reggie insisted that one of his friends, not he, had stolen the bike, but we no longer wanted our daughter hanging out with him. Liska, of course, was incensed.

"When I was younger I thought Mom and Dad were too strict," she says. "I wanted to spend time with Reggie but they didn't really like him. That made me mad. I think that's when we started having serious conflicts. A lot of times I would mouth off and say I wished that I never was adopted. I'd say that whenever I was really mad."

That was often. And our battle of wills over Reggie was complicated by Liska's relationship with the first African-American adult in her life, an elderly woman we knew as Grandma Mary. Mary was raising a granddaughter, Lisa, who was Liska's closest friend at school. Lisa also happened to be Reggie's cousin.

Throughout 1983 Liska lobbied for permission to stay overnight with Lisa and Grandma Mary. "Liska seemed to need a black adult in her life at that time," Gloria recalls, "and we were initially pleased to see her become attached to Lisa's grandmother."

Grandma Mary was an extremely religious woman who read to Liska and Lisa from the Bible and drove them to services at Saint Mark's Church. Weekend after weekend Liska stayed overnight with her new friends, not returning home until after a full day of religious activities on Sundays.'

Eventually our delight with the arrangement gave way to uneasiness. It began one Saturday night when we called Grandma Mary's house to let Liska know about some family plans, only to discover that Liska was not there and Grandma did not know where she was. "I didn't feel that the grandmother had sufficient parental control, and I didn't have confidence in her ability to know what the two girls were up to," Gloria says. "She didn't have the faintest idea where the girls were or what they were doing. I was really frightened for Liska's safety."

We imposed stricter rules on her visits to Grandma Mary's house and immediately noticed a new problem. Each time Liska returned home from a weekend there, she showed increasing disrespect toward us. Her remarks indicated she was picking up some antiparent and possibly even antiwhite feelings that lingered for days after every visit. At school she became insolent toward teachers and once was suspended for such behavior. Gloria arranged for some extremely helpful counseling after the episode, and it led to Liska's entering the Big Sister program and forming a relationship with a wonderful young African-American student at the university. Meanwhile, though, Liska continued to feel drawn to the home of Grandma Mary.

"Grandma Mary never said my parents or white people were bad," Liska says. "She was mainly a good listener. And she always wanted me to call home and tell Mom and Dad that I was okay."

Despite Liska's assurances, Gloria and I could not completely relax. We did appreciate Grandma Mary's interest in Liska, and Gloria tried to express her thanks on Christmas that year by buying

Grandma Mary a gold necklace with a cross. We were concerned, though, that some of her family's problems would harm our daughter. "For example," Gloria says, "I remember Liska coming home and telling about various children who were staying temporarily with Grandma Mary because their mothers were too strung out on drugs to care for them. I had to wonder whether that was a good environment for Liska to be in."

Then Gloria discovered that Lisa's father sometimes hung out at Grandma Mary's house when he needed money from her or a place to stay for a while. "I didn't like that situation," Gloria says. "He was always coming on to Liska and even to me when I'd go there to bring Liska home." Our breaking point came when Gloria discovered that the cousin, Reggie, had moved in with Grandma Mary. Unbeknownst to us, he had been living in the home while Liska was spending the night there. We were furious and put an end to the overnight visits at Grandma Mary's.

To this day Liska does not think our reaction was just. She was especially angry about favoritism she perceived toward our son Mike, who was heavily involved in bicycle racing in those days and could take off for many hours at a stretch, presumably training, without our insistence on knowing his exact whereabouts. And when he became involved with a girlfriend who was fifteen, like him, we seemed relatively cavalier about Mike's frequent visits, often late into the night, at her family's home. "I think both my parents were kind of unfair to my sister and me," Liska says. "There wasn't enough discipline towards my brothers and there was a lot towards Lynn and me."

Gloria and I find a grain of vindication, though, in Liska's current feelings about her old flame. "I really loved Reggie more than he loved me," she says. "He cheated on me a lot. I was so dumb."

Lynn today is a little more charitable than her sister in assessing our child-parent conflict. "I admire the way Mom and Dad raised us," Lynn says. "They did their best with what they had. A lot of people couldn't have done it — especially with me. Mom and Dad really didn't do anything wrong, but back then in my eyes it was *all* wrong."

Actually, our strife could not be blamed on anyone. It was an unavoidable endocrinological soap opera that all of us probably just had to live through.

Poor Gloria. By default, she usually had to play the villain. "I remember Mom having to handle most of the discipline and Dad being the communicator — when he was around. He was working a lot," Lynn says. "So Mom had all this on her. I just made things worse, and we'd both end up hollering. Dad never really did that. He was just so calm. He would come home and want to sit down and talk about the problem, going into complete detail. I just didn't want to hear it. I was always defensive."

It was a lot easier being the communicator than the disciplinarian — sort of like the United Nations peacekeeping forces going in after the combat troops already did all the dirty work. And I doubt that my ameliorative efforts ever accomplished much, although there was one incident that stands out.

One night I came home to discover that Gloria and Lynn, once again, had argued over some boy-related issue that is now long forgotten. In the heat of their skirmish Lynn had fired her nuclear weapon, the charge that Gloria did not really love her. Gloria had heard it many times, but for once she was far too upset to muster another response. She was emotionally exhausted. She could not face Lynn anymore. She needed help.

I chased everyone out of our family room and asked Lynn to join me there for a talk. She did not want to, so I had to order her to come in and sit down. Then, as she sulked on a couch, refusing to meet my eyes, I began a spiel that went something like this: "Lynn, I know you are afraid Mom doesn't love you. You've been haunted by that fear ever since you were a little girl. You are terrified that the day will come when she won't want you anymore and she will reject you, as your birth mother did, and send you away, as you feel your foster mother did. That fear is so great inside you that sometimes you can hardly stand it any longer, and you wish Mom would just get it over with and put you out of your misery by telling you to leave. Waiting for that dreaded moment is more than your heart can bear. Subconsciously, you even try to help Mom hurry up and reach that point by saying hurtful words and doing things you know will upset her. Does this make any sense?"

"I don't know," she said, still looking down.

"I've heard you say Mom couldn't possibly love you the way she loves Steve and Mike, because you're not her flesh and blood. Well, let me ask you a question, Lynn. Do you love Mom?"

"I don't know."

"Then let me answer it for you," I said. "Yes, you love her with all of your soul. That's why you act the way you do — because deep inside you're scared that your love can't be returned and you'll be rejected. So here is what you need to think about: since we know it's possible for someone like you to love Mom, who isn't your biological mother, why is it so inconceivable that *she* might love *you*?

"And let me put it another way," I continued. "Do you think I love Mom?"

"Yeah."

"And do you think I love your aunt Eloise and my friend Brian Lanker?"

"Sure. Who wouldn't?"

"Well," I said, "Mom and Eloise and Brian aren't my flesh and blood. Biological ties are no prerequisite for love in those vital human relationships. If we can love spouses and in-laws and friends outside our own biological families, why is it so hard to accept that we can love children who were not born in the family? Lynn, you're seventeen years old, for heaven's sake. If Mom didn't love you, do you think she would have stuck by you through all these years of you never being able to tell her, just once, that you even like her? Think about it. You've never told her that, have you?"

Lynn just shrugged her shoulders. Our talk was over. I felt frustrated, as I often did, with my apparent inability to get through to Lynn. Her unhappiness, and Gloria's anguish, seemed so unnecessary.

The next night, when Gloria and I went to bed, we found a long letter from Lynn waiting for us in our room. Lynn was always far better at expressing herself in writing than in conversation. Our collection of keepsakes is full of Lynn's notes and cards and lengthy missives, often apologizing for her behavior or thanking us for something or asking for special permission to go somewhere. This letter was special. After an elaborate explanation of her feelings about the prior day's argument with Gloria, Lynn ended with the following declaration: "I know I've never said this before, but 'I really love both of you.' "

After the lights went out that night, I could feel Gloria trembling beside me. When I reached for her, I touched her pillow, and it was damp. Maybe, I said to myself, that talk with Lynn was not such a waste of time after all.

For the next week or two, Gloria and Lynn had a détente of sorts, and I vainly flattered myself by feeling as calm and wonderful as Ozzie Nelson, as cool and wise as Bill Cosby. Sometimes, as television sitcoms would have you believe, Father does indeed know best, I thought.

That pink cloud went poof, however, when Gloria and I came home one night after a much-needed weekend by ourselves at the beach. We discovered that Lynn, who was supposed to have stayed at the home of a girlfriend during our absence, had actually spent the weekend partying at our house with a boy and another couple. Evidence of their merrymaking had not been fully eliminated, and the confrontation that ensued quickly escalated until all of us were right back where we had been a few weeks earlier. This time, Father did not know diddly. I was at a loss for words that could restore trust and calm things down.

The strain at home grew worse when I went to work at the *Seattle Times* in March of 1984, leaving Gloria and the kids to finish up the school year before joining me up north. For Gloria, those four months were nightmarish as she had to deal all alone with the two girls' emotional turmoil. Liska wanted to move in with Reggie and Grandma Mary. Lynn wanted to stay out all night with Mustafa. She ran away with him for a week, staying in a Vietnamese friend's apartment. After Gloria met with her and talked her into coming home, Lynn began skipping school and jeopardized her graduation. Just a couple of weeks before commencement, she left South High and accompanied a friend to an outlawed "Skip Day" beer party that resulted in a rash of car wrecks out in the woods. One of them killed a student. In a separate collision, Lynn suffered facial and ankle injuries and was hospitalized. The principal expelled three students after the tragedy. Seven others, including our injured daughter, were suspended. Lynn almost did not graduate. Where was the communicator when he was needed most?

"Normally, when girls go through that age, they don't think their parents know anything," Gloria says, "but because our girls were adopted they felt even more distant from us. They were probably thinking, 'Hey, these aren't even my real mom and dad, so how do they have any idea what I'm feeling?'

"Lynn didn't even think that we needed to be involved in her life. She said she knew what she was doing. Neither of the girls wanted to listen to anything I had to offer, even about safe sex. In the back of my mind I was always thinking, 'Please, God, just let them graduate from high school before they get pregnant.' I was so worried about that, and later about AIDS. They were both on birth control pills during their later high school years, but they were flaky about taking them regularly. I had to always keep on them."

The move to Seattle brought a pair of important changes in our daughters' lives. Lynn did receive her high school diploma and then chose to move in with Mustafa's family rather than join us in Washington. She went to work with Mustafa at a Eugene electronics plant, assembling components. Liska, meanwhile, dumped Reggie for Russell, the extremely likable and responsible son of an African-American minister in Seattle. To our great relief, she quickly began to snap out of the pouty behavior she seemed to have picked up at Grandma Mary's.

"I loved Seattle," Liska says. "And I loved Nathan Hale High School. If it had been up to me, I would have continued going there throughout my school years. Nathan Hale didn't have just white people. It had all different races — black people, Hawaiian, Mexican, Japanese, and Indians. I enjoyed it. I was so used to being the only black person at my previous schools.

"Everyone at Nathan Hale was real nice to me — especially Russell. He was a gentleman," Liska says. "I became friends with his sister and that's how I got to meet him. He played football. We ran track together and studied together. I taught him how to swim. We went to the zoo, movies, parks, the mall. He came over to my house and had dinner with my family, and I had dinner with his family. We went to a Prince concert, to the prom, and to a dance. Our friends thought that we would get married someday."

But a year later we moved back to Eugene, and Liska and Russell eventually became interested in different people. She did not resume her relationship with Grandma Mary and her granddaughter. Instead, Liska transferred to a high school in a different part of town and made friends with a different African-American girl, Lorraine Broadous.

"Lorraine and I, oh honey, we just had a good ol' time," Liska says. "We weren't troublemakers. We just liked to laugh with people. We liked being goofy. The Broadous family was really good. They were kind of a Cosby family, always making me laugh. It was like the second family for the African-American part of me. I learned a lot of things about my culture through them and how to cook a lot of African-American food. Lorraine's father worked for the railroad, and he was a minister. Her mother was a homemaker."

We were delighted with Liska's close friendship with the Broadous family and pleased that she seemed to be more serious about school after our return from Seattle. She also appeared to have finally accepted the fact that Gloria loved her unconditionally.

"I've always been close to my mother," Liska says, "but as I grew older we became even closer. It was easier to talk with her than with Dad. Mom doesn't take life as serious as he does. She has a lot of creativity in her, and she is an emotional person, like myself. Mom was brought up pretty much the way my father was, with strong beliefs and expectations, but she's fun-lovin' and has a good time. Like when holidays come along, she really, *really* gets into it. She goes all out. Other times, though, she's kind of quiet. She lost two people that she loved very much, her sister and her father. A lot of things are in her heart. I feel sometimes that she wants to get it out to somebody. That's why I wish we could have done more things together when I was younger, more mother-daughter things, like we do now. And I wish Mom would have talked to me more about certain things, like the birds and the bees. I found that out by myself."

Although Liska was no less preoccupied with the opposite sex after our move back to Eugene, she was at least content to abandon her one-boy fixation. That may sound hypocritical, since Gloria and I "went steady" in high school. We know from experience, though, how arduous life is for kids who marry at eighteen, and we did not want that for Liska — or for any of our children. Thus we were glad when she began dating a variety of young men.

Regrettably, though, on that November election night in 1986, I was sure one of those young men had smashed his way into our house and ransacked it before leaving with my wife's most precious heirlooms. As the two police officers left our house that night, they assured us they would be in touch if their investigation turned up a suspect or our missing possessions. I doubted we would ever hear back from them, though, and I was right.

For months I brooded about the treachery of the young African-American man I was positive had done the deed. He surely sensed that Gloria and I did not care much for him. He probably felt jilted by Liska. He had plenty of motives besides avarice for breaking into our home. And why, I wondered, would he get into Gloria's lingerie and fling it all over the house? The act seemed kinky and sick, as if he sought to inflict fear and revulsion along with the other punishment he was dealing out for us.

I did not give the young man's name to police; there was absolutely no evidence that he was the burglar. However, I devised a strategy for tricking him into revealing his culpability if he ever came over again. He never did, though. Liska, in fact, brought hardly anyone home the rest of her senior year of high school. I think she sensed a sad truth, that the symbolic rape of our home had somehow altered it. The Bates residence was no longer a warm and inviting place for our children's friends. Gloria and I felt violated. The event had changed us in unattractive ways, diminishing our trust in others and bringing to the surface some base human instincts that eventually left me shaken.

Many months after the break-in, I went to the Eugene City Hall to obtain a copy of the police report to attach to the theft-loss form accompanying our income tax return. A statement in the police document literally made the hair rise on the back of my neck. Officers had interviewed our neighbors, and a woman who lived across the street told them that on the afternoon of the burglary she had seen a suspicious-looking young man emerge in a hurry from our back yard, carrying a large black satchel. She provided a full description of the guy, including details of his baseball cap and the unusual jacket he wore.

I was astounded. Why hadn't she told us? Why hadn't the *police* told us? We knew the young man. There was no question about it. Liska had brought him home once to meet us. I remembered every detail of him sitting in our living room — cold and uncommunicative — as I took a look at his ball cap, his unusual jacket, and his disappointing grooming. Our burglar was indeed one of Liska's young male friends — the one and only *white* boy she had ever brought home.

Bitter feelings welled within me during the weeks that followed. What a fiasco it was, I thought, that so much time had passed between the crime and my discovery of our neighbor's report. Evidently the kid had long since moved out of state, and I was quite sure he would never even be questioned in the case. My frustration, though, was not the most powerful emotion I was battling. I was also overwhelmed with shame.

Why had I assumed all along that it was one of Liska's African-American boyfriends who had broken into our home? Why not the white kid? The rage and loathing I felt after the break-in had aroused in me an ancient, deeply buried capability for fear and hatred that I had not realized was there. Racism, I now know, is a malignancy that waits in remission inside everybody — *everybody*. Any of us, white or black, who claims to be immune to it is a fool — perhaps the most dangerous kind.

For a while I assumed that the crime against my home had brought out the worst in me. But I was wrong. The nadir was yet to come. All it needed was a nudge, and that was heading my way, courtesy of Bernard Lee, the Los Angeles thief who took away my youngest child, my freedom from fear, and my faith in people.

❧ 14 ❧

Heartaches

Dear Mom & Dad,
How's Eugene? Everything here is fine. I got a new job at
Elan's, a full-service French salon . . . Sofia and Zack are
doing great. They're over their colds. Sofia is completely
potty trained. It makes life easier . . . It's supposed to snow
late tonight. Too bad. It just finally started melting and
people took off their chains. Well, I'll let you know how
things are going.
Love,
Lynn

Letter from Lynn, age twenty-three
Seattle, Washington
February 16, 1989

THE MID-EIGHTIES BROUGHT US an explosion of high
school graduations — Steve in 1983, Lynn in 1984, Mike in 1986,
and Liska in 1987. Then came a totally unexpected intermission in
the formal education of our children. Today, most of them seem
eager for opportunities to resume studies, but in the late eighties I
found myself looking around and wondering what had happened to
my dream that all the Bates kids would go to college.

As it turned out, that was *my* dream, not theirs. All four children
were offered the same financial program: tuition, books, and fees
paid by Mom and Dad, with living expenses the responsibility of
the kids unless they chose to live at home. Steve and Mike enrolled
briefly in a Eugene-area community college but rather quickly decided they wanted to get out in the world first, sock away some
money, and perhaps return to school someday when they would
not have to live like struggling students. Lynn had no apparent

interest in academics after high school and seemed primarily interested in leaving home and enjoying the freedom to live entirely by her own rules.

"In high school I had no direction in life," Lynn says. "I was boy-crazy. For a while I thought I wanted to be in the Navy, and I passed all the tests, but after graduation I didn't want to join. I probably would have done really well in the Navy, but I liked Mustafa, and he kind of stopped me from going. I think my decision was a big letdown to Mom and Dad. That's what they really hoped I would do."

Instead, shortly after receiving her diploma, Lynn moved in with the Southeast Asian family of her boyfriend while Gloria, Steve, Mike, and Liska moved to Seattle to join me. Lynn's decision left Gloria and me disconsolate and changed her life in profound ways.

When I recall those unhappy days, I feel more sympathy for Mustafa Isfahan's parents than I do for us. Our family problems seemed minuscule compared with theirs. They had been uprooted from their homeland and nearly killed in a war that left many of their relatives dead or missing. Now the Isfahans were in a strange land with a culture that baffled and frightened them. Neither husband nor wife could speak much English after five years in the United States. All of their hopes for their future and that of their three daughters rested on the shoulders of their oldest child and only son, Mustafa.

He was an exceptionally handsome, muscular young man whose frequent, dimpled smile and keen intelligence gave him rather quick entrée into white U.S. society. He picked up English and American slang with astonishing speed and embraced his new country's popular culture with a gusto that alarmed his parents. Mustafa loved sports cars, rock music, Marlboros, Bruce Lee movies, and beautiful American girls like our daughter. The elder Isfahans feared they were losing their son. In their eyes, he was a young rebel spinning out of control in their scary new world. Already their plans for his future had been destroyed by the war and their escape as refugees to the United States. Mustafa was a Muslim, the faith of his Malaysian father, and as a young boy had been promised for marriage to a

Muslim girl in Vietnam. The upheaval in Asia shattered those plans. By 1984 Mustafa's parents must have been worried that their remaining dreams were in jeopardy, too. Lynn thinks that was why they invited her into their home — to keep Mustafa with the family.

"I stayed with the Isfahan family a year in Eugene and did not like it," Lynn says. "I don't think Mustafa's parents liked it, either, but he apparently had told them we would be married. That was not what they wanted. They did not really like me. They just didn't want a broken-up family."

Eventually Lynn found her own apartment and moved out of the Isfahan household, but soon afterward she discovered she was pregnant. She and Mustafa set up housekeeping together on their own. Not long after the birth of their baby girl, Sofia, Mustafa's parents and sisters moved to Seattle to join that city's burgeoning Asian Muslim community.

Although Lynn says her pregnancy was not planned, she looks back at it today as something that happened almost deliberately. "I wanted to feel like I belonged to someone, genetically, and that they belonged to me — having the same blood running down their backbone and sharing the same facial features," she says. "All my life I have felt that I belonged just to myself, and it was Lynn Bates and only Lynn Bates. I didn't know what it would be like to have a sister who looked like me or a brother who acted like me. When I gave birth to Sofia I felt that physical bond, for the first time in my life."

Mustafa was a highly respected worker at the Eugene electronics plant. He was promoted to advanced parts-testing work and earned enough to buy a bright yellow Porsche for him and Lynn and Sofia. Out of his parents' shadow, they enjoyed a lively, somewhat hedonistic, wholly young-American lifestyle. "It was then, after Sofia was born, that Mustafa and I had our happiest times together, living in our small apartment on West Eleventh Avenue," Lynn says.

When Sofia was ten months old, Lynn brought Mustafa and the baby to a Bates gathering at Odell Lake and introduced them to the extended family. My parents had not met Mustafa and had privately expressed disappointment in Lynn's decisions. Mustafa, however, quickly endeared himself to all of my relatives, particularly when we organized a work party to clear a pair of tall fir trees that had toppled into the lake near our dock during a winter storm. My brother Tom, always mindful of his macho reputation as the family's Duke of Earl, surprised no one by picking up an ax and wading out to the crown of the fallen trees, taking on the most difficult and dangerous part of the task. All of us, though, were startled when Mustafa grabbed a crosscut saw and followed Tom out into the water. There, working chest-deep in the icy lake, both of them cut away at the downed timber until each was semi-hypothermic, neither willing to be the first to wade back to shore.

"I remember Grandpa Bates being really impressed with Mustafa," Lynn says. "By the time that weekend was over, Mustafa was quite accepted by the whole family. It was a good experience.

"We got along very well then," she says. "His parents had moved to Seattle. There was no religious conflict. We had our own little group of friends and we all did things together. I didn't have to stay at home. Life was normal. It was just exactly how I wanted to live.

"Then we moved to Seattle, and everything started to change."

Mustafa accepted a higher-paying job with an aircraft manufacturing company. He and Lynn and Sofia moved in with his parents and sisters in a large, comfortable split-level house the family had purchased in west Seattle, almost directly under the flight path of jetliners taking off from Sea-Tac International Airport.

"I thought living with Mustafa's parents would be a temporary thing," Lynn says. "They wanted us to get married in a traditional Muslim ceremony at their mosque, and I thought that after the wedding we would live by ourselves, just like in Eugene. But I was wrong."

For the next two years, out of embarrassment and the hope that things would change, Lynn hid from us what was happening to her in Seattle. She wrote many letters filled with bubbly news about how well Mustafa was doing at work, how she was advancing at beauty college, and how quickly Sofia was developing. There was no clue, in our telephone conversations or in her visits to Eugene, that she was miserable.

By Sofia's second birthday, Mustafa was in his early twenties, settling down, and accepting adult responsibility as never before. He began shedding his youthful rebelliousness and reembracing the values and traditions of his parents and their faith. When he talked to Lynn about their move to Seattle, I'm sure he did not intentionally mislead her; Mustafa was too decent and honest for that. I think he was just beginning to return to the fold and did not realize the full extent of the changes that were awaiting him.

Lynn went through the Muslim marriage rites in Seattle without inviting us to the ceremony or even telling us about it afterward. "I thought it was neat, at first — just something I had to go through, and then Mustafa and I could get on with our lives," she says. "Now I feel they kind of suckered me into it without really telling me the truth about their expectations. I didn't know what was involved. It was like diving in blindfolded."

At the wedding, Lynn was surprised to discover she was being given a Muslim name — Sarigha — and that was how she was to be addressed in the home when Asian friends came to visit. During those visits Lynn was also required to wear traditional religious clothing — her head covered, her arms out of sight, her legs hidden behind floor-length skirts.

"When company came over I was told what to wear," she says. "I stayed out of sight and avoided mingling with their Muslim friends and relatives. They ordered me around and really kept an eye on me because I never prayed or studied the faith as they expected me to. I didn't have any interest in it. There was a lot of family pressure on Mustafa because I wouldn't go to religion school or study the Koran. The parents wanted me to. Mustafa got a lot of flak because of me. He didn't know what to do.

"Everything was totally different than the way I was raised. When I went outside of the house, I was supposed to cover my head. I couldn't wear shorts. I had to wear long sleeves and long skirts. When I refused to, Mustafa got even more pressure from his parents. They didn't like me going to beauty school. I couldn't really go anywhere without them wanting to know exactly when I would be back. I was permitted to go to the store if I was back in twenty minutes. I never got to go out and do things. The woman was expected to stay at home, while the men could do whatever they wanted to. If I was with one of Mustafa's sisters, then I could go to a store and stay a little longer. I was a prisoner."

The irony might have been hilarious if it had not been so painful. Here was Lynn at age twenty-three, a grown woman and a mother, being required to live by family rules far more prohibitive than the ones her adoptive parents had imposed when she was a defiant teenage girl. And now her complaint that the family's males enjoyed favored status had far more validity than it did when she used to think Steve and Mike had all the fun.

"Then I discovered that living with Mustafa's family was not a temporary arrangement," Lynn says. "I found out we were expected to live at that house until his parents died, and then *we* would own the house. That could take another twenty years. Meanwhile, the sisters would get married and go off, but Mustafa was to stay there with his parents and his wife and children and eventually own the house. That's the way the custom goes. I was *very* unhappy to learn this."

Still, Lynn kept her misery secret — even when Gloria and Liska drove to Seattle one Christmas and showered Lynn and Mustafa and Sofia with gifts. The Isfahan family greeted the Bateses warmly, and to all outward appearances Lynn and Mustafa seemed fine.

Lynn became pregnant with their second child and kept up her training at the beauty college. A few days after becoming a state-licensed hair stylist and cosmetologist, she gave birth to a baby boy. Gloria and I were extremely proud of Lynn and elated for her. We shared pictures of her and Mustafa and their children with all of our relatives, who swamped us with compliments about Lynn's apparent success, good fortune, and happiness. We still had no idea about her tragic conflict with her husband's native culture.

"Mustafa's family wanted to name our new baby Abubaka," Lynn says, "but I said, 'No!' It had to be a Muslim name, though, so I looked through their phone directory and found Zackria on the list. I thought at least I could Americanize it to Zackary or even Zack, so that's what I chose for our son."

Lynn says her relationship with Mustafa began falling apart as her self-esteem plummeted. She felt totally isolated, unable to have friends outside the Muslim family, and too ashamed to share her feelings with Gloria and me. Even within the Isfahan home, where the parents preferred that Vietnamese be spoken, Lynn felt left out, like an unwanted alien from a foreign land, "which is what I actually was to them," she says.

Race, interestingly, was a large factor. "I think the only reason they accepted me at all was because my parents were white," Lynn says. "That made them more at ease. They were more prejudiced toward blacks than whites. If I'd had black parents, they would have put a stop to Mustafa and me a lot earlier." As it was, Lynn says, the family continually pressured her to keep her hair straight and dyed black. With shawls over her head and with her face barely showing, "they tried to make me pass for Asian when their friends and relatives came over," she says. "No way did they want them to know I was really black."

Lynn's sense of African-American identity suffered horribly during that period. She was told constantly that blacks were inferior, that they were ugly, unintelligent, and undesirable. Family members frequently gave her ointments and powders they hoped would lighten her skin and remove her facial freckles, which they said were "bad marks." Lynn learned not to talk about African-Americans or to buy magazines with pictures of them. The family even disdained the black Barbie doll that we gave Sofia for Christmas. Mustafa's mother took the doll from Sofia and threw it away.

We did not learn of that incident, however, until much later. For our benefit, Lynn continued her charade of happiness and stability far longer than most people could.

"About a year later," she says, "when Mustafa's family prearranged a marriage for Sofia, I knew it was time to leave. I was so furious when they pointed out a little seven-year-old Muslim boy whom Sofia was supposed to marry. I thought it was ridiculous.

She was only three years old. And nobody asked *me* about it. I don't even believe in prearranged marriages, yet they went ahead and worked it all out with the little boy's family. Mustafa was torn. He finally sided with his parents. I flipped over it."

Lynn took Sofia and Zack and moved out. Three hundred miles to the south, in Eugene, we could not understand what had happened. Lynn had filtered information about her life so selectively for two years that we were stunned and crushed to hear she had left Mustafa and found an apartment in Seattle. When she hit us with this news in the spring of 1989, we were already reeling from the sordid melodrama involving Liska and Bernard Lee.

During the years of Lynn's travail, Liska had been a happy surprise to me. The child who had struggled in school all the way from kindergarten through twelfth grade — the one who needed almost continuous tutoring and countless hours of help from Gloria — turned out to be the Bates kid most interested in going to college. She lacked the grades required for admission to a university, so she enrolled at the local community college. Liska found a part-time job at Burger King and moved into her own tiny student apartment in the university district. The college work was very difficult for Liska, but she seemed to try hard at first, and she trained diligently for the track team. I felt proud of her and hopeful for her future. What we did not know, however, was that she had met Bernard Lee, a troubled young African-American man who would nearly destroy her life.

Lee thoroughly charmed Liska with his streetwise ways and talk of life in Los Angeles. Here, she thought, was a real man. She was sure she was in love with him and soon let him move in with her. Gloria and I surely would have found out about him, but before he had been with Liska a month he ran afoul of local police. They did a check on him and discovered an outstanding arrest warrant in California. He was sent south to face car-theft charges that landed him back in the state penitentiary at Chino.

Meanwhile, Liska's grades dropped so low that she could not reenroll at the community college. Gloria and I, still unaware of her love affair, assumed her problem was discouragement and perhaps a lack of self-discipline after her initial burst of effort with her coursework. We tried to get her interested in various career-training programs, to no avail. She was weary of school, she said, and wanted a break from it. She took on a second part-time job, which doubled her income, moved into a more expensive apartment, and began enjoying the Eugene singles scene.

One dreary winter day in 1989, Liska called us to say she needed help. She had been fired from her janitorial job on suspicion of stealing. The accusation was unfair and ungrounded, but she didn't know what to do, she said.

I called the custodial company that employed her and demanded to speak to the owner who had fired Liska. He seemed surprised to hear from her father and rather lamely verified that, yes, he had terminated Liska after a doctor complained that an expensive personal stereo boom box had been stolen from one of the offices she cleaned. I asked the man a few more questions, then made an appointment to meet him the following day.

Gloria accompanied me to the employer's office. The man was nervous and defensive. I could tell that he'd had no idea he would end up having to explain his firing of Liska to a couple of well-dressed, white professional people who happened to be her parents. What followed was a classic illustration of how the power structure sometimes treats those who are most helpless in our society.

I opened the conversation by expressing concern about his allegation against our daughter, whom I described as a highly religious young woman who did not steal and who already possessed a stereo boom box that we had given her as a high school graduation gift. Then I asked him a few questions. "Liska tells me she never worked alone," I said. "She always had a co-worker — a young white man. Why wasn't *he* fired?"

The boss squirmed and said he intended to fire the young white man, too.

"Also," I said, "Liska tells us the doctor's son and his pals often came by the offices at night and ordered your janitors to let them in, a practice that strikes me as unusual and worthy of suspicion, since narcotic drug samples are kept on the premises. Liska also says those kids came in the night before the stereo turned up missing. How can you be sure *they* didn't take it?"

The boss said there was no evidence of that, so the finger of guilt had to be pointed at Liska — and, of course, the white co-worker who had not yet been fired. And before I could utter the words "wrongful firing lawsuit," the employer changed his story and said the *main* reason for the terminations was unsatisfactory custodial work by both employees. There was no way, he said, that he would rescind his action against Liska.

Gloria and I went home satisfied that the guy was a jerk, that he had stereotyped our daughter as a thief, that he had discriminated against her, that we had sufficiently chastised him, and that she shouldn't be working in such a dead-end job anyway. Now we were left with the problem of her financial emergency. With ulterior motives, we invited her to move back home while considering her options. We saw this as an opportunity to help Liska refocus on some long-range goals and to guide her back into school or some sort of job training that would ensure her future.

When Liska moved home, though, we immediately saw that something was wrong. She had gained a lot of weight since the last time we had seen her, and she seemed unusually tired and listless. Liska would have napped and watched television all day if we had let her. We practically had to push her out the door to get her to her job at Burger King. She deflected all my attempts to talk about goals and career training. I became disgusted and could not understand her lethargy. It was Gloria, finally, who figured out that Liska was pregnant.

"Liska, isn't there something you want to talk to me about?" Gloria asked her one afternoon. "Don't you think it would be a great relief just to get it off your conscience and tell me about it?"

Just like that, Liska knew that Gloria knew. The two of them had a long talk. Liska says it was easy, once the secret was out. The hard part was telling me, and when I came home from work Gloria insisted that I hear it all straight from Liska.

Her news horrified me. Yes, she said, she was pregnant. Yes, she was pro-choice, and her choice was to have the baby. The young man who was the father did not want to have anything to do with her or the child, so she had decided to move to Los Angeles to join another young man, who loved her and wanted to marry her and adopt the child and become its father. His name was Bernard Lee. He resided with his mother and his brothers in Los Angeles. Unfortunately, Lee was living temporarily in a state prison on a grand larceny charge, but he had not really stolen anything — he had just altered license plates on cars that other men had stolen. Lee was actually a wonderful, loving man who just needed "a good woman to settle him down." She had saved enough money for a bus ticket and was leaving right away to move in with his mother, a good Christian woman like herself, while waiting for Lee's impending release from prison. Then they would find jobs, get married, and begin raising a family.

After listening speechlessly to Liska's lengthy explanation of her plans, I felt a nauseating, helpless sensation, as if I had just been told that my daughter was terminally ill and had only weeks to live. I had to fight to keep from hyperventilating. Or throwing up.

A strained moment of silence filled our house after Liska finished talking. I looked across the room at Gloria. The sorrow on her face made it hard for me to find my voice.

"Liska," I finally said, "this is insane."

Then, while battling the temptation to explode at her in a pious outpouring of indignation, I outlined my concerns, which were actually more like nightmarish fears. She had many options, I said. She did not have to have this baby. Or she could have the baby and put it up for adoption. Or she could keep the baby and stay in Eugene and continue her education. She did not need to move away and make her problems even worse by getting entangled with a convicted criminal. She had never seen south-central Los Angeles. She did not know what she was getting into. She was probably being conned by this man. She could not rescue him from his problems. He would ruin her life and the baby's, too. Yes, she was in trouble, but her decisions would only bring calamity.

"This is insane, Liska," I said again.

The next few days were like a bad dream as Gloria and I searched desperately for the right words to convince our extraordinarily strong-willed daughter that her plan was folly. We even enlisted the counsel of one of the women from Liska's church, who strenuously opposed Liska's idea and admonished her she was "thinking with her body parts."

Only those who know Liska could understand her reaction to our concern. She dug in. There was no changing her mind. She said she loved Bernard Lee. She showed letters he had written from prison, professing his undying love for her. She brought out letters from his mother, accepting Liska into their home and agreeing she was just what her son needed to straighten out his life.

Liska was twenty years old. Gloria and I could think of no way of keeping her, short of tying her up with rope. Reluctantly, I tried playing my hole card, the one I knew would hurt most.

"Liska, I hear what you're saying," I began. "You're willing to walk away from the people who love you most, and to risk everything — your health, your future, your baby, your life — on this guy who's behind bars. That's how desperately you want him in your life. But let me tell you something. I don't want him in *my* life. And don't call me a racist. There are plenty of great young African-American men out there in this country. You don't have to settle for this guy. There is no place for him in our family circle. If you accept him, you'll be rejecting us. You might very well be saying goodbye to this family forever."

Liska did not believe that. She insisted that after she settled Bernard Lee down, we would learn to love and respect him, just as we became fond of Mustafa Isfahan. She packed her bags and prepared to leave.

At first, I balked at even driving Liska to the bus depot. I did not want to contribute in the slightest way to what I considered to be a disastrous move by Liska.

Gloria was just as distraught as I was, but she urged me to accompany her and Liska to the depot. We had just two choices, the way Gloria saw it: we could totally reject Liska and her decision, and perhaps never see her again, or we could hang in there, disagreeing with Liska's move but keeping a lifeline extended to her for the day when she would need our help getting back.

On a rainy Sunday morning we drove Liska to the Greyhound station. It was silent in the car except for the rhythmic *swish-thump* of the windshield wipers. Gloria's eyes were swollen and red. I knew she had not slept the night before. Neither had I.

As Liska boarded the bus, I handed her an envelope stuffed with cash. She didn't want to accept it.

"I have money, Dad," she said.

"Take it," I said. "Keep it for a plane ticket to get home on."

As the bus pulled out, Liska waved sadly through her window, and I could not help thinking of the winsome little three-year-old girl who needed a father, seventeen years earlier, at the state adoption office — the first time I saw Liska. And I wondered if I would ever see her again.

Once in Los Angeles, Liska wrote to us almost every week. Her letters were filled with cheerful, marvelously naïve chatter about Lee, his family, and her new city. Parts of her initial letter set my teeth on edge: "Everyone here was surprised that Bernard could get a girl like me who would get up and leave her family to come and live with his, but they hope Bernard will change, because he said he loves me and would like to see things work out between us. Everyone is happy that Bernard now has someone who will keep him in line." She told us how Lee, still in the penitentiary, insisted that Liska tell people the baby was his, and how he wanted to adopt the child after their marriage. Then he and Liska would have two little ones: the baby and Lee's four-year-old son, who was known as Stink. Lee's mother was raising Stink. The boy's mother, a drug addict and prostitute, had abandoned him, Liska said.

Liska's letters rambled on about her pregnancy, the glorious Los Angeles weather, the heavy presence of police in the black neighborhood where the Lee family lived, and news about Lee's release from prison being delayed by disciplinary problems. In a lighter vein she also told us about frequent encounters with Latino men who tried without success to strike up a conversation. "I guess they don't know I got a D in Spanish class," she wrote. "Maybe I should wear a sign saying, 'No, I'm not Hispanic.' To top it off, Bernard thinks I look Samoan or Hawaiian. Why can't I just be *me*, plain ol' Liska Maril Bates?"

I sent her a long, carefully composed letter, telling her how much I wished "plain ol' Liska" would come home. I told her there was no shame in changing one's mind, and I used myself as an example. I described how I had decided to take a break from the newspaper business and try writing a movie screenplay and a book about the Pulitzer Prize. The big change was something I had contemplated for years, I told her, and now I was speeding it up because it was clear none of my children wanted to go to college, and I rather unexpectedly found myself financially free to pursue my writing ambitions. I had changed my mind about being managing editor of a newspaper, I told her, so maybe she could similarly change *her* mind about being involved with Bernard Lee. Liska responded with a long letter of her own, offering congratulations but sticking with her plans: "I'm glad you feel like you need a change from work, Dad. Let me tell you something: I have always been proud of you and the decisions you make. I'm glad God blessed me with a father who has a good, strong head on his shoulders. Believe it or not, Dad, I've always tried to compare my boyfriends to you. I always wish they could be more like you."

Liska's letters continued arriving faithfully, right on through July 14, when she gave birth to a healthy baby boy whom she named Terrell Michael Bates. The middle name was in honor of her brother Mike. She said the first name was that of a good friend back in Oregon.

The day after Terrell's birth, Gloria loaded the car with baby gifts and some of Liska's possessions and headed for Los Angeles. I was mortified at the thought of my wife driving alone into that part of the city. I could not break away from my work and go along, and I strenuously objected to her making such a trip without me. Gloria, though, can be as obstinate as Liska. "She needs me now," Gloria said. "There's no way I'm not going. Maybe I can even talk her into coming back with me."

I liked the sound of that possibility. Liska had been in Los Angeles nearly three months. Perhaps she was tired of waiting for Lee to be released. Maybe she was having second thoughts about him, and the arrival of her mother would trigger her yearnings to go home. It just might work, I thought, as Gloria gave me a kiss, told me to quit worrying, and took off by herself on the nine-hundred-mile journey.

Liska was moved to tears when her mom showed up but did not return to Oregon with her. Bernard Lee's release was imminent, she said, and she was not going to give up on him, despite my ardent plea to her over the telephone. A few days later, she responded with a letter that said, in part: "I guess what I'm doing is trying to find happiness. I know you're probably asking if I think Bernard will make me happy. Well, I know that when he and I talk on the phone we laugh a lot, and when I get his letters I feel good when I read them. I suppose that when you're in love, you'll do just about anything, but believe me, I know what to do if things go wrong. I'm not the type of woman who just lets a man run over her."

In mid-August, when Terrell was a month old, Liska wrote to us about his baptism at church and enclosed some snapshots. That was the last letter we ever received from Liska in Los Angeles. A few days after she mailed it, Bernard Lee was released from prison.

🌿 15 🌿

Escape from Los Angeles

Pick up the motherfuckin' phone, Liska. Think I'm stupid?
You can let that recorder go all you want. Keep the tape.
Give it to the parole officer. But see what it pay on your end.
The first person is your mom. The bitch that you call your
mom. I want her. I don't want your punk ass. I want you to
suffer for all this shit. I guarantee that. God as my witness,
that bitch goes first.

Recorded phone message from Bernard Lee
December 20, 1989

LISKA SOUNDED HAPPY in her first few telephone calls from
Los Angeles. Her man was out of prison, and the two of them and
their sons, Terrell and Stink, were starting from scratch as a family.
Yes, she said, in response to our repeated questions, Bernard Lee
was looking for a job and was enrolled in a rehabilitation program
aimed at helping him find one. Yes, Liska said, she and Terrell were
fine. Yes, they had enough money; Lee was receiving temporary
state aid while looking for work, and she was accepting welfare
checks for Terrell.

Gloria and I found ourselves dealing with more emotions than
severe anxiety over Liska's well-being. Both of us felt a sickening
sense of shame. Our daughter and her fatherless child were living
on the dole with an unemployed ex-con. Liska had become one of
Ronald Reagan's infamous welfare queens. We felt like failures as
parents. We suspected that critics of transracial adoptions had been
right: we were not cut out for the job.

For a while after Liska moved to Los Angeles, our shame was so
overwhelming that we tried to keep her new life a secret from our

families and friends. Maybe she would come to her senses and return to us before the whole world had to know about her awful choices. We never lied, but we refrained from discussing Liska, and whenever people asked about her, we mumbled vague replies that only magnified speculation and curiosity about our daughter. Eventually we began avoiding people altogether, and I started using Liska as an excuse to drink to excess almost every evening.

After Terrell's birth, though, she mailed out announcements and photos to my parents, Gloria's mother, and most of our other close relatives and friends. Liska was proud of her handsome baby boy, and she was not going to hide him from the family and allow his life to begin in an atmosphere of disgrace. I respected Liska for her aboveboard approach. My load of guilt over her life choices became even heavier as I struggled with regret for feeling so much humiliation at a time when the correct emotions should have been only love and concern.

Once Liska's announcements began arriving in mailboxes, well-meaning family members exacerbated the anguish for Gloria and me by bombarding us with anxious questions and harsh judgments of her behavior and our response to it. How could we allow such a thing to happen to poor Liska? Wasn't she practicing birth control? Why, one relative demanded, didn't Liska just get an abortion? Why had she been living in her own apartment when she "obviously couldn't handle the freedom"? How could we "allow her" to move in with a convicted felon? Why couldn't we talk her out of such a foolish decision? Did we try hard enough? Did we encourage her to go? She wasn't *really* accepting welfare, was she?

My personal torment increased as I perceived grave damage being done to the twenty-year record of racial tolerance in our extended family. Here we were, in the first half of 1989, just after George Bush and Dan Quayle had won the White House using television ads featuring the black rapist and killer Willie Horton. Now I felt that Bernard Lee was fanning racial fear within my family in the same way that Horton, with a lot of help from Bush and Quayle, had fueled ugly passions across America.

At the same time, news about Lynn leaving Mustafa was spreading among our relatives like a wind-whipped forest fire. Everyone liked Mustafa. They had fully accepted him. He was a hard worker and a good provider. His future looked solid. How could Lynn walk out on such a man? Like Gloria and me, our relatives had no idea about Lynn's unhappy life in Seattle.

My most unpleasant encounter during that period was with Gloria's mother, Mildred, who called while Gloria was driving to California to be with Liska and the newborn baby. Mildred knew nothing about Liska's problems or Gloria's trip to Los Angeles. I had to break the news, and the awkwardness was stupendous. After subjecting me to a rather ruthless grilling over the phone, Mildred broke into tears and said she could not believe her daughter was so foolhardy and reckless that she would drive all by herself into the most dangerous area of that big city. Gloria had always been a "funny duck," Mildred said.

The remark incensed me. For the first time in my life I found myself snapping back at my mother-in-law.

"You ought to be proud of your daughter," I said. "She's not a funny duck. She's a brave lady who will go to any lengths for the people she loves, and I think she's proving that right at this moment."

For the record, Gloria met nothing but friendly and helpful people in the predominantly black neighborhood where Liska was staying. Once Gloria returned to Oregon and described the trip to her mother, I sensed that Mildred was indeed proud, as she should have been. I never heard her say another unkind word about Gloria. And of all our relatives and friends, none showed any more genuine love and concern for Liska than Mildred did during the harrowing period that lay ahead.

Liska's telephone calls to us steadily decreased that fall as we continued to quiz her about Bernard Lee. Why, we asked, hadn't he found a job yet? What did he *do* all day long? Why was he always at home watching TV whenever she phoned us?

Once, when Gloria heard a child screaming in the background and asked about it, Liska said Lee had struck four-year-old Stink. Gloria was outraged. She demanded that Liska report him to authorities and leave before he began taking out his anger on her and the baby. Liska responded defensively and said Lee would not dare harm her or Terrell.

"Well," Gloria replied, "if he ever even raises his voice at you, get out of that house and call the police. And call us, too."

Liska insisted she was "a big girl" who could take care of herself. I knew she was no timid soul who would allow anyone to get away with violence against her or Terrell, but I still worried. In one of her letters she noted that Lee had won a trophy in prison for bench-pressing 285 pounds. She sent us a photo that supported the claim. His upper arms were as large as my thighs. Lee was a menacing-looking brute. I would not have wanted to be in the same room with him when he was angry.

By November, Lee had not found a job. He and Liska and the two boys still lived with his mother and brothers. Liska was evasive when we asked what was going on. She did reveal, however, that she was upset that Lee was going out at night and spending her money on crack cocaine. But in response to our furious outburst upon hearing this news, she said she had confronted Lee about his behavior and he had promised to reform. Liska rejected our pleas that she come home immediately. She remained confident, she said, of her ability to "straighten him out."

We did not hear from Liska again until the phone rang two nights before Thanksgiving. I took the call. Liska was at a pay phone at a convenience store a few blocks from Lee's home. Terrell was with her. She was crying. Lee had spent all of her money — her welfare check and the cash I had given her — on cocaine. He still had no job. He didn't want to marry her. He just wanted her money for drugs. They'd had a terrible argument. She threatened to leave him. Lee had struck her, saying he would never let her go. She was fed up and frightened. She wanted to come home.

My heart pounded. This was the call that for eight months I had been praying for, and I was ready for it — or so I thought.

"Liska, I want you to go straight to the airport," I said. "I'll have a ticket waiting there for you. Call as soon as you arrive, and I'll tell you which airline."

"But how will I get there?" she asked, still in tears.

"Call a cab, right where you are," I said. Then, with a sinking feeling, I asked the next logical question: "Do you have enough money for a taxi?"

"No," she sobbed.

"Is there anybody who'll drive you to the airport?"

"No."

"Okay, okay. No problem," I said, my mind whirling. "Get on a city bus, you and Terrell. I'm sure you can get there that way. It may take half the night, but at least you'll end up at the airport."

Liska said she did not even have bus fare. She had no money whatsoever. Lee had taken everything.

"Swell," I said. "He hit you, right? That's assault. Call the police and have him arrested. Meanwhile I'll drive down there and pick you up."

But Liska did not want to involve the police. She had a different idea. She would tell Lee that her parents wanted her to fly home for Thanksgiving and that while up there in Oregon she would ask for more money from her dad. She said Lee, faced with the prospect of Liska returning with cash from home, would gladly let her go and even drive her to the airport in his mother's car.

I did not like the idea of Liska spending one more minute with the man, but she insisted he had cooled down and she could safely return to his house. Reluctantly I agreed to her plan.

So Liska took Terrell back to Lee's home and told him the bogus story about flying home for Thanksgiving. He bought it. She began packing her things while waiting for my call with instructions.

Meanwhile, as I called airline after airline, I made a rude discovery. Every seat on every plane in and out of the Los Angeles area was booked for the entire week of Thanksgiving. She and Terrell could attempt to fly on standby, but that option struck me as too risky. I wanted them out of Los Angeles at once — before Liska changed her mind or suffered any further abuse from Lee.

Amtrak was also fully booked for the holiday period, but Greyhound had extra buses in service and had room for Liska and the baby. Unfortunately, the company would not let me buy tickets over the phone with a credit card. Liska would have to buy them with cash, at her end.

I wired the money to a Western Union agency not far from Lee's house, and then I called Liska.

"Just answer yes or no to my questions," I said when she answered. "Are you and Terrell okay?"

"Yes."

"Good. Is Bernard there?"

"Yes."

"Can he hear my voice?"

"No."

"All right. Here's the new plan."

I explained it to her, being careful to make sure she comprehended each step.

"When you collect the money, Liska," I said, "don't let Bernard touch it or even see how much I've sent, okay? If he tries to take it from you, *don't* let him. Tell him to be patient, that you'll be bringing a lot more money than that when you return. Got that?"

"Yes, I guess so," she said, forlornly. I could tell what was troubling her.

"Liska, I know you don't believe in telling lies, even little ones," I said. "But just this once you have to bend the truth, for the safety of you and your baby. God understands that. I know you'll still go to heaven. Okay? Can you do this?"

She laughed. "Yeah — for Terrell."

Never have Gloria and I felt more grateful for our blessings than we did late that Thanksgiving night at the Eugene bus station when a big Greyhound pulled in with our daughter and the grandson I had not yet seen. Liska was exhausted after the twenty-six-hour trip, but Terrell was alert and rested and ready to get acquainted.

Once we got home, Liska found her way to her room and crawled between her sheets like a little girl who had stayed up far past her bedtime. For a while, so Liska could go right to sleep, Gloria and I sat in our darkened living room and took turns holding Terrell, who soon fell into deep slumber. We remained there for a long time, neither of us speaking or having any idea what we were going to do next. For one night, though, it just didn't matter.

"Happy Thanksgiving," Gloria whispered.

"Same to you," I whispered back.

Lee's death threats, loaded with sulphurous profanity that filled the entire tape on our telephone answering machine, came five days before Christmas while I was in New York working on my book about the Pulitzer Prize. Gloria had accompanied me. Neither of us had ever visited the city, and we had been told Manhattan was an especially shimmering sight during the holiday season. We were not disappointed. Our arrival coincided with lovely snow showers that transformed Central Park and Fifth Avenue into enchanting scenes suitable for greeting cards.

Our holiday mood, however, was shattered on December 20 by Liska's urgent call from Eugene. Her voice quivered as she described the string of recorded messages left throughout the day by Bernard Lee. Gloria and I flew home the next morning, and thus began my adventures with the city police, the new shotgun, and the hapless paperboy whose footsteps on our driveway made me think Lee had already arrived to carry out his threats.

Much of his invective was directed against Gloria. She was the one who had been screening Lee's phone calls earlier in December and who had finally told him to quit calling because Liska was not going back to him. While we were in New York, his barrage of venom frightened Liska so severely that she refused to answer the phone.

(*beep*)

Liska, there's something for you to know. I have your address right here on the letter your sister wrote you. So you can run but you can't hide. You know I'll kill that white motherfucker that you call Daddy. But I want to kill his punk-ass wife first. White bitch! Like I said, I'll be up there soon. I'm on my way. It ain't too far. It ain't never too far. It ain't never too late. Bye.

(*beep*)

In yet another message, an enraged Lee said he had just punched little Stink in his anger, and our daughter and her "damn old white folks family" were to blame. "Liska, this is to you. My son suffered two broken ribs because of you," he shouted.

Upon returning from New York, I obtained a new, unlisted phone number for our home. Then I called Lee. Foremost, I wanted to check on his whereabouts. I also wanted to see if he had cooled off and to warn him against any further harassment of our family.

Lee was still at home. As soon as I identified myself, he demanded to speak to Liska. When I told him she did not want to talk to him, he unleashed a startling gusher of verbal effluvium, repeating all his earlier threats. He also added a new piece of information: Liska, he said, was carrying his child, and he would kill anyone who tried to take away his flesh and blood.

After I hung up on Lee, Liska confirmed she was pregnant. This time, she said, she wanted an abortion.

"Is this man just trying to scare us," I asked, "or is he capable of carrying out these threats?"

"He's capable," said Liska, still visibly shaken.

After getting no help from a Eugene police dispatcher, I tracked down and telephoned Lee's parole officer, who was equally unhelpful. It was the Friday night before Christmas, and he said he was trying to clear off his desk and get away for the holidays. "Lee's probably bluffing," the officer told me. "People who feel powerless commonly make those kind of statements but never act on them. It's like their only weapon against you. And if he *isn't* bluffing — well, that would be a violation of his parole and we'll have him picked up."

"Wait a minute," I replied. "Are you saying you won't do anything about these threats unless he carries them out?"

The parole officer said I had it right. Then, while trying to mollify me, he slipped up and mentioned that Lee had successfully served a previous parole from prison. When I demanded to know the circumstances, the officer clammed up. That's when I made the sardonic remark about buying a gun and he said it did not sound like a bad idea. He gave me the name of the parole supervisor who would be taking over his caseload for him during the holidays. "Call him if you have any trouble with Mr. Lee," he said.

"I thought I was *already* having trouble," I said as our conversation ended.

Then I called a former associate at the *Register-Guard* and asked for a favor. Using his police contacts, he obtained a criminal background check on Lee. His record was far more extensive than he had led Liska to believe. And his earlier stint in prison had been for shooting and wounding a white man in a street altercation in which racial epithets had been exchanged.

Lynn and her two children arrived at our home that Friday afternoon. Mike showed up, too, in the big white van he drove all over Oregon distributing merchandise for a small company owned by one of my uncles. Steve and his friend Paula Lincoln were scheduled to come over that evening, along with my sister Jill and her friend Dan Chenoweth, for a little pre-Christmas soiree. Gloria and I had decorated our home with unparalleled lavishness that season, perhaps unconsciously using glittering garlands and twinkling lights to mask the recent pain and fear in our lives.

Late that afternoon, as the house filled up with the aroma of delicious food and the laughter and happy jabber of our loved ones, I slipped away unnoticed and bought a shotgun.

As soon as the stores opened the following morning, a few hours after I had unintentionally terrorized our paperboy, I sneaked the 12-gauge Mossberg out of the house and took it back to the Bi-Mart for a full refund. Then Bernard Lee and I had our real showdown.

I made the first move by going downtown to the Eugene Police Department to talk to a command officer I had known through my years as a newspaper editor. I outlined our problem with Lee and described the frustrating responses I had received from the dispatcher and the parole officer. Then I played the answering machine tape. Listening to the entire thirty-minute recording all over again was a nauseating experience for me. My friend's face remained without expression as he listened, and I wondered whether he, too, was going to turn me away.

When the tape finally ended, the officer was silent for a moment, absorbed in thought. Then he handed the tape back to me and told me to make a copy for him. He said Bernard Lee had committed a hate crime against our family and would be charged under a new Oregon law making such acts a felony. He said the Oregon charge would automatically put Lee in violation of his parole. My friend said he would contact California authorities and have Lee picked up immediately. He told me to go home and quit worrying.

That evening, though, when I noticed a man sitting in an unmarked police car not far from our house, I knew Lee still had not been located. Was he somewhere on Interstate 5 heading north? I did not sleep well at all. Maybe, I thought, I should have kept the damn shotgun one more night.

The next morning, however, my policeman friend phoned with welcome news: Lee was in custody and was being returned to prison. California police conducting a stakeout had arrested Lee at dawn when he drove up to his mother's house in a stolen car — one he had almost certainly snatched for his trip to Oregon, my friend said.

Later, two uniformed Eugene police officers showed up at our house to do the paperwork on the case. They interviewed Liska at length and asked for the original copy of the answering machine tape. We mentioned Lee's abuse of the little boy, Stink, and asked that it be reported to California authorities. By the time the officers left, Liska had obviously descended into a state of deep depression. And why not? It was Christmas Eve and she had just helped send a man to prison — a man in whom she had once invested all of her hopes and dreams. I did not tell Liska about the stolen car or any of the other details of Lee's arrest, and she did not ask for any. She seemed to want to block out what happened, to act as if it had never occurred. That was going to be a very difficult, and probably unwise, thing to do.

A few days later Liska had an abortion, a choice she had once said she could never make. Today, her pain remains so great that she can scarcely talk about Bernard Lee and what he did to her life.

"At first I thought he was cool, but that was a mistake," she says. "He was royally bringing me down. I wanted to get away from him. I was scared of him. He was doing big-time drugs. I thank God I saw the light on him."

I wish I could say our lives mellowed out after that melancholy Christmas. Instead, we had more disappointments to endure as a family. Both Lynn and Liska seemed to find and embrace their African-American identities as never before — a development I welcomed as wholesome and desirable. But each of them, in search of the "right" black man, kept meeting the wrong ones.

Lynn took up with the owner of the hair salon where she worked. By all accounts he was a decent man, but I was flabbergasted when she brought him home to meet us. The fellow was at least thirty years older than Lynn, and he had personal problems that I could not believe she would want to add to her own. Liska, meanwhile, did something Gloria and I also considered unbelievable: she and Terrell returned to Los Angeles to move in with the family of the minister of the church she had attended there. She and the preacher's son had been corresponding for many weeks, she said, and their long-distance relationship had led to love.

Once again, no amount of reasoning and flat-out pleading from Gloria and me could shake Liska from her decision to go. "Forget about men for a while," I urged. "Let's talk about jobs and career training and a future for you and Terrell. If you want a man, there'll be plenty of time for that later. Your whole life is still ahead of you."

But Liska, true to her nature, stood by her plans. She was twenty-one years old now, she reminded us, and felt we were still lecturing her — a charge with validity, to be honest. History repeated itself, of course, and Liska returned to Oregon more confused than before.

Why, I wondered, did our daughters — long after their teen-age years — continue so desperately to turn toward men for their sense of identity and self-esteem? Was it born of their formative years prior to adoption? Were they subconsciously searching for the love they felt was missing in their lives? Were they acting out personality traits that Gloria and I had destructively and unwittingly instilled in them through clumsy parenting? Or was it all a reaction to the roiling forces of race, gender, and biology in the transracial adoption they had experienced?

My daughters and sons and Gloria and I have discussed those questions, and none of us knows the answer. Both young women, though, agree today that all of their significant problems as adults have resulted from past choices in men. And all of us acknowledge we probably would have benefited from family counseling. I know *I* could have used it. Instead, though, as the 1990s began, I simply disengaged.

I had never heard of the "disengaged parent" until I read about the psychological state long after I had been through it. Unable to deal with the problems of their adult offspring, some parents disengage emotionally. I did not realize I was probably doing exactly that in the spring of 1990 when I decided to pursue my new writing career in Southern California.

A pair of Hollywood producers bought the option to one of my motion picture screenplays that spring. They wanted to meet with me regularly to work on revisions, and that was all the excuse I needed to move a thousand miles away from my daughters' problems. Gloria and I did not want to live anywhere near Los Angeles, but we had always loved the San Diego area, so we moved there to the island of Coronado. Gloria found a job in the Coronado schools while I wrote my Pulitzer book, worked at the San Diego newspaper, and made a convenient arrangement with the film producers: our periodic script discussions would be at Laguna Beach, roughly halfway between Los Angeles and San Diego.

Our first year in California was undeniably good for our careers, our marriage, our health, and our mental outlook. Both Gloria and I were emotionally fatigued by the Bernard Lee episode and the continuing friction with Liska over what she should do with her life. And I suspected we were part of the problem; in constantly trying to help her, we had probably been holding her back. If Liska was ever going to get serious about her livelihood and future, we decided, it might happen sooner if we weren't always there, ready to bail her out with a checkbook and a ticket home.

In Coronado, while juggling both the writing and newspaper careers, I probably worked harder than ever before. That initial year was wonderful, though. For the first time in twenty-seven years of marriage, Gloria and I found ourselves with no kids around. Despite my workload, we had plenty of time for walks on the beach at sunset, moonlight ferry rides on San Diego Bay, and daily bicycle excursions through the floral-scented streets of Coronado. In a way, we felt like newlyweds enjoying life alone together before the childrearing years — an experience Gloria and I had missed out on by starting our family so young. This time around we reclaimed some of our lost youth by buying surfboards, getting suntans, and recovering our sense of humor.

Our new period of bliss lasted one year, ending when we flew back to Oregon on Easter weekend in 1991. First, we visited Gloria's mother at the nursing home where she had been confined after suffering a series of debilitating strokes. Mildred did not recognize me; she called me Dr. Fletchall. We were shocked at how her condition had deteriorated. She did, however, seem to remember Gloria. As we said our goodbyes, Mildred pulled her daughter close to the bedside and whispered in her ear, "I love you, Gloria." It was the first and last time my wife ever heard those words from her mother.

As we drove our rental car north to Portland for a dinner at my brother Tom's house, Gloria and I groped with feelings of guilt and helplessness. How could we go back to California and resume the good life while Mildred was suffering up here in the nursing home? Her second husband, Bob McCullough, was giving her lots of love, but his health was frail, too, and he could have used our help. Life was getting so complicated.

We had no idea just how complicated, though, until we arrived in Portland and assessed the situations of our daughters. Lynn, who did not make it to the Easter gathering, had broken up with her boss at the hair salon and was living with a new boyfriend who was jailed after beating her up. When he was released, they reconciled in what I feared to be a classic battered-woman syndrome. Liska, meanwhile, who came to the festivities with little Terrell, by then almost two years old, had moved into a government-subsidized rental home in northeast Portland.

Gloria and I were sorry to see that Liska was still unemployed, undecided about her future, and living on public assistance. We also were disturbed about her choice of neighborhoods — not because it was predominantly black, but because it was so crime-ridden. Broken car-window glass was strewn all over the street in front of her house. A short time before, two African-American teen-agers had been fatally gunned down in a store parking lot only a few blocks away. The neighborhood was dotted with boarded-up houses — an ideal breeding ground for the crack trade that Portland police were battling. Was this the environment Liska had chosen for raising our grandson?

Yes, Liska said. There were many nice people in her neighborhood, she explained. She had friends there. She did not want Terrell to be racially isolated, as she was as a girl. And yes, she said, she did indeed want to get out and begin a career to support herself and Terrell, but first there was a problem she needed to deal with: she was pregnant again.

🌿16🌿

Back to Yakima

Surprised? I'm seventy-eight years old. Nothing surprises
me anymore.

Grandma Grace, on her front porch
June 1970

HAD SHE STILL BEEN LIVING, Grandma Grace would probably not have been terribly surprised at the latest development in
Liska's life. But I did not possess my grandmother's longevity and
wisdom. I was not merely surprised, I was thunderstruck when
Liska, in a trembling voice, revealed her pregnancy as Gloria and I
drove her and Terrell to their home after the dinner at my brother's
house. My brain lurched crazily while I tried to process what I was
hearing. I had to fight to concentrate on traffic lights and pedestri-
ans and honking vehicles as Liska explained how she'd been raped
by a man she had met through the new guy in Lynn's life.

Gloria and I sat speechlessly in the car as Liska emotionally
described her situation, anticipating our questions and addressing
them one by one. She told us she had accepted my advice about
forgetting men for a while, and thus she had stopped taking birth
control pills. The pregnancy resulted from a date rape that she did
not report, she said. She forgave the man and thought they had a
future together, but he went to Mexico and had not been heard
from again. Meanwhile, she discovered she was pregnant. It was
too late for an abortion, and she did not want that anyway. She said
her previous abortion had caused her remorse that would never go
away. She also said she would never give this baby up for adoption.
"Being adopted myself, I identify with the baby," Liska said. "I
could never give it away." However, she said she intended to have a

tubal ligation after the birth so she would never have to face such a choice again.

Gloria and I flew home to California feeling sick at heart. By itself, her mother's plight in the nursing home was sorrowful enough, but the roads being taken by Lynn and Liska thrust us into a state of mourning.

Back in Coronado I wrote a letter that reveals how difficult it was for me to resist lecturing my troubled younger daughter:

Dear Liska,

This is a letter I've been meaning to write for some time, but I have been putting it off because I haven't known quite what to say. So let me just begin by saying I love you, and your mom loves you, and nothing is going to change that. I know you have trouble believing that — really *believing* it. You have had a hard time with that all your life, and maybe you always will. It's that way for many people who are adopted, especially at an older age. Some spend their whole lives questioning whether their adoptive parents *really* love them. Well, we do, Liska. And no matter what decisions you make in your current situation, we will still care very, very deeply about you. And that's a pretty good definition of love.

I'm not going to tell you whether you should or shouldn't keep the baby. Only you can make that choice. But let me give you some information to think about as you face this big decision:

1. Read the newspaper article I've enclosed. It reports the results of a study in the latest issue of the *American Journal of Psychiatry*. This study found that women who experience unwanted pregnancies seldom give up the babies for adoption, and many harbor resentment and anger toward these children for years. And these little ones are "much likelier to be troubled and depressed, to drop out of school, to commit crimes, to suffer from serious illnesses and to express dissatisfaction with life than are the offspring of willing parents." So Liska, if you keep this baby, it probably is not the best thing for the child or for yourself. The greatest act of love, in such cases, sometimes is to give the child up for adoption by a secure family.

2. You and Terrell live in poverty. That may be acceptable to you, but is it acceptable to Terrell? Do you want a better life for

him? Your efforts to climb out of poverty will be *at least twice as difficult* with a second child.

3. You *must* report the crime that has been committed against you. You have already made one poor decision by not reporting it right away. Don't compound the mistake by letting this man's crime go unreported forever. Yes, it may be too late to bring him to justice, but there should at least be a record of the fact that he has been accused of rape. What about the next time he sexually assaults some woman? Any attempt to convict him will be made more difficult by your failure to make a record of what he did to you.

4. You *must* get periodic AIDS tests, at least once a month for a year, or whatever a good physician recommends. You also *must* insist that the man who assaulted you submit to an AIDS test and share the results with you, if he can be found.

5. You should seek some professional counseling, whether you decide to keep the baby or not. Ask your doctor or nurse whom to call. Your mom and I will gladly pay for it. Please, Liska?

6. Whatever you decide — repeat — I will still love you. And I will still love Terrell. And I will love your baby.

7. You need to do a whole lot of praying. God loves you, too. Let the big guy show you the way.

Liska replied with a letter thanking me for the advice about AIDS testing, which she said she had already been receiving, with promising results. However, she rejected my other suggestions, including my plea that she reconsider adoption. "Let me lay something on your mind," she wrote. "When you got Lynn and myself, you were on the receiving end. My birth mom was on the giving end. You can never know what it feels like to give up your own child, and I do not ever want to know that feeling, either."

As I began comprehending what lay ahead for Liska, I felt myself losing whatever remaining shreds of paternal responsibility I still possessed. How could I help a daughter who did not want my advice? How in the world was Liska going to take control of her life now, with *two* babies and no job or husband? And what about Lynn's choice of men? Were both of my daughters somehow doomed to gravitate to the Other America of their biological parents? Were my grandchildren predestined to lives of poverty in the nation's black underclass?

Virtually overnight I completed the disengagement that had begun the year before. Part of me would never quit loving Lynn and Liska, but another part — a side I'm not proud of — wanted to banish them from my thoughts. I did not think I could handle the heartbreak that seemed inevitable.

For longer than I care to admit, it was Gloria who held our family together while I turned inward and tuned out the problems of my daughters. I quit writing letters to them or calling them or even getting on the line when they telephoned us. When friends or relatives asked how Lynn and Liska were doing, I would reply that I didn't know, which was the truth. As far as I was concerned, Gloria could wallow in their problems if she insisted on it, but I was finished.

Our quasi-honeymoon in Coronado was over, too. I buried myself deeper than ever in my work. I began drinking excessively again. I quit going to the beach. My only surfing now was psychological, on wave after wave of sour regret. The critics of transracial adoption had been right all along, I concluded, and the state adoption agency had erred in permitting Gloria and me to have the two girls. I was also convinced that we had neglected our two sons for years while absorbed in the woes of our daughters.

At the same time, I found myself struggling against a base human thought process — the same one I had battled after the break-in at our Eugene home five years earlier. The racist deep within me — the one I believe lurks inside every person of any color — was trying to get out. Every young black male I encountered became, for one ugly split second, a potential ruiner of my daughters, a threat to my family, an enemy to society. Every time I beat such vile feelings back into submission, my shame deepened and my abhorrence increased toward politicians willing to exploit such easily ignited racial fears and prejudices in all of us.

I spent the next two months in my morass of self-pity while Gloria made a series of trips to the Pacific Northwest to look in on her ailing mother in Eugene, to check on Liska in Portland, and to visit Lynn in Seattle. Gloria emerged during this period as the stronger partner in our marriage — the one with more personal courage. She was no less distraught than I was over our daughters' problems, and she was dealing meanwhile with far more intense feelings of grief and guilt over her mother. Still, Gloria was the one who found enough strength to keep our marriage and our family from coming unraveled while I remained disengaged.

I'm not sure exactly how Gloria thought of it, but I do know she pulled off a minor miracle when she decided I needed to get better acquainted with my first grandchild, Lynn's daughter, Sofia, who was approaching age five. After a trip to Seattle in June, Gloria brought the little girl home to Coronado with her, saying Sofia would spend a few weeks with us. The visit, Gloria had assured me over the phone from Seattle, would be a big help to Lynn as she trained for a demanding new job. I indulged Gloria in the plans, silently hoping the kid wouldn't disrupt my writing too severely.

Sofia disarmed me immediately upon getting off the Amtrak coach on a warm San Diego evening. She put her arms around me with a strong hug and said, "Hi, Grandpa," and I was amazed at how she had changed in the year and a half since I had seen her. Gone was the chubby little toddler I vaguely remembered. Sofia had grown into a beautiful, exotic, loving little girl with pale sandy skin, flashing green eyes, and wavy, shining dark-brown hair. At first glimpse she was a genetic mystery. A stranger might easily have guessed American Indian, Pacific Islander, or even Eastern European. Sofia, who was African-American, white European, Malaysian, and Vietnamese, defied any ethnic labeling except "twenty-first-century American," a product of the new melting pot that many demographers say is bubbling most vigorously today on the Pacific Coast of the United States.

Sofia's physical grace and intelligence were astonishing, too, as was her smile, which was frequent and charming. Even before we got home from the train station, my iceberg of disengagement began to thaw a little.

By midsummer I had become just like Gloria: completely infatuated with Sofia. Here, I said to myself, is a little girl who looks a lot like Lynn on that day we first saw her in the pet store, but this kid gives hugs. She speaks English and Vietnamese with equal fluency. She has the math and verbal skills of a nine-year-old. She's happy, witty, and athletic, learning to swim across the Coronado Municipal Pool on her first day of lessons. She's able to bond with people. She's cuddly, unlike her mother, who will always have trouble forming attachments. Lynn has done a great job with this child, I thought. And maybe *we* didn't do such a bad job with *Lynn*, who turned out to be a decent, hard-working, quality person herself.

Sofia was a gift, I now realize, even though we have no blood ties. She stepped into my life as a source of hope, a lifter of doubt, and an affirmation of the interracial adventure that I had come to regard as a sad mistake. By the time we put her on a plane for home, I was ashamed of the way I had withdrawn from Lynn in the face of my own disappointment. And I resolved to make it up to her and be a more loving and understanding parent.

As for Liska, I still had some problems to work through. How could I support her actions and decisions? How could I accept her new baby, the second one whose father I had never met and would never meet? How could I possibly help her save herself and her children from their sure slide into misery when she kept making what I perceived as wretched mistakes?

Shortly after Sofia's departure, Liska began having contractions, and Gloria took a flight to Portland to be with her and help with little Terrell. Liska had hoped I would come, too, but I had excuses — my Pulitzer book to promote, a screenplay to revise, a meeting to attend with a producer and a script consultant. It was all true, but any of it could have been postponed. I simply could not accept what was happening in Portland and did not want to be part of it.

Liska's contractions turned out to be false labor, but Gloria stayed with her in a waiting game that dragged out over three weeks. Liska and Terrell lived then in the cramped but cute upstairs apartment of a house occupied downstairs by a pair of Catholic priests. They were virtually the only whites in the neighborhood. Gloria, who rolled out a sleeping bag each night on Liska's living room floor, has vivid memories of her experience there before and after the baby came and refers to it warmly as her "Six Weeks in the 'Hood."

Upon Gloria's arrival in Portland, her white cabdriver set an unfortunate tone for the visit by describing Liska's neighborhood as "the bullet zone." He told Gloria she was lucky to arrive during the day because he would not drive into that area after dark.

Just after midnight on her second night with Liska, gunfire out on the street jolted them awake. Liska, while pulling her terrified mother away from the window so she wouldn't get shot, assured Gloria the shooting and shouting was just another domestic dispute between a neighbor couple who fought all the time. But as emergency vehicles came screaming to the scene, filling the neighborhood with wailing sirens, barking police radios, and blinding lights, Gloria broke into angry tears and demanded that Liska find a safer place to raise her children.

Hours later that night, Gloria was awakened again, this time by the sounds of someone digging in a yard near the shooting scene. Peering out into the darkness, all she could see was a flashlight being held on a man with a shovel. "At that point I really became upset," Gloria says. "I just knew someone had been killed, and police had already gone, and now somebody was digging a grave for the body. Then, suddenly, I heard a crackling sound and saw flames. Great, I thought. Now they're burning the body before they bury it. Why else would they dig a hole and light a fire at two in the morning? I was freaking out."

At daylight, upon hearing this breathless tale of murder and mayhem, Liska laughed. "She said, 'Mom, that was just the Tonkins next door, barbecuing a pig in a pit in their back yard. They do it every weekend.' I felt so out of it," Gloria says, "as if I was visiting a foreign country."

After that rocky beginning, though, she became charmed by positive aspects of Liska's 'hood, especially her African-American neighbors. "They were so friendly and helpful to Liska, and they extended their kindness to me, too, time after time, making me feel accepted and welcome," Gloria says.

She began to realize there were two ways to look at the neighborhood. You could focus on the littered yards of the one or two badly run-down houses that seemed to exist on every block, or you could look at the homes where the occupants were planting flowers, repairing fences, and painting their porches. You could dwell on the bullet holes in the windows at the local laundromat, or you could notice how hard many residents were trying to make a newcomer in their midst feel welcome and safe. You could move away because of crime and gang activity, or you could make a stand to save the neighborhood.

Gloria says she will never forget an African-American woman she encountered while out for a walk near Liska's house. "The lady smiled at me and said, 'You sure have pretty hair.' I thought that was so sweet. It was her way of trying to make me feel at ease in her neighborhood. There were many, many incidents just like that one, and before long, I *did* feel at ease."

In her second week there, Gloria joined people from Liska's neighborhood in a "Walk of Faith" to show solidarity against crime in their part of the city. She and the two hundred neighbors wore T-shirts emblazoned with pictures of Martin Luther King, Jr., as they walked en masse down the Portland boulevard named for the great civil rights leader. Then, gathering in the supermarket parking lot where the two teen-agers had been slain several months before, they formed a large circle, held hands, and sang "Amazing Grace" and "We Shall Overcome."

"Mom and I were always close, but we got even closer during those six weeks," Liska recalls. "We had our laughs, good times and bad times. The waiting was so hard. We went on walks and did laundry and went to doctor's appointments and worked on different exercises to prepare for the birth. Mom permed my hair, which was so funny. I couldn't get my head into the sink because of my big belly. We watched *The Young and the Restless* together and joked about when the baby was going to be born and talked for hours about what having another baby was going to be like.

"My mom is the best friend I have ever had. She has always been there for me. Even though she didn't give birth to me, I know I would not be here today if it weren't for her. I'm proud to be black, but I do wish that she could be my birth mom. I wish we could be blood-related, not just related through a piece of paper. That is how much she means to me."

Gloria called almost daily from Portland and kept me posted on her adventures in the 'hood. She told me about new friends with names like Shabree and Miasha and Dwayne and Lynn-Audrey. She described her introduction to sweet-potato pie and Popeye's chicken, and she said she knew I would love it, too, if I could find a way to come north to join her and Liska. There was still time, she said. This baby was in no hurry.

But I continued to tick off all the reasons why I could not break away from my work in California. Liska, of course, could see through my excuses, and she was hurt. She sent me a letter in which she said she was praying that I would someday understand her decision to have this second baby and to keep it rather than give it up for adoption. And while on the subject, she said she was thinking ahead to the day when she would explain to Terrell the nature of his interracial family:

> I don't think it will be hard to tell Terrell about my adoption. I plan to. It's not hard to talk about. I love being adopted because I love my family. I will break it down and explain that when I was three years old Doug and Gloria adopted me. Adoption is where some people sign some papers and bring this child into their lives. They raise that child and take full responsibility. I will tell Terrell everything. He will ask questions: "Why is my Grandma white? Why am I black?" I don't want him to see a difference. I want him to know that there are white people and black people, but I don't want him to lock on to different colors. I don't want him to favor black people. I want him to love everyone, like I do. I will tell all of my children about my being adopted. It's not a hard thing. It's not embarrassing. It's a beautiful thing.

Liska closed her letter by saying she had decided, if the new baby turned out to be a girl, to call her Kamaria, an African name meaning "like the moon." Liska said the baby's full name would be

Kamaria Grace Bates, in honor of Grandma Grace, unless I thought my grandmother's spirit, wherever she might be, would take offense at that use of her name.

Take offense? I set the letter down, unexpectedly moved. Would Grandma Grace take offense? Hardly. She loved Liska, and if she were alive and still in good health she'd probably try to get herself to Portland to help Liska through this difficult time. And where did that leave me? Feeling like the chump that I knew I was being. I thought about Grace's words to me almost twenty years earlier: "If I were you, I'd let the critics do all the worrying. You and Gloria just take care of raising those kids, and everything will turn out fine."

The next day I hurried to the San Diego airport and caught a flight to Portland, feeling like an Ebenezer Scrooge just awakened from a bad dream. Gloria had told me over the phone that Liska's contractions were getting close, and I prayed that I'd get to the hospital in time.

Gazing down from the plane at the gloriously green patchwork of Oregon's Willamette Valley, I smiled as I thought about one of Grandma Grace's interesting quirks — her belief in reincarnation, even though she was a strict Methodist. And now it occurred to me that a reincarnation of sorts might be about to happen, with Grandma coming back, at least in name, as a little brown baby girl — an irony that probably would have tickled the old woman.

Two days after I arrived, Liska went into labor at three in the morning. Gloria stayed in the delivery room with Liska and a midwife while I waited outside with Terrell. We played with toys in the hospital's kiddie room, took some walks in the deserted corridors, played some games, read some stories, and took a few naps, and I began to realize my grandson was a bright, affectionate, self-confident kid. Darker than his mother, with her good looks and long, curling eyelashes and a smile to melt the coldest of hearts, Terrell was also exceptionally smart. As Gloria had told me, he had already developed an impressive attention span and healthy inquisitiveness at age two and a half, thanks largely to Liska's efforts with books, preparing him for learning to read. He had a promising future.

Liska, I realized, had done a great job with Terrell. And maybe we hadn't done such a bad job with Liska.

Once again Liska's contractions proved to be false labor. I stayed in Portland another four days, then risked a quick trip back to California for a movie script meeting. Of course, that's when I missed the birth of Kamaria Grace Bates, a healthy and beautiful girl who looked much more like her mother than like Grandma Grace. Liska seemed to forgive me for missing the blessed event.

"You tried to be here," she told me. "That meant a lot. You showed that you still wanted to be a part of my life."

I did indeed. And not long after the birth of Kamaria, I returned to Portland and told Liska my new idea for the Bates Family Development Program, a work-study plan involving job training, education, and cooperative daycare, financed entirely by Gloria and me with the aim of ensuring that no member of our family would ever need government assistance. As Gloria listened, looking a little surprised at my bombshell, I explained that while all of us should appreciate what public aid had done to help Lynn and Liska and their children through some rough times, those programs were traps, and Gloria and I knew we could design a better assistance program at the family level — and I didn't mean just handouts from Dad and Mom.

All the details would be worked out shortly, I continued, but in the meantime I had one more announcement. I revealed I had an old, secret dream that I'd discarded long ago, but now I was resurrecting it in celebration of Kamaria's birth. All of us — Gloria, Steve, Lynn, Mike, Liska, and the grandchildren, too — were going to Africa. Together we would see the pyramids of Egypt and walk along the streets of Nairobi and gaze upon Victoria Falls and Mount Kilimanjaro.

Gloria looked shocked. I had never mentioned my thoughts about going to Africa, and I hadn't warned her about my announcement. As I beamed happily, waiting for waves of my loved ones' jubilation to wash over me, there was only a stunned silence, finally broken by Liska.

"Gee, Dad, couldn't we just go to Yakima?"

"Yakima?" I asked.

"I've always wanted to go see it," she said. "I'd like to see the hospital that I was born in and just see the town. I can't really *feel* anything about it because I've never seen it."

"You never told me you wanted to go to Yakima," I said.

"You never asked. Every time I see the freeway sign — YAKIMA, WASHINGTON — I want to turn off and go there. I would like to go to the hospital and stand in it. I'd say, 'This is where I was born.' "

I stammered a little. This wasn't the reaction I'd expected to my big Africa announcement. Why wasn't everyone as enthusiastic as I was? My feelings must have shown, because the awkwardness was excruciating.

It was Gloria, finally, who broke the tension. "Honey, all of us going to Yakima together *would* be a lot cheaper."

Neither Lynn nor Liska has ever shown a strong desire to attempt to find her birth parents. Gloria and I have encouraged them to try, and we've even volunteered to help, but both young women have always expressed reluctance. I have sensed their apprehension — fear that they might regret meeting their birth mom and dad, and concern that the reunion might somehow hurt Gloria and me. This most delicate of subjects, though, is probably best explored through the words of our daughters themselves:

LYNN:

"I think about my biological parents all the time. People say they understand, but they can't, really, unless they're in my position.

"When I was younger and thinking about looking up my birth parents, the possibility of hurting my adoptive parents was always on my mind. Now I don't think it would hurt their feelings. I *know* it wouldn't. I think I'm mature enough now to realize that. But right now I don't really care to find out about my birth parents, even though part of the answer is sitting right in my lap. I've known about my birth father for almost two years. Salem, where I was born, was a small city that had only five or six black families back then. I have met people there who say they know who my father was. They say he is in prison there. I'm afraid I'd be disappointed if I looked him up. Another fear is a negative meeting. Maybe he'd say, 'Who the hell are you?' I could probably handle it well and not take anything personally, but for now I'm not interested.

"I feel there is a reason behind everything that happens in life, and I really don't think I would be the person I am today if I hadn't been adopted. I think I'd be a lot rougher person. I'm not trying to put down my birth parents, because I have no way of knowing for sure how my life would have been different, but I feel I have had a good life with the Bateses. I know who I am. I'm not confused. I have a good family and my own goals. I couldn't have asked for anything better."

LISKA:

"I don't really think I want to find my birth parents, because there might be something I might regret. I don't hate them, because I don't know them. But they will always be in my heart, because there are always going to be unanswered questions. Sometimes when I'm walking down the street and see someone who looks like me, I wonder if it's one of my birth parents. Sometimes I do want to find out who they are, and other times I don't. I wish they would have, like, given me a picture or something. Then I would know who I look like. There is always that question: Who do I look like? I don't have the answer.

"Sometimes I'd like to know if there is any medical history that I should be aware of. Also, I'd like to know if I had any brothers or sisters, although I don't really want to find them because I'm happy with who I have.

"There have always been times when I have wished I could have continued staying with my birth parents and have them raise me, but I feel it worked out for the better. The parents I have now *are* my parents. I look at it as if they gave birth to me."

Liska got her Yakima wish. Gloria and I took her back to see the town where she was born, although the trip did not involve the big family entourage I had envisioned for the journey to Africa. I rented a van in Portland and drove the 190 miles to Yakima with Gloria, Terrell, Kamaria, Liska, and her friend Jimmy Pitts, a polite young African-American man she had met while shopping at the Portland food store where he worked.

I had never been to Liska's birthplace and thought the Yakima Valley looked like a beautiful green oasis in the middle of sagebrush country as we came over the rugged Toppenish Ridge on U.S. Highway 97. Liska, however, seemed unimpressed. I think she had been expecting a city skyline like Manhattan, or at least Seattle. Yakima turned out to be more of a cowboy town than she had anticipated. Liska perked up, though, when she began spotting Native Americans all over the place. "I'm part Indian — I might be related to one of them!" she exclaimed. "That man walking over there, he might be my cousin or something."

Gloria volunteered to stay at a city park with Terrell and Kamaria while Liska, Jimmy, and I got down to business. One of our stops was the Yakima Public Library, where I hoped to find a birth announcement for Liska in a 1969 edition of the *Yakima Herald-Republic*. Since we had no baby pictures of Liska, I thought perhaps we could at least find an old newspaper clipping as a memento of her birth and as a clue to her biological parents' identities. When Gloria heard my plan, she came up with an even better idea. Liska had been born shortly after midnight on January 1. Maybe she was the first baby to arrive that year in Yakima County. Small-town papers often make a big deal out of the first baby of the year, she reminded me. Maybe we would even find a newspaper story about the birth of Tina Lynn Jackson, who became Liska Maril Bates.

Sometimes, I said to myself, my wife is a genius.

Plowing through the library's microfilm with Liska and Jimmy peering over my shoulder, I found nothing on Tina Lynn Jackson's birth in the Yakima paper's January 1, 1969, edition. Liska was crushed until I explained that sometimes a birth announcement does not get published until the following day or even later.

With a noisy whir, I sent the microfilm projection machine speeding toward the newspaper's January 2 edition, aiming for the local news pages, where birth announcements normally appear. Liska grabbed my arm as I went past the January 2 front page.

"What was that?" she said. "Go back a page."

I slowly wound the microfilm backward to the page I had just skipped past.

"Look!" Liska almost screamed. People throughout the library's reference section turned their heads our way.

Now I, too, saw what Liska had alertly spotted on the front page of the Yakima newspaper edition that had been published the day after her birth. There at the top of the page was a large, prominently displayed picture of a nurse holding a tiny newborn baby who was looking directly at the camera with wide, bright eyes.

"Liska," I yelled, "that's *you!*"

In disbelief, the three of us gaped at the newspaper page. I quickly dropped a dime into the machine, made a photocopy, and began reading the photograph caption aloud to Liska and Jimmy as they leaned over my shoulder:

> MISS YAKIMA COUNTY 1969 — Nurse Mrs. Lester George holds the first baby born in a Yakima County hospital this year for the youngster's first look around at the world into which she arrived at 12:37 a.m. Wednesday in St. Elizabeth Hospital. The little girl, Tina Lynn Jackson, weighed five pounds 10 ounces at birth . . .

The caption went on to identify the baby's mother, who "was unable to show off her firstborn for the child's first public photograph because she may have the flu."

A couple of enormous teardrops landed on the photocopy as I finished reading it. Liska was weeping so hard her body was shaking. Jimmy put his arms around her. I gave her a hug, too. Everyone in the big room seemed to be watching, including the reference librarian who had been helping us. I thanked her and noticed her eyes were filled with tears.

"That's you, Liska," I said again. "Now we know what you looked like as a baby. You were a cutie, weren't you?"

She couldn't speak.

"And now you know who your birth mother was," I said. "We might be able to find her now, if you want to."

Liska just shook her head no, as tears kept rolling off her cheeks. After a moment, she managed to say something in a hoarse voice.

"I already have all the parents I need," she said.

The staff at Saint Elizabeth Hospital treated Liska like a visiting celebrity. They pinned a photocopy of her baby picture on a bulletin board loaded with other photos of infants who were born there. They gave her a 1960s file photograph of the hospital, showing how it looked when she was born, and an old picture of the physician — long since retired — who had delivered her all those years ago. And they gave her an extensive tour of the hospital.

Liska grew very quiet and somber when she walked around the recently remodeled maternity ward. It was clean and bright and modern and certainly nothing like what the hospital had been when Liska was born there twenty-three years earlier. Only one newborn infant was visible through the windows of the nursery. Liska peered through the glass. It was a white baby, and Liska seemed a little disappointed, as if she expected to see herself in there, a little brown baby Liska. Or perhaps she fantasized seeing her birth mother picking up the bundle and cradling it with love. Liska was silent as she resumed her stroll around the ward, a little subdued, pausing only once to say, softly, "This is where I was born."

Then she slowly turned and walked up to me and wearily placed her head on my shoulder.

"Dad?"

"What, Liska?"

"Is it too late," she asked, "to go to Africa?"

I put my hand on her head. It had been years since I'd done that.

Her hair felt just the way it did when she was little — curly, soft, and pleasant.

"It's not too late," I said. "You change your mind?"

"Yeah. Does that surprise you?"

I laughed. "I'm forty-five years old, Liska. Nothing surprises me anymore."

⚘ 17 ⚘

Love Is Colorblind

Dear Mom & Dad,
   . . . When I look back at all the times I said I wish you
never had adopted me, I feel so dumb. I want to be with
you. You're my life. As for the color differences, and what
other people might think, I don't care. You're *my* parents
and I'm very glad.

Note from Liska, age sixteen
May 14, 1985

GLORIA WAS BROWSING in an antiques store on April 29,
1992, when she heard the news bulletin that a jury had acquitted
four white Los Angeles police officers in the beating of the black
motorist Rodney King. Only two other people — the male proprie-
tor and a woman, both white — were in the store at Depoe Bay, the
tiny Oregon coastal fishing and tourist town where we had moved
to be closer to our children. As the man and the woman discussed
the verdict, the woman wondered aloud how anyone could be sure
Rodney King was actually injured by police, despite the famous
videotape that showed the beating.

"How do we really know he was hurt? I mean, do black people
bruise? I guess instead of turning black and blue, they just get white
spots," she said, laughing.

The store owner laughed, too, and Gloria walked out.

"I couldn't believe what I was hearing," my angry wife told me
when she came home. "I wanted to say, 'That's really inappropriate
and I'm bothered by it. Black people bruise just like anybody else,
you fools.' But I was too upset by the verdict, and by those two
people, to say what I was thinking. Now I'm *really* mad — at myself."

Gloria's incident, on the ugliest day of 1992, came back to me on the most beautiful day of 1992, the day of Lynn's wedding. In the reflective moments I had to myself while waiting to walk with her to the altar, my mind swam with memories of Lynn's life with our family: the forlorn foster child who arrived with only a cardboard box of ratty clothes, the beaming little ballerina in the dance recital, the happy Campfire Girl, the champion fish catcher of Odell Lake, the pretty cheerleader, the moody teen-ager, the struggling young mother, the talented hair stylist.

My thoughts drifted over dozens of such images, including the time nine-year-old Lynn took a bad spill on her bicycle while speeding down a hill. Yes, I thought to myself, black people do indeed bruise — and bleed and feel pain, although Lynn always tried harder than most to hide it. Her bike accident had been a nasty one, breaking a tooth and cutting up her face and hands. I realized it had been the last time I ever saw Lynn cry. She was tough, all right. But would she show any emotion on her wedding day? Not likely. Herbert was the one we were all worried about.

Lynn had become acquainted with Herbert Ray Johnson while cutting his hair at the salon where she worked. He was a thirty-year-old African-American man who worked at a Seattle ice-producing plant. Like Lynn, he was trying to raise children alone. His background was one of poverty, broken family, and very little association with whites — just the opposite of Lynn's life experience. Their goals, however, were the same. They wanted a stable family, decent jobs, financial security, self-esteem, and a good future for their children — pretty much what most of us want, the basic middle-class American dream.

As Gloria and I observed Lynn during the months of her engagement to Herbert, we realized that we'd never seen her so happy. Despite his totally different beginnings and some problems in his youth, we welcomed Herbert into the family. Naturally, we hoped Lynn wasn't repeating a mistake from the past by marrying into a subculture so alien to her that she would become miserable again, the way she had been with Mustafa's Southeast Asian family. But those concerns were assuaged by her obvious joy, which was so evident in a letter Lynn sent to Gloria a few weeks before the wedding:

Dear Mom,

. . . I don't know which is easier — raising children or watching them grow into their own world, hoping they'll make the right decisions in life and be happy. I guess in my case your mind can be at ease now. I wasn't exactly the perfect little daughter every mother wishes for. But I grew up and out of it, using you as a role model. Now I see you in myself in many different ways. Remember when I told you that when I had kids I would spoil them rotten and let them do whatever they wanted? I just laugh to myself, thinking how foolish I was. That's the beautiful part of growing up, though, and I hope my children — when they go out into their own lives someday — will think of me as I think of you . . .

The bottom line is, thank you for everything — for your love and support, for believing in me, for not giving up on me. I am very happy. I have a solid family and I am very proud. Life can only go uphill. Sure, we may slide down for a spell, but we won't fall. Thank you for being a wonderful, beautiful mother.

Love,
Your daughter, Lynn

On her wedding day, as I waited for our walk down the aisle, my main worry was no longer her happiness. It was whether Herbert could make it through the ceremony. The preceding night, at the rehearsal, he had become so choked up he could not focus on memorizing the ritual. Herbert was a deeply emotional man, more like Liska than like Lynn.

Liska was another concern for us at the wedding. When she had first heard about it and learned that Lynn wanted her to be the maid of honor, Liska had balked. She said she did not even know if she would attend the wedding. She was still carrying too much anger and resentment toward Lynn for a lifetime of perceived grievances, including a few involving Herbert. Only a few weeks before the wedding, after some peacemaking conversations with Lynn, Liska somewhat coolly agreed to attend and take part. Meanwhile, Gloria and I hoped Liska would be able to find a way to show happiness for Lynn and avoid tarnishing the joy of the occasion.

We also felt a little anxiety about Gloria's kindly, eighty-one-year-old stepfather, Bob McCullough. We wondered how comfortable he could be at a wedding where most of the people would be African-Americans. Bob, who had married Gloria's widowed mother in 1985 and had stayed close to us even after Mildred's death, had met our two daughters and knew they were black but nevertheless made comments from time to time that made us question his open-mindedness. More than once, for example, when spinning tales from his logging days, he told us about using a choker-cable hook called a "nigger lip." The hook's lip, Bob explained, was "fatter than the others." At other times, such as during the Los Angeles riot after the verdict in the Rodney King case, Bob made a sweeping declaration of his displeasure with "the Negroes in this country."

At first we decided against inviting Bob to the wedding, assuming he would not want to attend. One week before the day arrived, however, he handed Gloria a generous check made out to Lynn. "When I married Mildred, I figured I was getting granddaughters in the bargain," he said. "Give this to Lynn and Herbert and tell them it's from Grandpa and Grandma." We immediately apologized to Bob for failing to invite him to the wedding. A week later, he rode with us to Seattle, checked into a motel room next to ours, joined us for the wedding rehearsal, and dressed up the next day in his best summer suit for the nuptial service itself. Grandpa Bob, it appeared, was going to be just fine.

Another worry was the weather. We were staging the wedding outdoors, in the back yard of the Seattle home of Herbert's sister, Gloria Jean Usoro, a physical therapist, and her Nigerian-born husband, Uwem, an electrical engineer. All summer the Pacific Northwest had baked in the region's worst drought on record. As fate would have it, though, the first rainstorm of the season arrived in the Puget Sound area for the weekend of Lynn's wedding.

The night before the event, as rainclouds blew in over Seattle,

Uwem Usoro protected part of his back yard by erecting a wooden framework covered with clear plastic. If it rained, which appeared likely, our ceremony would not be an artistic success, but at least it would go forward.

The rehearsal that night was chaotic. Rap music pounded and about twenty children frolicked in the yard as the minister, the Reverend Donald West, gamely tried to get the wedding party organized. Don was the pastor of a Protestant congregation composed mainly of Cambodians, including the family who lived next door to the Usoros. Lynn and Herbert asked Don to officiate after the white pastor of their own church made insulting comments to them when they approached him about getting married. Don, who also was white, seemed entirely comfortable with the predominantly black members of the wedding party. I'm sure, though, he had never in his life experienced such an uproarious rehearsal — one in which the tearful groom could not get through the practice. Each time Herbert tried, he broke down. He explained that he was "too happy" and could not believe so many good things were happening in his life.

"Go ahead and be happy, Herbert, but you're *not* going to cry in the wedding," his sister scolded. "You hear me? You are *not* going to cry."

On the wedding day, Gloria and I arose at dawn to find Seattle covered with fresh puddles of rainwater under a dark and threatening sky. The wedding was going to be a wet one. Dejectedly, we wondered if the unfortunate weather was an omen. We were only hours away from a wedding in which most of the white guests had never been around many black people and most of the black guests had never been around many whites. How was this going to work out?

As Gloria and I frantically decorated the yard that morning, with an enormous boost from our son Steve and his friend Paula and some of Herbert's relatives, the sun burst through those gray clouds and the sky turned bright blue, lifting our sagging spirits. Finally, a *good* omen. Maybe, I said to myself, this wedding will somehow come crashing into place.

It did, of course. Life imitated the movies.

The guests sat in chairs on the lawn facing a little canopy where vows would be exchanged. The structure and much of the yard were draped generously with bedsheets that Gloria Jean Usoro had dyed purple and pink, the wedding colors selected by Lynn and Herbert. Flowers, balloons, and crepe paper of similar hues completed the look, almost magically transforming a scene that had looked impossibly funky only a few hours earlier.

The rites began with Herbert's daughter and son, Shantera and Herbert Junior, lighting candles. Then others in the wedding party took their places as a boom box played Percy Sledge singing "When a Man Loves a Woman." I watched from inside the house as Herbert and his best man, Michael McMurray, proceeded to the altar, followed by little Zack, the ring bearer, then Liska, and finally Sofia, the flower girl. As maid of honor, Liska looked very pretty in a new purple gown, but I noticed she was unusually somber, as if determined not to overdo her support for this union by displaying any feelings about it.

Then it was Lynn's turn — and mine. A recording of the traditional wedding march blared as we stepped out of the house and headed down the aisle. Lynn wore Gloria's white wedding dress, which had needed only minor alterations, performed by my brother Dan's wife, Chris. With her hair in long braids and beads, crowned by a lovely floral wreath, Lynn looked beautiful. All heads turned our way, of course, and as we walked I surveyed the smiling crowd. There were my parents, John and Patricia, watching Lynn with shining eyes, and Dan and Chris, and their sons Nicholas and Jeffrey; my sister Jill and her daughter Caitlin; Steve and Paula, Grandpa Bob, Gloria, and almost no other white people, except for Herbert's boss and his wife, the minister, and a couple of white friends of Lynn's and Herbert's. Everyone else was African-American, most of them relatives of Herbert's. He came from a huge family.

In the traditional Christian ceremony, Lynn was given in marriage by Gloria and me; Herbert, whose parents were deceased, was presented by his maternal grandparents, Conrad and Ruth Deloney, who had flown in from Arizona.

Herbert's heart-on-the-sleeve emotions were legendary among members of his family. When it came time for him to repeat his vows, the audience — Gloria and me included — noticeably tensed. Herbert, however, after a shaky start, performed admirably, making it through with a big smile and even a bit of flamboyance.

Then came the surprise: Lynn, the tough kid who never let herself show emotion, broke down in front of seventy people. As all who were watching seemed to hold their breath, many struggling with their own emotions, the minister paused while Lynn fought to compose herself and go on with her vows. Gloria lost it during the silence. So did Liska, standing behind her sister and facing the audience. Nobody had expected this from Lynn — especially not me. These tears were far happier than the last ones of hers I'd seen, when she was thrown off her bicycle, but I was sure they also had much to do with release from pain.

Black people do indeed bruise. Just like me.

Epilogue

. . . Dad, first of all, don't let your expectations go down the
drain. Like the great Dr. Martin Luther King, Jr., said:
"Even though we face the difficulties of today and tomorrow, I still have a dream." His dream is slowly but surely
coming together, and you have helped it by accepting two
African-American children into your home. Your dream for
me is going to take time, but I promise when you die you'll
know we have made it together. I believe that your miracle
has been witnessed, and I know my miracle was the day you
and Mom came into my life.

Letter from Liska, age twenty-two
Portland, Oregon
August 14, 1991

FOR ME, LYNN'S WEDDING unfolded as a metaphor for Amer-
ican society, reflecting the extraordinary fragility of race relations in
this country. Our joyful day in Seattle did not begin, or end, as a
love feast between Caucasians and African-Americans. Some of
Lynn's white relatives felt snubbed by the blacks. A few black
members of Herbert's family thought the whites were standoffish.
The reception after the ceremony was stiff and strained for some of
the guests from either side. I overheard a few well-intentioned but
clumsy remarks, some made by whites and some by blacks, that
could have been construed as insulting if anyone had chosen to take
offense.

After the last piece of cake was consumed and the punch bowl
drained, I felt relieved that the reception was winding to a close.
Some out-of-state guests said their goodbyes and slipped away, and

Gloria and I and Uwem and Gloria Jean Usoro finally began to relax a little.

"Whew. We did it," I said to Uwem.

"Yeah," he said. "We sure did."

Then something unexpected happened. A dozen or more children from Herbert's side of the family moved the rented folding chairs off the lawn and began dancing to rap, rock, and hip-hop blasting from the same boom box that had played the wedding march. The kids were great dancers and put on a good show, to the delight of gawking members of the Bates family. Then Herbert danced with Lynn, and after I cut in, Steve and Paula and Liska and her friend Jimmy Pitts got out on the lawn. Just like that, a party was under way. The real celebration had begun.

What a shame, I thought, that some folks had needed to leave early. But as I was regretting that there were not more Bateses around, my brother Tom, just six days after undergoing surgery on the spine that had ached since his football days, showed up with Eloise and their children, Melody, Alex, and John, and a friend from France. Several friends of Herbert's and Lynn's arrived late, too. Herbert's relatives threw some chicken on the barbecue and brought out the booze.

True to my new healthful ways, I had just one drink, but the libations helped loosen up the rest of the crowd to a welcome degree. In the hours that followed, several good things came together.

Liska and Lynn reconciled in an emotional private moment. Our photograph of the two of them embracing will be cherished.

Liska's friend Jimmy told me he wanted to marry her and become Terrell's and Kamaria's father.

Uwem Usoro listened enthusiastically to my plans for going to Africa and suggested several places to visit. I agreed to take some clothing and medical items to his relatives in Nigeria.

"Your daughters are going to love it there, and so will you," he said. "How long have you been planning the trip?"

"About twenty years," I said.

All over the yard, as the smell of roasting chicken filled the air, blacks and whites who had never celebrated with people of the other race found out what it could be like. No one enjoyed the experience more than Grandpa Bob, who put aside his cane and got up and danced with our African-American host, Gloria Jean Usoro. "I never thought I'd live long enough to go to a wedding like this one," he told me later with a grin and twinkling eyes.

As the sun went down and the party warmed up, I plopped wearily beside my happy wife, who sat holding Kamaria while Liska danced. Almost in wonder I watched the festivities and tried to make sense out of what had happened. The wedding and this spontaneous celebration, I decided, were examples of integration — positive instances that demonstrated the value of interracial synthesis as a step toward harmony for a diverse and badly splintered society.

I thought about our family, too, and realized that integration is not really what happened to Gloria and me and our children. Through the adoption of Lynn and Liska, we moved beyond that and achieved assimilation — and not the controversial, unilateral kind affecting only blacks. For us the process cut both ways, with whites changing, too. Over twenty-three years, two African-American girls grew up with a special understanding of both races, black and white, and with a valuable ability to function in both worlds, bridging two cultures. At the same time, their lives touched those of Gloria and me and Steve and Mike and perhaps two dozen other white people, Bateses and Burtons, who "grew up" along with Lynn and Liska. In our family, relationships have transcended race.

I don't think transracial adoption will ever become preferable to same-race placement of children — not in my lifetime, anyway. But I do strongly feel that adoptions like ours are an acceptable alternative and should not be outlawed or even restricted, as some critics seek. If there is any hope for race relations in this nation, we need to be unafraid to embrace precisely the kind of social engineering that allowed Gloria and me to become the parents of Lynn and Liska.

Would we do it again if given the chance? That's easy. Sure we would, and we'd do it better — not that we're sorry about the way things turned out. To the contrary, we are extremely grateful for the many blessings our family counted in the days after the wedding.

Lynn disclosed plans to quit the beauty business and to further her education, aiming for a career in a field that doesn't involve hair.

Liska and Jimmy enrolled in job-training programs and announced their engagement to be married.

Mike returned safely from the Persian Gulf, and Steve became a supervisor for the building contractor who employed him. Both sons revealed plans to resume their college educations.

Gloria and I announced details of our family-level assistance program and set up a fund to help ensure the education and career training of all of our children and grandchildren. Proceeds from this book will be placed in that fund and also will help finance our long-deferred journey to Africa.

Our good friends Mike and Sandy Thoele, like us, are still together and immensely proud of the way their interracial brood has turned out. The Thoeles share our concerns about American society and wonder who will step forward on the national stage to provide the direction our country has sorely needed. Will President Clinton accept that role? We have high hopes. "I think racism is an issue that responds to leadership," Mike Thoele once told me. "Even someone as unlikely as Lyndon Johnson can beat it back. And with almost no effort at all, people such as Ronald Reagan and George Bush can make it fashionable again." Hear, hear.

My spouse and I have no illusions about tidy, fairy-tale endings, and life continues to mix our blessings with setbacks. Like America, we are somewhat more cynical today, a little less idealistic, a lot more world-weary than we were back in 1970 when we thought we could handle just about anything life chose to send our way. But we have a surprising store of resilience, and we still have plenty of determination and hope. Granted, like the country as a whole, we've realized that some of our dreams for our children have not come true. So we're making new dreams. And rather than wallowing in our disappointments, we're choosing instead to look ahead with optimism, rejoicing in how far we've come as a family.

We know in our hearts that it isn't too late, for us or the country, if we all remember not to leave the party before the real celebration begins.